YOUR OWN
ALLOTMENT

If you want to know how…

How to Grow Your Own Food

A week-by-week guide to wild life friendly fruit and vegetable gardening

Planning and Creating Your First Garden

A step-by-step guide to designing your garden – whatever your experience or knowledge

How to Start Your Own Gardening Business

An insider guide to setting yourself up as a professional gardener

howtobooks

Please send for a free copy of the latest catalogue:

How To Books Ltd
Spring Hill House, Spring Hill Road, Begbroke
Oxford OX5 1RX, United Kingdom
info@howtoboooks.co.uk
www.howtobooks.co.uk

YOUR OWN ALLOTMENT

How to find it, cultivate it, and enjoy growing your own food

Neil Russell-Jones

SPRING HILL

Published by Spring Hill Books
Spring Hill House, Spring Hill Road,
Begbroke, Oxford OX5 1RX, United Kingdom.
Tel: (01865) 375794. Fax: (01865) 379162.
info@howtobooks.co.uk
www.howtobooks.co.uk

The right of Neil Russell-Jones to be identified as author of
this work has been asserted by him in accordance with the
Copyright, Design and Patents Act 1988.

First edition 2008

British Library Cataloguing in Publication Data
A catalogue record for this book is available from the
British Library

ISBN 978 1 905862 19 1

Cover design by Mousemat Design
Illustrations by Deborah Andrews
Produced for How To Books by Deer Park Productions,
Tavistock, Devon
Typeset by Pantek Arts Ltd, Maidstone, Kent
Printed and bound in Great Britain by Bell and Bain Ltd, Glasgow

NOTE: The material contained in this book is set out in good
faith for general guidance and no liability can be accepted
for loss or expense incurred as a result of relying in particular
circumstances on statements made in this book. The laws and
regulations are complex and liable to change, and readers should
check the current positions with the relevant authorities before
making personal arrangements.

Contents

About the author

Neil Russell-Jones (BSc (Hons), MBA, ACIB) is an author and management consultant. He has been gardening and growing vegetables for years, having carved two gardens from scratch out of the builder's yard left following new construction.

He has an allotment plot in south-east London, which he tends with his wife and two daughters. He is also the treasurer for the allotment society, which is run on organic principles; and he maintains the website. The whole family works on the allotment, generally, but his two daughters have their own special area of the allotment where they grow what they choose, and his wife also has a herb garden. The very first crops (potatoes) came from the children's plot.

He has written many books and papers on a variety of other topics, including a leading-edge paper in the 1990s on 'Environmental Banking'.

He has also written a sci-fantasy trilogy (*The Loud Moutain*) with his children, which is currently under consideration by several publishers.

This is his first foray into real green issues.

He has been lecturer on the CASS EMBA course, and a special advisor for the Prince's Youth Business Trust in the areas of strategy and marketing.

You can contact him at neil.jones333@ntworld.com

The allotment website is www.dulwichallotment.org.uk

Preface

There has been a marked increase in interest in and demand for allotments. People are focusing increasingly on green issues, the environment and well-being; and the increased interest in allotments is symbolic of a reaction to concerns about the quality and healthiness or otherwise of mass-produced food. There is also concern at the lack of choice in the produce offered: for instance, few of the many interesting and tasty varieties of apples that once abounded in the UK are now available.

A number of factors started us on our venture into the world of allotments. My family and I wanted to know where our food came from; how it was produced; and also to ensure that the 'carbon footprint' was as small as possible. We had both been brought up in or near the countryside – rather than in cities – and remembered things as they were (or might have been – nostalgia is rose-tinted). We wanted our children to share the experiences that we remembered.

There is nothing like plucking peas straight from the pod; or picking a strawberry and popping it into your mouth. The flavour of sweetcorn taken off the plant and cooked within minutes cannot be matched by corn flown thousands of miles which has turned to starch; and the intense pleasure of harvesting, cooking and then eating your own potatoes has to be experienced to be appreciated. My wife Catherine is a fantastic cook and we wanted to be able to cook our own produce – fresh. I have included one or two of her recipes in the chapter 'Enjoying the Fruits of Your Labour'.

I had been gardening for many years, firstly with my parents, where I looked after their garden until I moved away, and then in my own homes. As I was always being moved around by my employer I had to create two brand-new gardens out of the dumping grounds left behind after the construction of new houses. Prior to our present house, I bought a house that had belonged to two elderly sisters. Although it had a lovely, mature garden they hadn't been able to cultivate it properly, so I also had to rescue that one. When I met Catherine we moved to our present house.

We decided that, as we had no garden to speak of, and as we were unlikely to move to the country (because of schools and work) for many years – if then – we would apply for an allotment. With both new houses the first crop that I planted was always potatoes to clean the ground. An allotment would give me a chance to try some larger-scale vegetable cultivation.

This book is based on my real first-hand experience of trying to get an allotment; of being allocated what was basically a run-down field or jungle; and the process that I went through (and am still following to some degree) to tame it, bring it under control and put it back into useful production.

We went through the process of finding out about sites, obtaining a plot and then dealing with it. This book will examine the key steps involved in finding, obtaining, starting and then maintaining an allotment, and is based on our experiences. It contains information to help you in your search, to understand what you have got and what you will be able to do with it (or not). It will look at the items usually grown on an allotment and what can go wrong, as well as sharing tips and experiences.

I will discuss some of the issues that I encountered and, I hope, help you to avoid some of the pitfalls and mistakes. Throughout the book I will give real-life examples drawn from our plot and the larger site; and some little tips in a fun way from Sammy Scarecrow, the scarecrow my children made for one of our fund-raising days.

An allotment is not a *destination* – it is a *journey*. You never arrive – you just keep on going.

This book will help those wishing to grow their own food, but who do not have a vegetable or fruit garden and are seeking an allotment. You will find nothing in here on growing lawns and very little on ornamental shrubs. Of course, the principles for good management apply equally well to those *with* gardens and growing lawns and shrubs!

Each chapter will examine a key area – all based on organic principles – of which the fundamental principle is:

Look after the soil and it will look after you.

This is the theme that runs throughout this book: and I shall return to it on several occasions.

This book will (like Gaul, for the many classicists among you) be in three parts:

I: A Good Grounding – The Basics

Introduction; applying for an allotment; getting started; the basics; preparing the ground; organic principles.

II: Know Your Onions – The Plants

Plant life cycle; heritage plants; vegetables; fruits; herbs; flowers, trees and shrubs; permanent beds.

III: Maintaining the Allotment

Dealing with pests; composting; protecting and supporting your plants; harvesting; storage and preserving; seed collection; propagation; useful tips; contacts.

This book is dedicated to Catherine my wife. Without her I would not have achieved so much – nor enjoyed so much happiness.

Part I

A Good Grounding – The Basics

1

All About Allotments

This chapter will explain what an allotment is; give a brief overview of the allotment movement and how allotments came into being; and explore a couple of questions – 'Why do you want to grow your own food?' and 'Why do you want an allotment?' – which, although they may overlap, are not the same. Having answered these questions to your satisfaction, and if you are still keen on the idea, you can then go forth and seek an allotment.

When we went for an allotment I decided that I would apply the techniques that I have been practising as a management consultant heavily involved in change programmes. That is, to understand everything that is necessary; to relate that to the current situation and the future desired state; and then develop a plan to get there. This may sound a little bit like jargon, but it is just logical (Mr Spock) and accordingly the book is structured along those lines – finding out the basics; understanding the plants and crops; and then the practical implementation and day-to-day management once you have got the allotment going. Taking time out at the beginning to find out what you have got, think things through and then plan – rather than jumping in with both feet and a spade – can reap rich dividends later on.

Although this book has a primary focus on food, that does not mean that flowers, trees and shrubs are unimportant, nor does it mean that they should not be grown. Our own society, many years ago, was originally called the Dulwich Chrysanthemum and Horticultural Society. Over the years the emphasis has changed and so has the name – with 'Horticultural' moving forward to displace 'Chrysanthemum' – and now it is more commonly known just by the initials DHCS. What you grow is, of course, up to you and, as long as it is within your objectives and the rules of the allotment society, that is fine. Our society's lease, for example, has clauses within it (stipulated by the lessor) that nothing can be grown that is over 6 feet in height, thus precluding trees and large shrubs, which compete with vegetables anyway in terms of light, water and food.

All plots should have some flowers. They are not only beautiful to look at and to smell, but they also attract beneficial insects that you need for pollination purposes. In many cases they also repel pests.

The principles that are discussed generally apply equally well to all plants.

What is an allotment?

An allotment is simply a piece of, usually public, land set aside for the express purpose of being rented to individuals to enable them to grow food. The historical standard size is 10 rods. A rod in this context is an *area measure* equivalent to $30^1/_4$ square yards (not to be confused with the old *linear measure* (rod, pole or perch) which is 5 feet 6 inches) and so the standard size is just over 300 square yards. This size was originally derived from that considered as adequate to feed a family of four annually. Nowadays it is common for plots to be divided into smaller ones: half- or third-sized plots are typical. People now have less time, or allotments do not represent their only/main source of food, or they share. In some cases allotment sites have subdivided the plots just to get more people in, or to reduce waiting lists and times.

Most, but by no means all, are owned by local authorities. In Dulwich, where we live and our site is located, the situation is most unusual: many of the local allotments are not publicly owned, but rather belong to the Dulwich Estate, a charitable foundation set up by Edward Alleyn (an Elizabethan actor and theatre owner) in the sixteenth century to support education. He purchased much of the land in and around the village of Dulwich, and there are at least five allotment sites within its purview. Our site falls within its jurisdiction.

The rent paid by allotment holders varies enormously across the country, driven by demand and the local situation and economic factors. But, wherever it is, it is always very good value and rarely exceeds £100 annually for a full plot. Economic pressures (or greed), however, are causing many local authorities to look at the potential values of allotment sites and there is a trend towards selling them off for development. There is more than a whiff of corruption attached to this.

> Recently a site in London was completely closed (with government acquiescence) because a tiny proportion of it was allegedly needed for a road for the (supposedly 'Green') 2012 Olympic Games. The council used this as an excuse to get rid of the whole site – providing a meagre new site elsewhere in return. You couldn't imagine that happening had the road run near a government minister's house. This trend is very sad but there are several organisations and societies whose objective is to fight closures and sell-offs.

Below are extracts from a London Assembly publication looking at the state of allotments: *A Lot to Lose: London's disappearing allotments October 2006.*

It takes a very good look at the state of allotments in London: it does not make happy reading. They are disappearing extremely quickly. It is available here: http://www.london.gov.uk/assembly/reports/environment/allotments-main.pdf

> The last major survey of allotments was carried out on behalf of the National Society of Allotment and Leisure Gardeners in 1973. It revealed that plots across England were disappearing at a rate of 9,400 per year. It also found that the number of people waiting for an allotment site had more than doubled since 1970. Within London, the survey identified over 36,000 allotment plots, of which almost 31,000 were in outer London, and a waiting list of 1,330. Over the last ten years, the number of allotments in London has decreased at three different levels.
>
> - Firstly, the number of sites has diminished. A decade ago, there were 769 sites in London. Now, data from all 33 councils suggests there are 737 – a net loss of 32 sites, or 4.2%, across the city. The majority of these were in outer London in boroughs like Bexley and Hounslow, which our map shows are fairly rich in allotments per head of population. However, provision has also decreased in

inner London, with for example Lambeth losing three sites. It is important to note that this is a net loss: we identified 39 sites that have disappeared over the last ten years while seven new sites have been established in the same period. However, these new sites tend to be considerably smaller than those they have replaced, for example a single two-plot site in Tower Hamlets. Statutory sites are among those being lost. In the twelve months to February 2006, five applications were made to the Secretary of State for disposal of sites in London – two in Croydon, two in Harrow and one in Bromley. The first four were to be sold, and the last retained as open space. All five disposals were approved.

- Secondly, the number of individual plots has shrunk. Within the 20 councils for whom complete data was available, there are 20,786 plots, compared to 22,319 in 1996 – a reduction of 1,534. In percentage terms, the loss of plots (6.9%) has been significantly greater than the loss of sites. At first glance, this may appear puzzling. However, it reflects our finding that allotment sites, instead of being done away with in their entirety, are often chipped away, a handful of plots at a time. It is this insidious loss – five plots shaved off at the periphery to allow a new road to be built – that is the real threat to allotment provision in London. The apparent disappearance of plots is especially worrying when set against a backdrop of diminishing plot sizes. In sites where there is high demand, it is increasingly common to split newly vacant plots in order to get two people off the waiting list – perhaps two new gardeners who would find a full-sized plot too much to cope with. This suggests that the amount of allotment land which has disappeared is greater than the reduction of individual plots would suggest.

- It is at this third level, land area, that the disappearance of allotments is most difficult to measure, as many boroughs were unable to provide accurate and up-to-date information. However, we estimate that the 1,534 plots to have disappeared over the last decade are equivalent to over 87 acres of allotment land – equivalent to 54 football pitches. Among the boroughs for whom information was available, the largest areas were lost in Barking and Dagenham (over 13 acres) and Merton (over 15 acres).

The erosion of allotment provision is a cause for worry. One of the key objectives of DHCS is to raise awareness of the issue through open days and produce stalls, as well as outreach to the local community and schools.

History of the allotment movement

In the seventeenth and eighteenth centuries a major demographic shift took place in the UK. The rural poor started to drift to the towns and cities in search of work in factories – usually becoming the urban poor. This was the time of the industrial revolution in the UK and it totally changed the socio-demographic profile of the population. The majority of people, instead of working in agriculture and related trades – became industrial workers. They often lived in appalling conditions – the infamous back-to-backs with no sanitation, heating (except for fires), water or gardens.

Given the low wages it was difficult to feed a family   this was before birth control and so the birth rate was high – but unlike in the country where children soon grow into hands to work on the land, in cities they are just 'another little hungry mouth to feed'. Land was set aside for food production and 'allotted' to families to grow food – allotments. It is, therefore, largely an urban phenomenon – although there are allotments everywhere, including the countryside.

It is estimated that there are 300,000 allotments and about 30sq miles under production in the UK.

Why grow your own now?

Historically there was little alternative to growing your own food. If you were very rich you could, of course, employ others to grow food for you. In the eighteenth and nineteenth centuries there was nowhere to do the weekly shop. Most food came from the plots outside the cottages or from the kitchen garden of the large country houses. Allotments were a response to the needs of the working people who became urbanised. Food shops largely grew up in the latter part of the nineteenth century to serve the rising urban middle classes of the UK who fell into neither category; and agriculture progressively adapted to meet this rising demand.

Nowadays the choice is fantastic – food is available anywhere and every-where in the UK at incredibly low cost. In many cases, however, this price is too low as mega-retailers are continually seeking to drive prices down – resulting in many farmers going bust or selling up. The UK milk industry is a good case in point: dairy farmers are quitting in droves as they cannot make a living out of it any more. It is a similar story with beef production. There is also a knock-on effect in social and demographic terms. In addi-tion, as we lose domestic production, it can leave us more vulnerable to the whims of international politics and trade.

It also comes, of course, with a non-monetary price. Many items are grown on large industrial agri-business farms across Europe or even further afield, where techniques have been developed to allow for mass sowing, uniform ripening and mass harvesting, often at the expense of taste and flavour (the cotton wool wrapped in yellow wax that purports to be a French Golden Delicious is neither golden nor delicious). Or they are imported from across the globe, travelling long distances to reach us and, therefore, stuffed full of preservatives; or picked to ripen en route away from the plant and making a huge 'carbon footprint'. Either way it is less than ideal.

Fresh in many cases, therefore, merely means as fresh as it can be, given the circumstances. This is not to say it is a bad thing necessarily – as global trade is generally good for all – but importing food that is also, or could be, grown locally does seem illogical – even to give a wider choice.

There is very little true, crushing poverty in the UK anymore, and few need to grow food in the same way as in earlier centuries, but the demand for allotments is, after a depressing decline in the 70s and 80s nevertheless, rising.

Objectives

For many people growing their own produce meets many objectives, including:

- They can be sure of where it came from and what is in it. You are in charge of chemicals and can determine exactly what goes in (ideally zero, of course!).

- They can choose exactly *what* to grow (not necessarily what *will* grow or grow well, however; that is random, depending on your location, soil, pests, diseases, weather and luck).

- They can experiment with new and interesting varieties, unusual crops, intercropping, new techniques, etc.

- They can 'get back to their roots' and 'commune with the land'.

- It helps to deal with the stresses of modern life.

- It is a fun and rewarding experience (if hard work sometimes).

- It is a good family activity – providing quality time together.

- It leaves a smaller carbon footprint, which is important to many.

- It provides a great deal of healthy exercise (digging, walking, cycling).

And so, lacking space at home, they choose to have an allotment.

Politics and agriculture have long been linked – the Corn Laws in the eighteenth century; the wasteful and heavily subsidised European Common Agricultural Policy (CAP), which encourages use of pesticides and creates large unwanted mountains and lakes of produce; the general subsidies allocated by many countries to farmers; the difficulty in getting real free trade to help third-world countries, etc. Growing your own is another way of reducing the political element in your food.

Why do you want an allotment?

It is important for you to think through the reasons why you, personally, wish to have an allotment. Some of them might be as listed above; you may have others of course; but you do need to be really clear because it is a major *time commitment* and an undertaking involving a great deal of *effort*. Some people on our site complain that they don't have enough time to work on the allotment – but they won't down-size!

You might find it helpful to draw up a balance sheet of pros and cons.

Allotment – pros and cons (examples)

Pro	Cons
● Good exercise	● Requires commitment
● Out in the fresh air	● Hard work
● Social	● Initial outlay may be high
● Interesting foods	● Needs constant effort (weeds don't go
● Environmentally sound	on holiday)
● Family fun	● Needs planning
● Relaxation	● Food not necessarily cheaper than
● Communal	that bought in

You should set your own pros and cons out and then weigh them up – before applying.

When it comes down to it though, the reasons why you want to have an allotment don't really matter too much, as long as you are sure that it is what you really want to do and you will *give the commitment* necessary.

Bear in mind the following, however:

- Allotments are not a fashion accessory – they are for producing food (and maybe flowers in some cases).

- Do not try to take on more than you can manage. As the size increases arithmetically, the effort required increases geometrically.

- There are only so many hours in a day/week and the more tired you become the slower and less efficient you become. You want it to be enjoyable as well as practicable – so that you *want* to do it, rather than feeling that you *have* to.

- A full plot is definitely too much for one person in today's demanding full-time work environment, as you will have to commit many hours throughout the year – often when you don't want to or when you least feel like it. It is better to take or down-size to a smaller plot, or share. Families find it easier to work full plots as they are many-handed. We are four and even then it is a stretch in May to August when everything is growing. Also, you will not be able to consume what you grow and it will either have to be given away or go to waste, which is just pointless.

- By and large the food isn't cheaper than in supermarkets – but it should be better.

- You will get more out of it, and it will enrich the experience of being an allotment holder, if you *get involved* in the allotment society, whether by attending work days, open days and social events, giving produce for sale on produce days, or by volunteering to help in the administration. Human beings are by nature gregarious and the social interactions are as important a part of belonging to a group or society as the output from the allotment.

- If you do not keep the allotment up to the standards required by the site/society then you will probably lose the allotment and it will be allocated to someone else on the waiting list.

- NINO – Nothing In: Nothing Out. Crops need attention and looking after – but putting in worthwhile effort will be rewarded by very worthwhile output.

For most people, an allotment is challenging, hard work – but also fun and rewarding.

Abram Maslow studied people and what motivated them; and came up with his famous 'Hierarchy of needs', ie what drives people to do things.

Maslow's hierarchy of needs

Self actualisation doing your own thang!

Ego needs Personal worth, respect, autonomy

Social needs Belonging, friendship

Safety needs Security, protection

Basics Food, shelter, warmth

As needs are met you move up and satisfy others, ie what drives your behaviour changes.

Having an allotment actually meets several of these layers:

- the basics – food;
- social needs – by belonging to the society and working with friends or family;
- self-respect – personal worth;
- and possibly self-actualisation – growing your own food!

So having an allotment can also meet several of the needs that humans have – in part anyway.

You do it your way

Whatever people may say, it is important that you manage your allotment in your own way. Do what suits you and your likes, dislikes and objectives: within the constraints of what you can do, neighbourliness and the local rules. You will adopt and adapt what you see, hear and experience into your own way of doing things. Just because one person says do it this way doesn't make it right. Others will say something else. Use your common sense and develop a feel for things. Learn from your mistakes (learn also from the ones I made that I share here) and the old hands, and have fun and grow great food.

Having decided that you would like an allotment, you now need to try to get one – and that, unfortunately, isn't as straightforward as it once was.

Getting an allotment

Getting an allotment is not easy; although it is easier in some parts of the country than others. Ten or even five years ago there was only very limited interest in allotments, and the movement was in danger of dying on its feet. Many holders had died, there were insufficient new members wanting plots, and many sites were moribund with derelict and abandoned plots. Cheap food for all, coupled with busy lifestyles (or laziness), meant that demand for allotments generally fell. These were probably the driving factors behind the rising level of disposals by local authorities.

In recent years, however, allotments have become very popular again. This is probably due to increased awareness of green issues, quality of life concerns and a desire by people to take charge of their food sourcing, partly from increased exposure on TV and in other media. As a result, demand has soared and waiting lists in many areas have increased exponentially. This is a good thing in many respects, as it means that the allotment movement is vibrant and that pressure is exerted to keep existing sites, as well as on plot holders to maintain theirs properly – and perhaps to create more. But it can mean that you may have to wait for some time.

The first thing that you need to do is to find out where your local allotments are. It is a good idea to try to get into the nearest, as it is less trouble getting there, and less distance to transport things. You could probably walk or cycle, as many on our site do – and indeed as we do, although not every time. It is, however, difficult to cycle carrying flagstones or a large bag of sand or fertiliser or a garden spade, so other forms of transport will be needed from time to time.

Where is my nearest allotment? And who do I contact?

The best thing I found was an internet search (what else, of course, nowadays?). Putting in 'allotments' usually gives you a list of local sites, and often whom to contact at the council. You may also have seen some allotments as you travel around. If not, then look at local maps, or ask in local shops or libraries.

Go to the allotment sites when you have found them and talk to someone, anyone. They will usually give you the name of the lettings officer – often the details are displayed.

People are more likely to be around on allotment sites at weekends and in the evenings in summer early autumn.

You can also ask them about the site; what sort of people have plots, what grows well, waiting lists, etc.

On our site we have a list of the committee and their email addresses/telephone numbers. These are also on our website.

Talk to as many people and visit as many allotment sites as you can. Many have websites. DHCS does and ours is www.dulwichallotments.org.uk Many have said it is an exceptionally useful one, so have a look!

Websites will usually give you details of the allotments and how to get onto the waiting list. Contact your local authority – this will be your parish, town, borough, city or district council. When I started my trawl I couldn't find any local allotment websites (some did exist, but I guess that search engines do not often look for them!) – but I managed to get a list of addresses of local allotment sites from the council website, although it was hopelessly out of date, and wrote to or telephoned several.

Contact the National Society of Allotment and Leisure Gardeners (NSALG). It can give you details of local sites – or put you in touch with other like-minded individuals if you want to start your own.

NSALG contact details:

Telephone: 01536 266576
Email: natsoc@nsalg.org.uk
Website: www.nsalg.org.uk

Applying – waiting lists

Once you have contact details of local sites, you should write or call and explain that you are keen to obtain an allotment, and would like to join the waiting list. They will either give you the bad news on the spot or write to you telling you about the waiting lists. In our area I was staggered to find that most have waiting lists of literally hundreds of people, with time to obtain plots measured in years rather than months (one quoted up to five years!). Many lists are even closed to new entrants. This reflects the upsurge in interest – as well as the closures of other allotment sites.

Don't be downhearted. Place yourself on the lists wherever you can. I put myself down for five different allotments and, gratifyingly, one came back in a couple of months (the one I have now). Another one (which was very full according to the lettings officer) came back a couple of months after that. Out of courtesy I contacted the other sites and let them know that I had obtained an allotment. Most people don't do this and of course it inflates the waiting lists, giving a false impression of true demand.

Take what you are offered

If you are offered an allotment that is smaller than you want then nevertheless take it. Let them know that you would like a larger one, if that is the case; but it will get you started and it is easier to change when you are on the inside looking out than to wait on a list until a larger plot comes free – which might be never.

Allotment holders change throughout the year. Some find it too much; some get tired of it; some die – they don't retire; others move away. A few holders are thrown out because they haven't kept their plot up to the required standards.

We have a strict policy on this and the plots are inspected on a quarterly basis by the committee members to ensure that they are being worked and kept up to scratch. You receive a warning, and if there is no improvement by the next inspection you are out! We also take into consideration how much people put into the society and of course their personal circumstances.

So although the lists may seem long, you can move up them quite quickly sometimes. In addition, when a plot becomes free many on the list have obtained one elsewhere, lost interest, moved on or died (yes, the lists are that long!). So it may not be as bad as you (and they) think.

Creating a new site

If there appear to be no allotment sites in your area – all is not lost. You can go further afield of course, with all the travel disadvantages that that would bring, or you could try to get a new site created. I have not tried this as I didn't need to, but I would certainly have done so had it been necessary. I imagine, though, that it would be quite a long slog and require a great deal of persistence and effort. This does not mean, however, that you shouldn't try. The NSALG would, I feel sure, give advice and assistance to you if you followed this path. There is a requirement that authorities must provide allotments if there is demand.

If local people feel there is a need for allotments which is not being met, they can get together a group of any six residents who are registered on the electoral roll and put their case to the local authority.

All councils in England and Wales (with the exception of Inner London) have to, by law, provide allotments. Any group of adults over the age of eighteen and registered on the electoral role can group together to request the council provide one. Source: NSALG

My local authority wants to dispose of allotment land; what can I do?
If you discover this then the first thing to establish is whether the allotment is *statutory* (provided for the specific purpose of being used as allotment land) or *temporary*. If an allotment authority wishes to sell a statutory allotment site it must have the consent of the relevant Secretary of State dealing with Local Government who will first, *in theory*, want to be satisfied that certain conditions have or will be met or have been taken into account. I would get in touch with the following:

● NSALG so that they can get involved and give support and advice;

● your local MP (or equivalent in Wales and Scotland);

- your MEP;

- the parish and other subsidiary bodies;

- the local councillor;

- the local press;

- local community associations;

- green organisations;

- allotments are very green and that is a hot political potato at the moment so in order to make a lot of fuss I would also get in touch with the relevant shadow Secretary of State;

- anyone else that you think would help (well, known people like David Attenborough or David Bellamy, or even David Beckham if you know them!).

Further information can be found on the Department of Communities & Local Government's website.

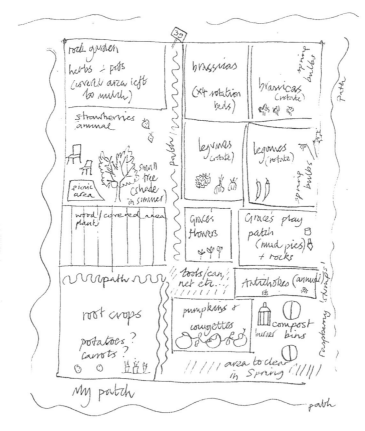

2

Our Allotment

A few words about our particular allotment and its site. We now have a plot that is some 130 feet long by about 20 feet wide, ie pretty much the standard sized plot of 10 rods, mentioned previously. We didn't get it all in one go; first we were allocated the 'top' part (which was furthest away from the path and on the boundary of the site) – around three-sevenths. This was a real nightmare. It hadn't been worked much for several years and was showing a good crop of brambles, buttercups, thistly plants and other, unidentified, growths. We received it around Christmas/New Year time – a little late for digging over – but we were very glad to get it and made a start straight away. You can see from the photo what it looked like!

The first thing that we did was to measure it and draw out a plan of what we had. My children did that while Catherine and I attacked the jungle. We also took some photos as a record of what it looked like to begin with. We didn't actually have many tools to speak of at that time. Our London house only has a tiny garden area – mainly a small patio with a small border – so all we had was a pair of secateurs, a trowel, a small hand-fork, a medium-sized garden fork and one small watering can. We also had, bizarrely enough, a rake, which must have been a legacy of a previous owner.

Our second activity, therefore, was to visit the local garden centre where we bought a spade and fork, two sets of secateurs and some loppers (essential for thick growth – the leverage is fantastic) and several sets of thick gardening gloves (one pair each). There were lots of sharp, barbed things growing on the plot: 2 inch-thick bramble stems have wicked thorns about an inch long; very hard, sharp and vicious! Thick trousers and tough boots were a must: not shorts or mini-skirts with plimsolls.

Armed with these, and several big, tough bags for the things we cut off, we manfully attacked the jungle. We were helped by the fact that at that time of the year little was growing and most plants lay dormant. This took some time and a not inconsiderable effort but there was a fabulous sense of well-being and of real achievement afterwards – as well as a deep tiredness as we sat at home with a cup of tea and a slice of cake in front of the fire.

We still needed to tackle whatever lay *under* the soil of course – and we knew that there were many root systems where we had hacked off the growth above ground. Having a bonfire afterwards was also very cathartic (only allowed on our site after dark) and warming.

A few weeks after we had been granted our initial plot we decided to call on a real expert for his opinion – Catherine's father. At eighty-nine he had been gardening for twice as long as we had been alive, just about, both in the UK and Africa where he worked for the Government. His previous garden was huge – half an acre – and had been incredibly productive for fruit and vegetables before it became too much for him and he and Catherine's mother moved and down-sized to a smaller area (still thirty times bigger than our home garden). We had just double dug it so the soil was well and truly exposed for him to see.

He looked at the soil, bent down and picked some up, crumbled it in his hands and stood for a minute thinking, or asleep. We waited with bated breath. 'Aye well,' he said in his Lancashire accent and turned round. 'I think that the soil is good and you will have a very productive plot when you have cultivated it.' So that was a relief.

First steps

Having cleared the site, we did two things in parallel: we planned what we wanted to grow – drawing up a sketch; and we *double dug the whole plot*. (See Double digging). There are arguments for and against digging (see Dig V No dig) but it is, in my view, *essential* for a newly acquired, neglected plot. Perennial weeds lurk, quiescent, underground with massive and extensive root networks, just waiting for you to drop your guard – when they will spring up like the Teeth of the Hydra in *Jason and the Argonauts*. There is no other way of getting rid of them organically, quickly, other than by physically digging them out. It is possibly not so critical to double dig every year thereafter – but definitely worth it every four or five years or so, or when you decide to remove permanent crops.

As we dug we incorporated masses of manure into the soil as it was in a pretty poor state; and decided to use the top half of the initial plot – which had been particularly infested with perennial weeds – for early potatoes: to 'clean' it, drawing on my previous experience of cleaning building sites.

At the bottom of the plot we allocated an area each to the children – about 10 feet by 4 feet – where they could grow what they liked; and a herb bed for Catherine: but in the main we had decided that we were going to grow fruit and vegetables, with a smattering of flowers. By March we had, by dint of a massive effort, more or less tamed the plot, and had started planting onions, potatoes and some fruit bushes – and were ready to prepare areas for sowing seeds (see photo above).

Another step forward

In April, after the annual allotment year ended, we were lucky enough to receive the other part of the plot. This was a completely different proposition. The previous holder had initially started with enthusiasm, we were told, but had progressively faded out. He hadn't been, it seemed, terribly interested in vegetables, and although he had grown some at some time (we kept finding self-set and residual growths); he had covered much of the plot with fixed plants (rhubarb, blackberries), shrubs, trees, ornamental items such as bamboo and lots of herbs. Many had gone 'wild' and original delineations of beds and between different plants had been destroyed by expansion of plants, invasion by weeds and the general ravages of the elements. The mint, raspberries and strawberries had been particularly successful at colonising large parts.

A key feature of this part of the plot was, however, that the soil was, generally, in much better condition: whether because the bottom half was better drained (which was definitely the case); or because the cultivation had been more effective in years gone by wasn't clear.

Due to the timing of the allocation, it was not a good time to take the same approach as we had with the initial plot. It was the wrong time to dig it over as the soil wouldn't benefit from the action of the winter weather. Things were growing away with incredible vigour (a feature of weeds) and we didn't have a plan for it as we were busy with the initial part and hadn't really expected to receive that part just at that time.

We therefore opted for a partial attack, later on preparing a plan for the next year. We chopped the huge and rampant growth of blackberries back to a manageable size (70 per cent reduction). The plants had become moribund and this would give good, new, vigorous growth. We also dug a few parts of the plot over where the soil looked workable and created a few beds. The rest we left to fend for itself, occasionally tackling a piece when we had time.

There was a massive clump of bamboo at the very front of the plot, which was about 8 feet high, well over the limits allowed under the terms of the site lease. I cut that back to a more acceptable height – fortunately without disturbing any pandas – and ripped out the suckers, by means of which bamboo propagates. These had infiltrated the surrounding area and were making a break for the plot next door. It doesn't surprise me that pandas find it hard to breed or even survive very successfully living on bamboo. Bamboo is horribly hard (blunting and resisting the secateurs – so I had to resort to loppers) and lacking in nutrients; a bit like very twiggy cucumber in terms of food value-added – without even the liquid. I used the branches I lopped off to make canes – naturally.

I didn't want to destroy the small trees that were there, because trees are vital to bio-diversity and the environment, but decided to move them to the site boundary to plug a few gaps in the hedge. As the best time to move them is in autumn they were left *in situ* for the time being. This was actually a bit of a nuisance due to the root systems and the fact that they got in the way of our plans – but it seemed the greenest and most environmentally friendly option.

Some of the shrubs I cut hard back to tidy them up. A dogwood, although having branches of a very pleasant red, was extending its roots across a lot of the surrounding area from where it was placed. I cut it right back to the ground – after which it would spring up again – and I also chopped back the root system. Some very wild and rambling roses were given a 'short back and sides' to tidy them up. They did give us some very lovely blooms later on though.

A voyage of discovery

We found many strawberries all over the place, so we created a bed for some and sold the rest on produce days. We created a new raspberry bed, buying in new stems and transplanting a few older plants there as well. We placed one of our 'three sisters' sites in the new part of the plot as well and created an asparagus bed – finding out later on, as the growth pushed through, that there was the sad remains of a similar bed not too far away struggling to compete with a whole panoply of wild plants and invasive weeds.

That still left an awful lot more for later on in the year. We put the rest of the front plot on the 'do later' pile and got on with the other portion, occasionally attacking particularly high or noxious weeds and growths just to keep it tidy.

The lurker in the soil!

As the year progressed, something that hadn't been apparent earlier on became obvious – the new plot was totally overrun with convolvulus. The previous holder thought it was pretty (give me strength!). Convolvulus is an incredibly vigorous and tenacious plant that grows like wildfire and binds itself to other plants, hence its other name: bindweed. It is so bad that its common name actually contains the word weed. It eventually strangles the plants that it has grown round – a real pest!

The *Henry Doubleday Encyclopaedia of Organic Gardening* told me that it was Hedge Bindweed (*Calystegia* (convolvulus) *sepium*) and that it was extremely difficult to eradicate, spreading by underground, white, brittle stems that you can't even see, and that it is probably not worth trying to get rid of it where it is established. Bindweed roots can reach a staggering depth of 30 feet!

Thank god the soil isn't that deep. We took miles and miles of its roots out as we excavated – but it is still there. This is one of our longer-term projects or crusades – eradicate the bindweed.

Each piece will grow into a new plant if given a chance, and spread to other plot-holders' land, who will hate you. Burn every piece you can find.

Our site

Our society is not on a large site, having about 50–60 plot-holders depending on your definition. Many are half plots. We are extremely lucky with the location as it is very secluded; fully enclosed by hedges and fences – which keep out unwanted visitors (dogs and vandals) – and well situated for sun, generally. It is bounded by woods on one side which favours good wildlife – even if some visitors (pigeons) are not so welcome as others (frogs and toads) – and the very interesting Cox's Walk is another of our boundaries.

The soil is typical London clay, but although it is heavy to work, and holds water too well, it is also full of nutrients which, with the addition of manure and compost to unlock them, provide an excellent growing medium – unfortunately for weeds as well as our own produce. There are also a couple of small ponds which give a welcome haven to amphibians and others which are the 'good guys' as far as slug control goes, and encourage dragonflies which can be seen flying all over the site. Ponds are essential to organic growing – see Part III.

The allotment society has been in existence for over a hundred years and one of the prize possessions is a magnificent mahogany shield with solid silver badges for 'best allotment' going back to 1907. The site itself used to be known as Alleyn's Nursery in the nineteenth century and goes back even further – history as yet untraced, but we are looking into this.

Who will you meet on allotments?

The old stereotype of Northern men in cloth caps keeping racing pigeons or 'East Enders' with whippets has changed. On most sites the holders are an extremely eclectic mix of all sorts of people and with far more women. This is good as it changes the perspective and brings new dimensions to sites. There are also many more family-run plots and therefore children.

On our site we have, among others, retired print workers, secretaries, a conservation officer, artists, nurses, the unemployed, a doctor or two, the odd accountant, teachers, a surveyor and many others (even a management consultant and author!). They are from many different colours, creeds and nationalities, including English, Welsh, Scots, Irish (North and South), Turkish, Bengali, Dutch, Spanish, Sri Lankan, Latin American and others I have no doubt forgotten. We also have plots that are run by families – sometimes several generations, couples, friends that share, and so on.

It is a good mix and most get along fine and pitch in with events and fund-raising, although there are a few backsliders, Marleys and Scrooges.

This will probably reflect the site that you eventually end up with, although rural sites will probably be more homogeneous than inner-city sites.

③

Getting Started

Carrying out a diagnosis

Once you have obtained your plot it is essential to find out what you have got. You must carry out a **diagnosis**. When you go to a doctor, he or she does not know what is wrong with you and so they carry out an investigation into your problem: the diagnosis. What are the symptoms? How do you feel? What happens if you do X or Y? Then they prescribe medicine or treatment, ie what you need to do to solve the issue.

In business situations or when starting anything new it is the same. The first thing that you do is find out what is going on. You must understand the situation thoroughly. You must do this for your plot because it will tell you what is there, and allow you to understand the limits or constraints on what you can and cannot do. Otherwise you will try to grow things that will not thrive or you will be overtaken in the growing stakes by well-established weeds, and you will suffer disappointment and become downhearted.

Constraints example

If you have ever wondered why freight trains seem to go on for miles while most passenger trains have only a few coaches despite the power and size of the engines pulling them, it is because of one of the key **constraints or limits** on carrying people: the length of platforms. Your train cannot be longer than the available platform, generally speaking, or the passengers cannot embark and disembark safely. Freight trains are not subject to that constraint and so they can load the engines up. When I was working in Kazakhstan (yes it is a real place and not made up by Borat) a freight train went through a level crossing, scaring the camels (Bactrian) and took about 15 minutes to go past.

Your diagnosis

This exercise is essentially about examining the key aspects of the plot and the surrounding site, etc. You need to understand the implications of what you have got as it will constrain what you can do – you can't grow brassicas easily in acidic soil. You then need to match your findings with what you want to do, and produce a plan to effect that – reflecting your discoveries. This may mean changing your original ideas on what you were going to grow, or changing aspects of the plot make-up where you can (eg, improving the soil).

What shape is your plot?

Plots come in all shapes and sizes depending on the configuration of the site. We have all sorts of shapes on our particular site. Some are long; some broad; others squeezed in between paths and the boundary. Most are, of course, (ir)regular rectangles, but there are plenty of other shapes.

What shape is your plot?

Typical shapes are regular rectangles, as below…

…but can in fact be any shape – depending on the site dimensions

Whatever the shape, however, it does not constrain *what* you grow. It will impact on some things, though. You cannot grow a 20 foot row of beans if your plot is only 10 feet wide. But you could have two 10 foot rows.

Diagnosis

What do you need to know?

This involves the following:

- Understanding the dimensions of the plot, ie what area do you have to play with?

- Where am I in relation to the water supply? Water is heavy and you will get to know watering cans extremely well in the course of your allotment experience.

- Where is North?

- What grows around me?

- What soil type do I have?

- What is growing/has been grown before?

- What is the climate – generally; and the specific micro-climate for the site?

Getting to know your plot

Why do you need to know these things? Well it is absolutely vital to know where North is. This is because sunlight is one of the three key elements for good plant growth (see Understanding the Basics). You must, therefore, find out where the sun is in relation to your plot, and how it moves across the plot/site. Most sunlight is received on the south side of an area and if there is, for example, a row of very high trees to the south of your plot your sunlight will be very limited indeed (to say nothing of the soil depletion from the trees' roots).

Draw a sketch of the plot and mark where North is. Visit the plot at different times of the day to see how the sun and shade change. A good way to do this is to take a chair and sit on the plot on a fine day: with a supply of drink, and something to read (such as this book), making notes on the sun's position from time to time. Working without working!

In the diagram below there are two plots shown on the same site: plots A and B. The differences between them are apparent when the path of the sun and the situation of the trees are plotted.

Geographical location

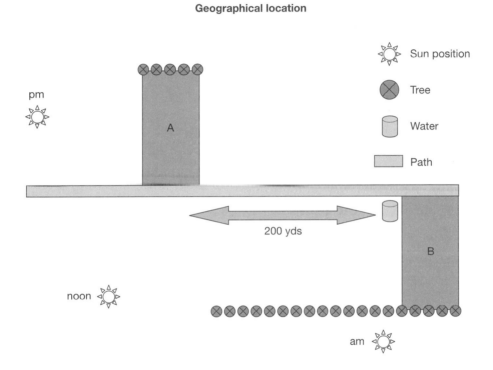

Plot A has trees on the NNW aspect of the plot and none on the southern aspect and therefore receives full sun. Plot B, however, has several trees on the SSE side and therefore will be in shade for much of the morning. So crops grown in the bottom area will receive a lot less sunlight than others. Depending on the type and height of the trees it might be even worse – nothing grows under beech trees, for example.

On the bright side, however, Plot B is very near the water source, whereas the plot holder for A has to lug it 200 yards or more: and he (and you) will be spending a lot of time watering in the hotter, drier months.

What is the soil like?

The soil is what your crops will grow in. It is essential, therefore, to understand the composition and the implications of this. You are going to have a
long relationship with your soil – so get to know it. Understand what it can
do for you; and what you can/need to do to improve it. As the Bible says,
each man must eat a peck (a quarter of a bushel – two gallons) of dirt
before he dies. That is a lot of dirt, so make sure yours is healthy!

At the beginning of this book there is a phrase:

Look after the soil and it will look after you.

This is, if you like, the bedrock of organic gardening (pun intended). There
is nothing more important than looking after the soil. It provides the growing medium through which food and water are absorbed, and a home for
all those beneficial micro-organisms that make soil a good place to grow
crops. Focus here then is priority number one. Treat the soil well.

Where soil came from

The soil that you find on your allotment will be a result of two things:

- the *geology* of the location (the make-up of the rocks); and

- what has *happened to it* over time through natural growth, cultivation
  and other things.

The first determines the physical make-up of the soil, sometimes called the
texture; the second determines its **structure**. You cannot change the fundamental soil type or texture, but you can alter the structure by adding
organic matter.

The more you work your soil, the better you will understand it. It is best,
however, to start to analyse and understand your soil characteristics
straight away, as this will save you time and trouble later on (planting
acidic-loving blueberries on a chalky site is doomed to failure).

4

Getting to Know Your Soil

Soil is so important that I am going to devote a whole chapter to it. It is the be all and end all of your site. Get to know all about it; its strengths and its limitations.

What is soil?

Soil has arisen over millions of years through the erosion of rocks by the actions of weather (rain, ice, sun, wind, etc) and the vicissitudes (good word huh?) of nature (earthquakes, submersion by the sea, glacial activities, uprising land, etc); from chemical activities as different elements mix in; and the enrichment with organic matter produced by animals (manure) and the results from the death and decay of living organisms (animal and plant). It takes about a thousand years to create an inch of soil from rock.

The above accounts for about half the volume of soil; the other half is a mix of air pockets and water. The composition of the rocks that have been eroded down forms the type of soil and also affects the proportion of air and water. In some circumstances, soil can hold *about 1,500 tons of water per acre* (3,800 metric tonnes per hectare).

The main types of soil

The main types of soil are:

- Clay.

- Silt.

- Sand.

- Chalk.

- Peat.

Each has different-sized particles (granularity) and therefore each type holds water and air in different proportions.

Clay is composed of the tiniest particles which are infinitesimally small; almost dust when separated out. These fine particles, when wet, stick together in clumps to form a solid mass. Lifting a very full spade of wet, sticky clay can seriously damage your back – so be careful. Dry clay metamorphoses into a hard, solid mass which is extremely difficult to work (take it from me). It is, however, very fertile, containing many nutrients – but they are locked up and difficult for plants to access.

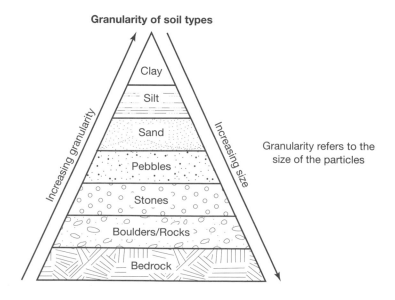

Granularity of soil types

Clay
Silt
Sand
Pebbles
Stones
Boulders/Rocks
Bedrock

Increasing granularity

Increasing size

Granularity refers to the size of the particles

Silt is composed of slightly larger particles than clay. It is often laid down by rivers, and estuaries and flood plains benefit from it (eg in China the Yellow River basin and in Egypt the Nile delta). Not only does silt hold water well, but as the particles are larger it drains better than clay. It is also, however, very fertile like clay and an excellent growing medium – so it is the best of both worlds. That is why despite the obvious dangers from living in areas subject to massive flooding by large and dangerous rivers, many people fight to live in alluvial plains.

The word desert is from the Ancient Egyptian 'Deshret' which means essentially the 'Red land', ie pure sand – without the fertility given by the annual flooding of the Nile; which land they termed 'Black land' and is where they grew their crops in a thin ribbon following the Niles course. It was the need to predict and tame the annual Nile flooding for the fertile, alluvial soil it deposited and the fresh water for irrigation; that gave rise to the Egyptian civilisation. Even today the majority of Egypt's 80 million inhabitants still live in a thin strip that runs along the Nile – the rest is still desert.

Sand is composed of small pieces of rock, often quartz or sandstone, but still very small grains – just as you see on the beach, where it is great for sandcastles. Sand, however, although it is dead easy to dig, as a soil is very poor at holding water and often contains few nutrients, so it is not at all fertile. It is particularly susceptible to being blown away. It also creeps as it is driven by the wind, eating up good soil. This is a severe issue in some areas, especially when coupled with erosion. It is highly likely, for example, that China's capital city Beijing will disappear under the Gobi Desert in the foreseeable future as it is advancing rapidly across China! This is, however, unlikely to occur on your allotment – at least not soon! In hotter, drier climates sand may be all that there is. If climate change continues as predicted then perhaps southern parts of the UK will have to come to terms with sand!

Pebbles and stones are larger pieces of rock that haven't yet been eroded or worn down and are often present in soil. They can help drainage, but can cause problems for plants. Some areas seem to grow stones, particularly after rain, which washes soil off them and they appear to have risen through the ground, like plant shoots. You could spend your entire life taking them out – but it isn't necessary. In general plants can cope with them, although new seedlings will suffer if you don't prepare their seed bed properly.

Rocks and boulders are very large and not usually found in soil, but occur where soil is poor and top soil thin, eg on hills.

Soil is usually a mixture of types

Of course, soil can be a mixture of the different types of soil and different particles, and most soils do indeed contain a mixture of the different types, but it is the predominant type that will give the soil its name. For example, soil that has a greater proportion of sand will be called (with remarkable imagination) a sandy soil. All soils except peat are composed of broken-down minerals.

Sometimes it is easy to see what type of soil you have – in some cases it is less obvious. There are a few simple tests that you can do to establish types.

Loam sweet loam

Take a handful of soil, add some water and try to roll it into a ball. If it easily goes into a sticky ball or a sausage shape then you probably have **Clay** (groan).

If the water drains through easily then it is probably **Sandy** (slight groan).

Silt lies in between these two extremes (sigh of relief).

Look also at the composition of the soil.

Soil that is a good mixture of clay, silt and sand is called loam – and fortunate is the gardener who has this on their allotment.

Chalky soil will usually be 'thin' or shallow with white lumps of chalk (or flint) in it; soil from 'Downs' is often like this. Chalk arises only where the land was once part of a seabed. It is the result of a process in which the dead shells of billions of sea creatures have been deposited, over millions of years in an almost unimaginable process to form what is called sedimentary rock.

This soil will be alkaline (see below) and some plants just will not grow in it so don't bother planting them. Brassicas, however, will love it (groan – unless you like sprouts!). Indicator plants include cowslip, primrose, clover and daisies.

Peaty soil tends to be very dark, very acid, extremely wet in winter – and can be very dry in summer (groan). It is, however, and paradoxically, very rich in organic matter, because the acid conditions in which it occurs prevent the organic matter from decomposing. Because of the high levels of organic matter, unlike clay, peaty soil cannot be rolled into a ball. Brassicas hate it. If it dries out then it can be the devil to get moist again. It used to be used as an additive to other soils, but as this destroys natural peat habitats this is now considered a poor gardening procedure and not organic. Adding organic matter to it in quantity, however, makes a fine soil (hooray).

Loam is a good mixture of all components and is what everyone wants (cheering, stamping of feet, loud applause and popping of champagne corks!).

> Clay soil is often referred to as 'heavy' soil.
>
> Sandy soil is 'light'.
>
> Loam is 'medium'.

Our site (as is most of London) is clay and therefore requires masses of organic matter to break it up, make it easier to work, and release the nutrients. When this organic matter has been worked in, however, it does provide a great growing medium. If the soil has a grey look, then it is probably anaerobic – not a dance workout but a lack of air – and needs to be turned over and broken up to allow air in. Adding organic matter at the same time will also help.

There are three levels of soil (the scientific word for them is 'soil horizons'):

- Top soil.
- Subsoil.
- Bedrock.

They can vary in depth across the country and even locally.

The key characteristics of each are as follows:

- **Top soil** – the level that you first encounter. It is usually darker in colour because it contains the organic matter. It can range from 2 inches (5 cm) – if you are really unlucky – to 24 inches (60 cm) depending on the geological history. Intense cultivation involving the incorporation of lots of organic matter will increase the depth of the top soil. Poor cultivation and erosion by nature and the elements will reduce it. The depth of top soil in an allotment or garden can give you an indication of the effort that has gone into creating it, when you compare it with the surrounding uncultivated soil.

  It takes a year of intensive digging and incorporation of organic matter into subsoil to create one inch of top soil. So if your top soil is, say, ten inches deeper than that which surrounds it, then it took, as a minimum, ten years to create it. If you allow that it probably wasn't always cultivated with that level of intensity, then it probably took even longer. Deep-rooted crops such as parsnips and carrots like around 12 inches to 15 inches of top soil – so if you started from scratch with subsoil it would be years before you could grow them.

- **Subsoil** will be indicated by a change in colour to a lighter shade. This is because it will contain little organic matter – but will hold water. Deep roots will often penetrate into this level. The nature of the subsoil will affect drainage: sand will drain freely – clay will not. It takes an estimated thousand years to create an inch of subsoil – so looking at the depth will give you an idea of how long it took to create.

- **Bedrock**. Where soil levels are shallow then you may encounter bedrock, which is no good for cultivation. In this case, raised beds will probably be a very good idea (see later).

To find out the relative depths, a simple way is just to dig a hole. It varies as to how far you need to go, but a yard (metre) should suffice. As you dig you will see the different layers and you can measure their respective depths.

A note on Latin names. Even if you took Latin at school, as I did, then the Latin names are still a bit of a mouthful. I give them in some cases to be helpful because they are a global standard terminology. Asking for a plant using the local name may result in blank looks in other countries – or even in different parts of the UK – but the Latin names are standard. Don't worry: you don't need to know them – you can always look them up.

This is the list of the Latin names in the classification of a tomato:

Kingdom:	Plantae
Subkingdom:	Tracheobionta
Division:	Magnoliophyta
Class:	Magnoliopsida
Subclass:	Asteridae
Order:	Solanales
Family:	Solanaceae
Genus:	Solanum
Species:	S. lycopersicum

No, it doesn't mean anything to me either – except that it is a plant!

But I love its Latin species name: Lycopersicum – Wolf Peach!

Note that there may be variations in soil type across the allotment, especially if some parts have been cultivated differently from others. On our plot, although the top soil is generally at least a foot deep, surprisingly in one area it was only a few inches deep and unwittingly I dug lots of clay subsoil to the surface, which was really unhelpful for the crops we grew there initially.

One of the benefits of understanding your soil is so that you can make sure you either put the right crops in that will thrive there or you strive to alter the soil to accommodate others.

If you have *clay* soil (as we do) then some crops – potatoes and the brassica family (cabbages, sprouts, broccoli), for example – will love it. This is curious as potatoes hail from the mountains of Peru where the soil is almost certainly not clay, but clay is packed full of nutrients and potatoes, like all members of that family (solanaceae), are hungry feeders. Plants to look out for that indicate clay soil are docks, thistles, plantains, buttercups and bluebells. If I didn't know it before, when I saw all of those growing I knew it would be clay soil on my plot.

If you have **sandy** soil then others – for example roots such as beetroots, parsnips and carrots – will love that. This is because they adapt to particular environments and the closer that you can get to their environment or pre-ferred growing soil the better they will grow. Broom and gorse love sand.

Of course – almost anything will grow in **loam**!

You have probably noticed the recurring theme – adding organic matter will improve your soil, whatever type it is! If you only take one thing from this book, take this.

What grows around me?
Looking at what is growing on the plots around you – especially those that are not very well cultivated – will tell you what plants like to grow in your locale. Be nosey!

Large nettles and thistles mean that your soil is likely to be rich. Lots of brambles, convolvulus and buttercups mean that you are likely to be infested with difficult to eradicate perennial weeds and a clay soil (and don't I know it!). Heathers mean the soil will be acid. If you see healthy brassicas then it probably means that they will thrive, although you obviously need to check if they have been given helping hands, such as massive liming, etc.

If you can't see any of a particular type of plant that you might normally expect to be grown on allotments – eg carrots or tomatoes or potatoes – then ask why this is the case – if they haven't told you. If there are lots of raised beds, then this might also indicate a problem with the soil – or disease.

Also asking your fellow plot-holders what they find works well helps; however, it cannot be taken as gospel, as what works on one particular plot may not work on yours due to a whole host of factors (soil history, disease, pests, etc).

Analysing soil

A good way of looking at the mixture of sand, silt, clay and organic material that you have is to use the 'soil and water in a jam-jar' technique – which is very simple.

- Fill a jam-jar one-third full with soil.

- Add water until the jar of soil is almost full.

- Stir thoroughly.

- Let the mixture settle for about an hour.

You should now be able to see what mixture you have as they will form different layers.

Soil analysis

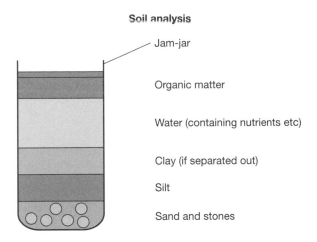

Jam-jar

Organic matter

Water (containing nutrients etc)

Clay (if separated out)

Silt

Sand and stones

The heaviest particles will be sand. Any small stones or pebbles will also fall to the bottom.

The next level will be silt, as these particles are smaller than sand and less dense, so they float a little above the bottom. Clay, if separated out, will appear above the silt. If you have thick clay then you will probably just get a clumpy collection at the bottom. On top of these layers is the separate water level. This is unlikely to be clear as it will contain dissolved nutrients, etc. Finally, floating on the top like jetsam and flotsam, is the solid (ie not decomposed) organic matter.

If you measure the relative height of each layer you can get a feel for what your soil is composed of – ignoring the water element which you added. For those with a mathematical bent, you could then draw a pie-chart.

This is also a great thing for your children to do. You could also get a class during a school trip to do this from several plots and see if there is any difference (with plot-holders' permission and appropriately instructed and supervised.)

Carry out this experiment with soil from several areas of your site, to get an overall feel and avoid any unusual 'local conditions'.

Soil can also be just about any colour. Depending on the contents it can range from creamy-white through yellow, red, brown and black. (As noted above, a grey colour means it is lacking in air.)

What else is in my soil?

Soil does not just consist of eroded rock, air and water. It obviously contains nutrients (we hope) in different amounts depending on the type. You may in some cases find lots of stones. These can also affect the way crops grow (see Preparing the Ground). There may well be 'rubbish' from previous plot-holders that has been buried – this must be taken out.

When your site has a skip, get there early: you will be surprised how quickly it fills up!

An initial exploration of our site led us to discover a veritable cornucopia of rubbish. We found pieces of broken glass where old cold frames used to be; bottles and bits of wood; plastic bags and carpet remnants subsumed into the soil; and occasionally paving slabs that had been a path of some sort but had become overgrown (hitting those with a spade or a fork is an interesting experience!).

Most well-run allotment sites (like ours) will organise communal skips on a few days throughout the year and this is extremely useful in clearing the plot. Prepare by getting the rubbish in a heap ready to go at the end of your plot nearest to where the skip will be. It pays to be careful when digging things out, as you may find such items as water pipes that may or may not be still in use.

Air and water

As mentioned earlier, air and water are contained in the 'gaps' between the particles of soil. The size of these gaps (granularity) determines what is there. The larger gaps usually contain air, but not usually water. It is normally the smaller gaps that hold the water, and this is where the roots take it from. Soil with a good balance of larger and smaller gaps, eg silt and loam, will drain well but also hold water in a way that facilitates take-up by roots. Waterlogged or very wet soil arises where water has replaced air in the larger gaps and it will not drain away. A good indication of waterlogged soil, or poor drainage, is standing pools of water after rain. Our plot, when we got it, was a good example of this. One year later, after the incorporation of masses of organic matter, this was no longer the case.

Organisms

More important, however, is the fact that the soil is full of living organisms. Most of these organisms are beneficial, breaking down organic matter or aerating the soil. Some, however, are pests. The organisms present will include not only those that you can see with the naked eye – earthworms, centipedes, woodlice, beetles and, unfortunately, slugs and millipedes – but will also include – in their millions – micro-organisms: bacteria and fungi. A gram of soil will contain 10 million bacteria! Good, rich organic soil that promotes a soil organism bio-diversity will ensure that the good organisms far outweigh the harmful ones and keep their depravations in check.

One of the perverse consequences of indiscriminate usage of pesticides and herbicides is that it kills off many of the good creatures as well. Of course, it is those creatures we regard as pests that come back faster than the 'good guys', and then find that their life is easy as the natural balance has been disturbed in their favour, ie their natural predators have been killed off as well. Organic gardening is designed to redress this imbalance and ensure that the beneficial organisms and animals are there to keep the pests in check naturally.

NB: Slugs still need special attention! See Problems – pests.

The pH measure of the soil

What's this then?

A lot of gardening books talk about the pH of the soil. Most of us will remember this from chemistry as the measure of alkalinity or acidity. It is not necessary, however, to be a chemist to understand it. (Phew! I hear you say.) The pH just tells you what the basic nature of the soil is. This is useful because some plants prefer slightly acid conditions (eg blueberries, strawberries, potatoes) and others (brassicas) prefer soil that is alkaline.

The scale runs from 1 (extremely acidic) to 14 (extremely alkaline), with a pH of 7 representing neutral – where acid and alkaline balance perfectly. We all tested substances in school using litmus paper which changes colour: red being acid, purple alkaline and light green or amber neutral.

For those who are interested, pH stands for *potency of Hydrogen* and is recorded on a log scale. So between, say, 6 and 7 it is ten times the difference, but between 6 and 9 it is thousand times the difference. This clearly will have an impact on how plants grow!

It is also an indicator of the presence or absence of nutrients in the soil. The type of soil will determine what is available to your crops. Most nutrients or minerals are more likely to be available in soil that is of a slightly more acidic nature. Highly acidic soils, however, are more likely to lack calcium and potassium, whereas alkaline soils are less likely to contain iron and zinc.

If you look at a geological map of the UK it will show the broad (very broad) soil types found across the UK. You will see that there is a large lump of what is called Weald clay around London (which is where we live), surrounded by chalk. We then have the downs before running into the rest which is pretty much hilly and or mountainous.

This landscape will affect your soil.

Some approximate indicators of pH

Extremely acidic	2.0–4.5	stomach acid, lemon juice, vinegar
Highly acidic	4.5–5.5	beer, tomatoes, carrots
Slightly acid	6.0–6.5	milk
Neutral	7.0	water, blood
Slightly alkaline	7.4–8.2	eggs, sea water
Highly alkaline	8.2–10.0	sodium bicarbonate
Very alkaline	11.0–14.0	ammonia, lime, battery acid

(Note that despite being called battery 'acid' it is in fact alkaline!)

Most UK soil has a range that is somewhere between 4 and 8; and most plants prefer to grow in a range of 5.5 to 7.5. Vegetables, in general, like a pH of between 6.5 and 7.0 (slightly acidic to neutral), whereas fruit generally prefers it to be slightly more acidic (say 6.0 to 6.5). Brassicas like it to be in the range 7.0 to 8.0.

What makes soil acidic or not?

It is largely the presence (or absence) of one thing – calcium – the basis of chalk and limestone. This can be leached out by rain, especially in sandy soils, and it tends to be replaced by more 'acidic' elements such as aluminium or iron. As a general rule, therefore, soil formed in areas with higher rainfall is more acidic than those formed in drier areas.

Cultivation also tends to increase acidity because the deterioration of organic matter releases carbon dioxide which forms acidic solutions.

These statements are not, however, absolute.

Some plants have adapted to survive in more extreme levels of acid and alkaline, eg peat (acid) – loving ericas and heathers or rhododendrons. And if you see reedy grass or lots of moss it is also probably peaty with poor drainage, whereas rosemary and grapevines love chalky soil (alkaline) – the Champagne region is pure chalk.

What does this mean for me?
The soil pH also affects plants in other ways. Potatoes can suffer more from blight in alkaline soils, whereas this is a positive factor for the brassica family, as it helps to reduce incidence of clubroot. When rotating plants, liming is frequently carried out just before brassicas are planted out – but never for potatoes.

As a rule of thumb – if you have scum on your water then it is hard and your area is alkaline; but if you have soft water then it is likely to be acidic.

Earthworms do not like very acidic conditions, nor do many of the micro-organisms that cause the beneficial decomposition of organic matter. This is one of the reasons why peaty soil is full of un-decomposed organic matter.

Testing pH
You can buy a kit from a garden centre or shop to test the pH. It is very easy but I have never bothered, although it might be useful if there is a history of issues with soil acidity. If you do test the soil, remember to test it from several different locations as recent activity in a particular area of your plot may affect it (eg if an area has been limed or manured this will swing it one way or another).

You can use litmus paper, by mixing a solution of soil with distilled water (pH 7.0) and then inserting the strip (just as in chemistry lessons). If the soil is alkaline the paper turns blue – if acid red.

You can also buy (or better still borrow, if you can) an electronic pH meter. Here you put the rod into the soil and it measures the pH.

One way to test the pH could be with hydrangeas (no they are not a football team). They produce pink/red flowers in alkaline soils, but blue flowers if the soil is acidic – fine if you want hydrangeas! Perversely, the hydrangea flower colours are *the opposite way round* from those of the litmus test!

A useful reason for knowing the pH is to assist in diagnosing issues with plant growth. Often the things that you see are symptoms. You might diagnose magnesium deficiency, but it may be that the real reason for it is because of the pH of the soil, not a lack of the mineral. Your actions would, therefore, probably be different if you knew that it was the acidity of the soil preventing the minerals release, rather than a basic lack. Similarly, knowing that your soil is alkaline would deter you from adding lime, as that can hinder the release of nutrients.

Here is a general analysis of the acidity or alkalinity of different types of soil:

pH indicator	Soil type
4	Upland peat
5	Pine forest and heathland
6	Deciduous forests
7	Agricultural farmland, fenland
8	Chalk and limestone soils

Notice that very few soil types fall outside the range 4–8.

Below is a list of some plants and their tolerance of/preference for acid or alkaline soil:

Acid	Alkaline
Blueberry	Asparagus
Carrot	Beetroot
Citrus fruits	Brussels sprouts
Cranberries	Broccoli
Endive	Cauliflower
Potato	Grapevines
Radish	Leeks
Rhubarb	Onions
Strawberry	Shallots

Note that providing the pH is not too extreme (outside 4.0 to 8.0) – most plants will be OK although they might not thrive depending on their preferences.

(5)

Digging

This is exactly what it says – digging over the soil. The pros and cons are listed below.

Dig v No dig

There are two schools of thought on digging. Some people swear by it: others never do it. They claim that it is not from laziness but because it is better for the soil, as digging doesn't occur in nature. This is not quite true, as anyone who has seen pigs and other animals in action grubbing up soil will attest. Even cows will cut up soil as they walk on it if it is wet. Of course, rabbits, moles and other burrowers also disturb the soil – but you don't want them in the middle of your plot!

It is obvious that there are arguments for and against and it is up to you what you decide to do. There are no real rights and wrongs, however – it is the results you achieve that count.

There are two main types of digging. They are known as 'single digging' and 'double digging'. The difference refers to the depth that you dig – not that it is twice as hard – although obviously greater effort is involved in the latter. A single dig is the depth of a spade – a 'spit'. Double digging goes down twice as far as this – two spits (or a 'phlegm').

On our site you will see both approaches. The pros and cons are as follows:

Dig v No dig

Dig

Pros

- Breaks up the soil
- Aerates the soil
- Improves drainage
- Brings pests to the surface where they can be eaten
- Buries weeds
- Allows incorporation of organic matter deeply
- Lets you pick out perennial roots
- Good exercise!

Cons

- Involves some effort
- Can release dormant seeds
- May bring sub-soil up if you are not careful

No Dig

Pros

- No effort required
- Doesn't not disturb relationship between top soil and subsoil
- You do not compact the soil by walking on it
- Can improve drainage
- Claimed to be more 'organic'

Cons

- Will not get perennial weeds out
- Will not break up the soil, especially if it is heavy, eg clay
- Needs masses of organic substance

Digging technique

- Mark out the area to be dug.

- Divide it in two with string and mark out the dividing line.

- Excavate a trench across half of the area about one and a half feet wide.

- Throw the soil onto the area just in front of where you are digging, turning it upside down to expose roots to the air and bury any weeds.

- Take out roots as you go.

- Chuck in some compost across the trench and even it out.

- Dig out the next foot and a half of soil immediately behind the first, working backwards from the end and throwing the soil on top of the compost, turning it over to bury plants and filling in the first trench.

- Carry on until you get to the end of the first half, then work back down the other half.

- When you get to the last trench in the second half, use the soil from the first trench on the other side to fill it in.

- Don't break down the clods.

- Leave it to be weathered over winter – let the rain take the strain.

Double digging is similar except that you use a slightly wider trench. You then either dig out the soil to twice the depth or you dig down one spit and then loosen the soil with a fork before adding the compost.

Double digging breaks up the harder, more compacted soil below one spit depth. This improves the drainage and allows the roots of crops to penetrate deeper and more easily in search of moisture and nutrients. You will also get bigger crops. Long-rooted crops need over a foot, so if you have a hard pan of soil within that depth their growth will be severely stunted.

On our plot, when we tackled the top part I double dug it, taking out two spits *and* then loosening the soil below that as well, before throwing in masses of manure – sort of two and a half times, or triple digging. We took out enough roots, it seemed, to fill a skip – and the perennials still kept coming up later on!

Tips

- Take it easy. Do not try to excavate the whole plot in one go – you will do yourself serious damage and come to hate digging (of course you might hate it anyway).

- 10 to 20 minutes to begin with is fine, then take a break and do something else – gentle weeding, cutting back shrubs, have a cup of tea or hot soup on a cold day, etc.

- It really does pay to go through a stretching routine *before* you start – not afterwards as most do.

- Straighten up from time to time and rest.

- Making two insertions – one at 90° to the first – will make it easier to extract the soil.

- Let nature work for you. Gravity will pull the soil off the spade if you let it (as long as the soil isn't so wet that it sticks).

- Use a good-quality sharp spade. (For much of the plot I used a fork as it was the only way to penetrate the soil.)

- Do not overload the tool that you use. This is especially important when using a fork as it tends to take out very large clods when the soil is wet.

- The best time to dig is in late autumn – all crops have been harvested and the soil is not too wet; and you will have four to five months for weathering of the clods. We had to dig in January which was much harder as the soil was very wet and it was colder – it kept me warm though. It also meant that we had less time for weathering – and in one or two parts (those that I dug last) this did cause a bit of a problem when we came to plant as the soil was still rock hard and hadn't been broken down adequately.

- Try not to bring up too much of the subsoil. This is infertile and will take some time (years) to break down fully, requiring the addition of yet more organic material. On the other hand, afterwards you will have increased the levels of top soil considerably!

- Leave the soil in big lumps – it exposes a greater surface area to the elements.

- The earlier you finish the digging the more time you will have for the weather to get to work by soaking, drying, thawing and freezing the clods so that they break down.

In spring, after nature has done its job, you will need to flatten the lumps out. I usually do this by bashing them with the back of a spade or fork. If you are really lucky and have light soil, you might only need to rake it.

Raised beds

For many who follow the No dig philosophy, raising up their beds is part of the *raison d'etre* (nothing to do with Lazarus!).

What is a raised bed?

It is quite simply a part of the ground under cultivation that is raised up from the normal ground level. This might be just a few inches or so, or for a disabled gardener it could be several feet.

If you like, it is a very large container.

For those adopting the No dig philosophy, virtually any bed soon becomes a raised bed as more and more organic matter is progressively added.

The reasons advanced for using a raised bed are as follows:

- Drainage is improved – especially true where the predominant soil type is clay.

- It will warm up more quickly than the surrounding ground.

- It can be (slightly) easier to cultivate (less far to bend).

- They can look neater and tidier than traditional beds (depending on who looks after them).

- Work can be carried out from the paths between the beds, avoiding compacting the soil.

- Concave beds have a slightly increased surface area.

- Less need for digging.

- Crops can be planted closer together, although they will probably be smaller as a result.

- Harvesting can be easier.

- It can be easier for those with age-related problems or size issues.

- It can be very visually appealing, especially if you plant trailing plants such as tumbling Toms, lobelias or nasturtiums at the edge to fall gently over the sides.

There are some disadvantages:

- Initial cost is greater – edging is required to hold the soil in.

- The edging must be raised as the bed rises.

- It needs replacing periodically.

- It can be labour intensive to set up.

- They have a tendency to dry out.

- Lots of organic matter is required every year, which is costly.

- Weeds (perennials) can be a problem, especially in the early years.

- Paths between raised beds become increasingly compacted as they are walked on and never altered or dug over. In my view this is not really an issue unless and until someone else takes over the plot and gets rid of the raised beds.

- They can only be four feet wide, otherwise you cannot reach the centre.

If you decide to utilise raised beds as part of your plot, it is important to include these in your plan. Key considerations are:

- They are usually 10 feet by 4 feet to facilitate access and make it easier to walk round them.

- Paths between them are usually covered in gravel, woodchips or bark, etc to stop them being eroded and getting muddy/waterlogged (they can be paved but that is expensive!).

- Paths should be wide enough to walk along – possibly wide enough for a wheelbarrow for moving organic matter, or a wheelchair if you are disabled.

- Choose an open, sunny position.

- Run the beds north/south to stop shading of plants.

- If they have to run east/west then grow taller crops on the north side – furthest from the sun.

- Choose your edging with care – functionality v beauty v cost.

- Mulching can help to maintain moisture levels as raised beds dry out quickly.

- Plan for rotation – it still applies – and remember the needs of the plants going in the bed next (eg brassicas: lime – potatoes: organic manure) – never together.

- For gardeners in wheelchairs, consider an arrangement where the bed is very much higher – rather like a table so that the chair can fit partially underneath to make access easier.

- Don't forget about drainage – raised beds can become waterlogged.

Improving the soil

There is no soil so bad – nor none so good – that it cannot be improved.

What does this mean?

It means putting in lots of organic matter. Whether it is manure, compost, leaf mould, seaweed, spent mushroom compost or a mulch doesn't matter – all organic material will rot down and decompose and add goodness.

It is a quasi-artificial/natural way of making what would normally happen in the outside world happen on your allotment (see Part III, Composting).

Get into the habit of keeping all compostable scraps separate from your rubbish and putting them into a compost heap. It can all go onto your allotment.

All soils can be improved:

- Clay soil benefits from organic matter as it breaks the heavy lumps down.

- It also encourages the release of the nutrients that are locked within clay soil.

- Sandy soil benefits as the organic matter bulks up the soil and allows it to retain more moisture and nutrients, which come from the organic matter.

- Loam – which is already good for crops – of course becomes even better.

- Adding organic matter to chalky soil improves it by adding bulk and reducing the alkalinity.

- Adding organic matter to peaty soils reduces the acidity and helps to release locked-in nutrients.

- It also makes water retention better in both peaty and chalky soils, allowing plants access to nutrients in a form that is accessible to roots.

- It helps enormously in preventing diseases, as it is more likely that the right minerals will be there to help the plants fight them off.

- It encourages beneficial animals and micro-organisms.

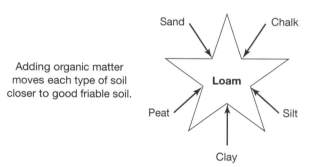

The holy grail of soil – loam

Adding organic matter moves each type of soil closer to good friable soil.

Although I have used neither, I have added details on permaculture and hydroponics, as these are in use in some areas. One of our nearest local allotment sites has a permaculture display.

Permaculture

This is a way of living that uses many organic principles. It is about blending the way humans live with nature. 'Permaculture uses the diversity, stability and resilience of natural ecosystems to provide a framework and guidance for people to develop their own solutions to the problems facing their world, on a local, national or global scale. It is based on a philosophy of cooperation with nature and caring for the earth and its people.' www.permaculture.org.uk

At its simplest, permaculture is about observing your surroundings to assist you in making choices and using as few resources as possible to achieve your aims. For example, placing things used most often in the garden nearer to your home so you can use time resources and energy more efficiently. It meshes well with organic principles. For example, it is about using output from one activity as input into others, such as using potato peelings as compost, thereby minimising wastage.

History

In the mid-1970s two Australian ecologists, Bill Mollinson and David Holmgren, started to develop ideas for creating stable agriculture systems as a positive response to the agri-business methods – rather like the organic movement and the Soil Association in the UK. They called this approach 'permaculture' and published it in *Permaculture One* in 1978. They then started to design permaculture plots. Since then it has spread all over the world and there are lots of courses and many people have adopted the permaculture lifestyle.

The ethical basis of permaculture is:

Care of the earth – provision that all life systems continue and multiply – fair shares for all life. There is only one earth – share it wisely and responsibly.

Care of people – giving people access to resources necessary to their existence, and looking after people at both community and individual level.

Setting limits to population and consumption – by governing needs, resources can be used to further the first two principles.

Hydroponics

This is a method of growing plants just using water, or rather mineral nutrient solutions, instead of soil. Plants can be grown with roots in water (hence the name from Greek for water – *Hydro;* and work or toil – *Ponos*) or in an inert medium such as perlite or gravel. Although it sounds like a modern process, it goes back hundreds of years. In fact, Babylonians and Aztecs used something like it.

The basic premise is that plants absorb the nutrients that they need through water within soil, but that soil is not actually needed – it is just the medium for access to nutrients. You can therefore introduce the nutrients via a mineral-rich liquid and the plants will grow happily. Almost any plants can grow this way. Watercress is a great example. Surprisingly, the mineral nutrient solutions were developed in the 1800s!

The earliest book on the subject was written by Sir Francis Bacon as long ago as 1626, published posthumously in 1627 and called *Sylva Sylvarum*. In 1699 John Woodward published his analysis of spearmint and found that it grew better in less-pure water than in distilled water – as there were nutrients in less-pure water. In the 1860s two German scientists developed the nutrient solutions and it became called 'solution culture'. This is now the term for hydroponics that doesn't use an inert medium (perlite, gravel). The name, however, was only coined in the 1930s changing from aquaculture to hydroponics, although why they changed it from Latin to Greek isn't clear to me.

Although the higher yields initially claimed for hydroponic crops are now thought to have been played up or exaggerated, there can be a great benefit as it gives plants access to the right amount of water, nutrients and oxygen and reduces the likelihood of over- and under-watering – the biggest issue for growers of plants. It requires special equipment and techniques so is probably not for regular allotment holders.

Growbags

A growbag is a useful way of cultivation which makes the soil type largely irrelevant. It is simply a plastic bag full of a growing medium (it varies depending on whether you are growing tomato/potatoes, squashes or citrus or other types of plants). You lay it flat on the ground, cut two diagonal slices that intersect in the middle of the bag, slot in the plants, firm them in and water them.

Note that growbags are not usually very deep, so they need intensive watering and feeding, and they will not develop deep root systems. They are particularly popular for tomatoes. You often see them on patios and window ledges. They are fairly uneconomical for allotments, unless you have disease present and are growing plants susceptible to it, or parts of the allotment are so poor that it will take years to improve them.

Containers are similar except that you fill them up yourself. (Make sure that there are holes for drainage, and plenty of stones or pots over the holes to facilitate drainage but stop from the soil being washed out.) We have used them very successfully on our patio at home for growing tumbling Tom tomatoes (which we also grow in hanging baskets) along with other herbs and plants. They hang over the edge and bask in the sun. They are deeper than growbags, so although they tend to dry out less easily, they still need looking after and feeding. They are not really necessary on allotments, however. A raised bed, you could say, is just a very big and flat container.

6

Climate

At this point I can hear many of you saying 'Why is climate important?' The answer is because it directly and continually affects your plot, and you cannot do anything about it.

Understanding climate and its impact on your allotment

What you can do, however, is to *understand* it. That is:

- how it will affect you;

- when it has the greatest effects (beneficial or otherwise); and

- what that means for you and your plants.

Then you can plan.

Your plan should aim to capitalise on the beneficial aspects and militate against the negative aspects as much as possible. Climate varies enormously, not only across the year – particularly in temperate 'seasonal' zones such as that in which the UK is situated (winter, spring, summer and autumn (or leaf-fall)) – but also across the country due to location, eg mountains or hills, plains, proximity to the coast, and where the prevailing wind blows from.

It would be very unusual for the climate to vary much across your site, but the impact on particular parts might be affected by local factors, eg trees might shelter one part more than others or a low wall may cause excessive turbulence.

The UK is a group of islands and therefore we experience far more climatic variations than our continental neighbours or those in the USA, although perhaps less extremes of temperature.

Parts of the country are very much wetter (the west usually receives more rain) – while some are very much drier (East Anglia). Even in small areas there can be variations.

For example, rain clouds are blown into southern Hants. They hit the Purbeck Hills and are forced up, dropping their water as rain to allow them to rise because dry clouds are lighter than moisture-carrying ones. As a result, the land in front of the Purbecks is very wet. One of my friends, whose family used to farm there, said that it was so wet in winter that they had to move the cattle to fields many miles away where it was drier. Behind the hills, however, it can be bone dry for much of the year. The profile of what grows well, therefore, can change just over the brow of a hill. (This will also affect the pH of the soil – see above.)

Some effects of climate:

- **Rain** will leach out nutrients and, if allowed to, wash top soil away. If rain water doesn't drain and is continually standing then it can cause quagmires to form. Of course, rain is nature's watering can and frequent light rain is just what you need throughout the year. In June 2007 there was a long period of terrific and torrential rain that caused a lot of damage to crops and widespread flooding. That wasn't what was wanted.

- **Wind** will dry plants out as it picks up moisture and carries it away. Plants that are exposed to a continual strong wind are often misshapen and stunted – see those on sea shores on the edge of woods for good examples. On the coast, winds are often salt-laden and this will affect plants – unless they have adapted, eg tamarinds.

- **Frost** will kill tender plants and ruin crops by literally nipping them in the bud if they are at that stage when the frost falls. Cold air is also heavy and will lurk at the bottom of hills or where it is trapped. If you have a sloping plot then cold air will flow down and if it meets a wall it will keep the frost in. Try to make gaps in whatever perimeter you have to allow cold air to flow away.

- **Temperature** Plants usually start to grow when the ambient soil temperature reaches 6° Centigrade, and then stop if it falls below this. Temperature falls 1° Centigrade with every 170 yards [150 m] increase in altitude – so 'spring' comes later on hillsides and winter arrives earlier. It is the same issue as you go further north.

Getting to the bottom of temperature. In olden times a farmer would drop his trousers and sit on the soil. If it was not warm enough to sit on comfortably he wouldn't sow. Perhaps best not to try this on your allotment!

Our situation

In Dulwich where we live we are surrounded on all sides by hills. These are not especially high but the local area has a micro-climate that can be completely different from the surrounding areas. It is a lot more sheltered, but strangely enough more prone to short hailstorms. I went off to play golf a few years ago at Beckenham, just over the hills (but not far away) and after two holes three inches of snow had fallen! When I returned to my house in Dulwich, Catherine and her parents were sitting outside in the sunshine – and refused to believe me when I said it had snowed two miles away – but the hills protected them from the storm.

The allotment site, though, is pretty well sheltered and winds are not usually an issue. It does tend to rain quite a lot though, so the plan needs to take that into account. With no rain though, being clay based, the soil dries out very quickly. The whole site is on a gentle southish-facing slope so that water generally runs down. Our plot is at the top end but, due to the composition of the soil, wetter at the top than below. However, the site is also famous or infamous (if you hold an allotment) for springs and streams (in the eighteenth century the area was noted as a spa area and the gentry would come to take 'Dulwich waters') and these can suddenly pop up where you don't expect them.

Some parts of the UK are far colder, or colder for longer (eg the north), while others bask in an almost subtropical climate (the south-west, Scilly Isles). Higher land tends to be colder than low-lying areas, and more northerly areas receive less light as days are slightly shorter. This affects the growing season as all plants need warmth and light and some (those from hotter climates) need very long growing seasons indeed. These latter need to be started off inside, or in heated greenhouses, to allow them a head start so that they are ready to benefit from the UK summer when (if) it arrives.

Some areas suffer frequently from sporadic, intense gusts of wind, which can devastate an allotment, or rather the plants. A string of beans on poles can act as a sail – catching even the gentlest Aeolian zephyr – and, as they tend to be shallow-rooted, if not properly staked the whole kit and caboodle can take off in a gale, which is irritating to say the least.

Of course, even when you have looked at the local climate you cannot plan for all eventualities – unforeseen and unusual events will occur (late frosts, torrential rain in August; long dry spells) – but you just have to take those in your stride.

Climate change

We have all noticed that the climate seems to be warmer than a few years ago – certainly the winters seem to be less severe and wetter rather than the snowy, icy winters of my youth in Wales and the Midlands. Whether this is a man-made phenomenon or due to the very long-term, natural rhythms of the world, which we don't understand fully, is unclear. It does mean though that, if the climate *is* warming up, you need to factor this into your planning.

Milder winters may mean the following:

- Pests and bugs that were historically killed off by cold are now more likely to survive.

- The beneficial action of frost on newly dug-over soil will be reduced.

- You may be able to work more on your plot.

- Some animals (insects) that used to migrate overseas for winter may now over-winter here.

- Some may come here that in the past found it too cold (some mosquitoes).

- Plants that like winter (eg parsnips) may not thrive as well, especially in the south.

- Conversely, some plants may be easier to grow in the northern parts of the UK.

Hotter summers may mean:

- The growing season may be extended.

- More delicate plants may be more easily grown outside (tomatoes, grapes, squashes, melons). I have certainly found this, and sweetcorn, squashes and pumpkins in particular love being in the UK. Be careful though: even a sniff of Jack Frost nipping at their toes or rather their roots and leaves will kill them stone dead! So don't plant them out too early. They haven't yet adapted to that particular aspect of our seasons.

- There may well be a lot less precipitation, but it might be in the form of thunderstorms or hailstorms, rather than gentle rain – which can flatten crops in one go.

- More/different pests may migrate here.

Fauna and flora change?

Climate change could mean a change in the animals that live here – different amphibians and other predators. The effects on, say, ladybirds are unknown. We also do not know what will happen to temperate flowers and plants. The UK has something like 90 per cent of the world's bluebells living in our temperate woody glades: will that be the case in the future or will we, or our children, miss their little blue flowers in early spring? That would be a tragedy.

In the longer term it may mean that the entire eco-system of the UK becomes more like the Mediterranean is now. Certainly in the south, if you believe some pundits, but we don't really know for sure. Best thing then, is to plan for incremental change and make allowances (eg more watering!), possibly experimenting with different plants.

Planning

Your diagnosis will tell you what your current soil situation is. This lets you understand what you can do and what you have got. You can then compare your situation – ie what is feasible – with the things that you want to grow – your objectives. This will point you towards what you can do and what you need to do to make other things grow more easily.

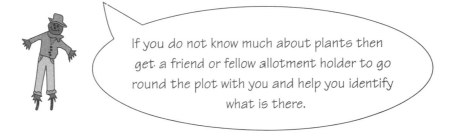

If you do not know much about plants then get a friend or fellow allotment holder to go round the plot with you and help you identify what is there.

You may have to change your ideas or alter them somewhat.

You should also carry out some contingency planning, ie what will I do if this or that happens? For example, how will I manage if there is a drought during my annual two-week holiday in Clacton?

Key steps

First identify all the plants that you can. It is easier from May onwards as, until then, many do not poke up through the surface; but you should do it as soon as you get the plot.

'If in doubt – take it out.'

Planning

```
┌─────────────────┐                          ┌─────────────────┐
│                 │      ══════════▷          │                 │
│    Diagnosis    │                           │   Objectives    │
│                 │                           │                 │
└─────────────────┘                          └─────────────────┘
         │                                            ▲
         ▼                                            ║
┌─────────────────┐                                   ║
│   What do I     │                          Gap      ║
│   need to/      │                                   ║
│   can I do?     │                                   ▼
└─────────────────┘                          ┌─────────────────┐
         │                                   │                 │
         ▼                                   │                 │
┌─────────────────┐                          ┌─────────────────┐
│                 │      ═════════▷           │     New         │
│   Achievable    │                           │   Objectives    │
│     plan        │                           │                 │
└─────────────────┘                          └─────────────────┘
```

Draw a plan of what you have, marking the positions of the plants.

Now decide what you want to do with them and divide the plants into three groups. Those you want to:

- keep *in situ;*

- move elsewhere;

- get rid of altogether.

Depending on your plans, these groups will vary. You may decide, as we did with our initial plot allocation, to take everything out (of course all were pretty much weeds) and make a fresh start.

Alternatively you may decide that some plants will fit in with your plans and decide to keep them *in situ*. We did that with the blackberry plants on the second part of our plot (although I cut them back very hard). We left the front of the plot as it was for the first year, which had red-hot pokers, bamboo and some beautiful old-fashioned geraniums. These are blue and bees love them (we would never get rid of those).

As a temporary measure we left the cardoons *in situ*. These are massive plants, related to globe artichokes, grey in colour with huge leaves. They are quite monumental in plant architecture terms, as they grow to over 8 feet high and the foliage can be up to 4 foot wide.

Cardoons were very popular with Victorians so their kitchen gardeners often grew them. You can eat the lower shoots but they need blanching – which is a performance. Our thinking was to let them develop the long spike (inflorescence) flower so we could harvest the seeds, and then decide if we really wanted them. I couldn't see it myself as they take up a lot of room for not much output. Interestingly enough, we were inundated with requests from other allotment holders to have the Cardoons if we didn't want them ('there's nowt so queer as folk').

We tried to transplant a couple but they didn't take. They also reproduce, however, by seeding smaller 'daughter' plants next to the roots, and we were able to give those away.

You may decide to move other plants. We moved many strawberries into a new plot (although they didn't like it very much) and later on moved the trees out and into the boundary hedge.

Thirdly, draw a new plan of what you want to grow. Keep this as a reference – it *will* change.

There are no hard and fast rules – it all depends on what you want to do. The only real constraints are your imagination, the location and the type of soil – but remember that putting in organic matter will improve the soil greatly.

(7)

Understanding the Basics

This chapter considers some very basic concepts which you must understand to make the most of your allotment.

They may seem obvious, but often it is the simple things that are ignored
or forgotten and failure or severe issues can result. Attention here can save
a lot of bother later on.

What makes plants grow?

For *how plants grow*, ie the life cycle of a plant, see Part II. Here the external environmental factors that facilitate growth are considered.

There are three things that are absolutely necessary to make plants grow.
The presence of all three in the right quantities – or their absence – is the
difference between good growth and no growth – with partial or poor
growth in between. They are:

- Food.

- Light.

- Water.

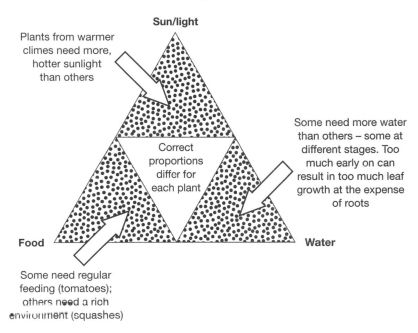

Key elements for plants

Sun/light

Plants from warmer climes need more, hotter sunlight than others

Correct proportions differ for each plant

Some need more water than others – some at different stages. Too much early on can result in too much leaf growth at the expense of roots

Food

Water

Some need regular feeding (tomatoes); others need a rich environment (squashes)

All plants need food, light and water, but different plants need them in varying proportions. Those from hot dry locations can survive on a lot less water, eg some Mediterranean herbs, and indeed over-watering will kill them. Similarly, those from wet, or wetter, environments must not be allowed to dry out.

Plants also have different requirements at different stages. During germination most plants do not need light – in fact, most will not germinate when light is present. (Note that lettuce is an exception to this rule, so do not sow it deeply at all.) They also need moisture to help start the process, but not to excessive levels or they will rot.

Once through germination, however, they need full light almost immediately.

We saw the light

One of our major failures with growing from seeds initially was a failure to grasp this issue: or at least to understand that what seemed like full light to us wasn't for plants. Leaving new seedlings in the dining room, where it seemed very light, was a great mistake. The light from windows – even full-length French windows like ours – is in fact a lot less than you think, and many of our initial attempts grew very spindly and 'weedy' seedlings because there was insufficient light.

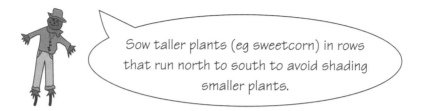

Sow taller plants (eg sweetcorn) in rows that run north to south to avoid shading smaller plants.

As a result we bought a small and cheap plastic greenhouse as a propagator which was a fantastic investment and changed the percentage of our success-to-failure ratio immeasurably in the plants' favour. You still have to remember to move the newly sprung shoots to a higher level in the greenhouse to maximise the light that they will receive.

Make sure that you do not take one of the three elements from your other plants by planting without thinking. For example, large trees will suck in nutrients and stop rain water from falling down as well as shading out sunlight.

Food

The food that plants need is not same as for us. They can't nip into kitchen for a bacon sandwich!

Plants take the food that they need – nutrients – directly through their root system via the water in the soil. They do this through the small hairs on the root – the root follicles. They absorb water in which the nutrients are dissolved.

When we eat food we use it to fuel our daily movements, ie it is converted to energy. Any excess in humans is stored as fat – eat too much or the wrong type of food and the results are obvious for all to see. Plants are the same: they need the right food in the right amounts at the right time.

What are the nutrients?

These are all the things that life needs to support it – the same things that we need, just in a different form and in different amounts.

The four key nutrients are **nitrogen, potassium, phosphorous** and **magnesium** (chemical symbols **N, K, P, Mg** respectively for those that are interested).

- **Nitrogen** is key for growth of leaves and shoots and is only found in living things, and therefore organic matter is vital to ensure a good supply. 70 per cent of our atmosphere, however, is composed of nitrogen and some plants (legumes) can take it from the air and fix it into the soil.

- **Potassium** is critical for flowers and fruits and is a general booster.

- **Phosphorous** helps promote strong, healthy roots.

- **Magnesium** is vital for chlorophyll (see Photosynthesis), which makes plants green.

Plants convert these nutrients into energy using the sun. The scientific name for this is photosynthesis (*photo* means light, *synthesis* means change: Latin). Most of the photosynthesis is carried out in the leaves, but in fact any green part of the plant can do this as long as there is light.

It is important to know what these nutrients do, as a deficiency in one or more will manifest itself in a symptom, and can be treated by adding the mineral to the soil (see Problems).

Feeding

Plants need to have a good supply of food – so the soil must be fed. (Potato and cucurbit families are very hungry crops, and love to be planted on compost heaps.) This involves putting in organic matter, and some organic fertilisers (eg blood, fishmeal and bone), but also rotating the crops as some take nutrients out and others (eg legumes with nitrogen) put them back. Again, do not over-feed. This will usually result in too much leaf growth at the expense of roots and stems.

Other nutrients that are important include calcium, sulphur and iron.

Light

As the god of plants might have said 'Fiat Lux' (let there be light); and there was light and it was good.

Light is essential to good healthy plant growth. But it must be in the right proportions. Too little light results in spindly, 'weedy' seedlings that will flop over or not grow properly.

Light also means warmth and this is essential for good plant growth. Seeds need warmth for germination (there are exceptions) and it is the warmth of the sun that makes plants grow strongly. Again it must be in the right proportions.

Too much sun will either scorch the plants or result in desiccation. It is the same for us. We get vitamins from the sunshine, and we all feel better with a bit of 'sun in our bones', but over-exposure can mean we get sunburnt, blisters or sometimes sunstroke, especially if we have fair skin. Being Welsh, I have very fair skin and I can burn under a 40 Watt light bulb – or even on a cloudy day in October.

Optimise the light

You must ensure that you plant crops where they receive the right amount of light. Putting 'tropical' sun-loving plants in shade is a waste of time. This is why you need to understand the climate and where the sun will shine most. Putting plants that require dry conditions in waterlogged or boggy soil is doomed to failure.

Plants that need lots of sunlight include tomatoes, squashes, melons, gourds, grapes and many herbs. Some flowers – mesembryanthemums and gazanias, for example – just love to be baked in the hottest part of the allotment that you can find. For plants that originate in warmer climes (melons, courgettes, squashes) a greenhouse, cold or hot frame or propagating tray can usefully help you extend the season and give them a head start so that when it warms up they can be put outside to romp away. Although some plants have adapted to shady environments, eg ferns, not many vegetables have.

Note that if your area is affected by pollution, this will reduce the amount of light received.

Sunlight in the UK

If you were to draw a line north-east from Newport in Wales to Scarborough then you would effectively be dividing the UK in terms of sunshine. Areas below that line get far more than the areas above it.

Furthermore, if you were then to draw a line from Dunoon or Greenock in the west of Scotland across to Inverness, then above that line the sunshine decreases even further. It will come as no surprise to find that the average temperature also decreases above these lines as well; although Northern Ireland is consistently warmer than its situation would indicate, presumably because it receives the benefit of the Gulf Stream. This body of warm water flows from the Gulf of Mexico across the Atlantic and hits the UK, which is one of the reasons why our winters are more mild than those on the continent at the same latitude.

If you have a south-facing wall then that is a great place to plant crops that need sunlight. In Victorian kitchen gardens that is where they used to grow succulent fruit such as peaches and nectarines. Our neighbours planted a passion flower on their side of the fence – and it grew over to our side. Because our side of that wall was south-facing we always got far more of the pretty flowers than they did.

Phototropism

Plants have a homing device that tells them where light is. If they do not receive adequate light then they will grow towards whatever light they get. The scientific name for this is phototropism (from Greek *photo* – light; and *tropism* – movement). You can see this in seedlings. After they have pushed through, if they are in a place where the light is much stronger from one direction – eg in a room with windows – then they will bend towards the light. They do this with remarkable speed – in only a few hours. If you do not do something about this then they will fall over, and certainly not grow properly. Either move them into full light, or turn them through 180 degrees. This must be done every day as they bend very quickly back.

When a bank refurbished a branch in West London they planted trees in the foyer for ambience. They looked very nice at first but then they started bending over towards the source of light and the bank had to dig them up and put them on a revolving platform to fix the problem – which was very expensive!

Water

As essential to plant life as it is to human life. While we can go some time without food, without water we can die very quickly – particularly if it is hot or we are involved in great exertions. Plants are the same – they need extra water when it is hot and dry. Dehydration is the biggest risk for marathon runners – not hunger or calorie deprivation. Humans are composed of around 70 per cent water – so are plants.

The rigidity of plant stems comes from the water that plants hold in their cells. Lack of water is very apparent in that wilting seedling that collapses over the side of the pot and then shrivels up into a brown dust.

Some plants have adapted to very little water, eg cacti and other succulents (but not many vegetables), and others to living in water. In fact, plants first evolved in the sea so it is probably more correct to say that they have evolved to do with less water – and to live with fresh water rather than salt – which will kill most land-based plants (there are exceptions, eg mangroves).

Note that too much water can also kill a plant – literally killing it with kindness. As the soil becomes waterlogged (water in the gaps that are normally filled with air) the plant cannot take up the nutrients and air that it needs.

Also, damper conditions – especially where there is lots of foliage which restricts airflow – will encourage the development of fungal diseases.

Rainfall in the UK

Generally it is fair to say that the western parts of the UK receive more rain than others, that is Wales and the West Country, northern England (west of the Pennines), most of Scotland and Northern Ireland.

The reason for this disparity is because the prevailing water-laden winds are from the West, and the rest of the country lies in the rain shadow of the several mountain ranges that run down the spine of England, extend to the West Country and make up most of Wales and Scotland.

The position of Ireland also shields the Western parts of the UK from some of the fiercer rain storms that blow in.

360° degree rainfall

This is not to say that rain doesn't blow in from other directions – we receive it from all points of the compass throughout the year – but the prevailing rain-bearing winds come from the West. Note that snow tends to come from the North and North-east and when it hits warmer air then this too can turn to rain.

Our climate is very curious. We describe June as 'flaming' but in fact that is when the phenomenon known as the European monsoon occurs. It is not quite on the scale of that in, say, India – but in 2007 it brought wide-scale and damaging flooding to many parts of the UK, particularly Northern Ireland, the Midlands and Yorkshire. I have also seen snow in June (in Nottinghamshire), and some days in autumn can be as warm as, if not warmer than some, in summer.

When to water

In dry times you **must** water or *your crops will die*. Do not water at noon or mid-afternoon (which incidentally is when it is usually hottest), but in the early morning (ideally) or late evening (although here there is a possibility that the increased humidity will encourage slugs and other pests which are more active at night) so that the water has time to sink into the ground before it is evaporated. Of course, when you are busy you will have to water when you can. Try to water the roots and not the leaves.

When not to water

On the other hand, excessive and constant watering will also inhibit the development of a strong root system. If water is always easily obtainable at or near the surface then the plant will not put down deep roots: then, when it is dry, it will not be able to search out water in the deeper reaches of the earth where it will still lie, nor will it have good enough anchorage to hold it into the earth to withstand strong winds.

Watering when it is hot will also bring the roots to the surface, where they can be scorched by the sun. Remember that when it rains (natural watering) it is generally cloudy or overcast – this prevents the sun from scorching wet plants. Also frosts may kill roots lying near the surface, so you do not want to encourage them to be there.

Water tips

For some very thirsty plants (eg marrows) it is often a good idea to sink a plastic bottle with the bottom cut off (ie open at both ends) or a tube, six inches or so into the soil, so that when you water it goes down to the roots, rather than lying on the surface to be evaporated or to encourage the roots upwards instead of downwards. Pumpkins and squashes develop massive root systems so they do not need this.

As a gardener one of your key criteria for success is to ensure that your plants receive the right proportions of the three vital elements – light, food and water – when they need them.

Tools for Your Allotment

Tools are essential and you will not be able to manage the plot at all without them – there is a minimum even for 'no-dig'.

There may be some tools that you will need because of your own particular plot (eg if you have a grassy area you will need shears/sickles, etc). For those with lots of tall grass and weeds you may decide that a scythe is the answer. I always find that wearing a black, hooded cloak puts me nicely in the mood for using it! Of course, if you are feeling idle, you could use a strimmer...

Whatever you end up with, you will need somewhere to store your tools on site – unless you are going to cart them there and back again every time you visit (see Sheds and Tool Stores).

The tidy gardener cleans, oils and hangs up the tools every evening when he or she has finished – or so I read once somewhere.

Essential tools

The tools you will *need* include:

Spade One of these is essential for digging; also for chopping up roots and for moving 'stuff' from one place to another. You will almost certainly need one, even if you espouse the no-dig philosophy. Choose a good make with a sharp blade that suits your body shape. Test it in the shop before you buy it (for size and balance – don't try to dig up the shop floor) and make sure it is not too short or too long. They have different-shaped handles – 'YD', 'T' or 'D'. Everybody has their own preferences. I prefer a 'T' but we have a 'YD'! Note that continental and USA spades are often longer with no handle. I really don't think that it makes a ha'p'orth of difference what the shape is and you will adapt to whatever you have pretty quickly.

Go for a spade that feels balanced when you hold it. Move it around a bit to get the 'feel' for it. Most have wooden shafts, although there are other (sometimes more expensive) versions with tubular steel. The shaft should be about 30 inches (70 cm) long. Some spades have flattened tops that make it slightly easier on the sole of the foot. I don't believe that is really necessary, unless you are doing an awful lot of digging.

Don't just go for the cheapest or most expensive – if in doubt go to a couple of other places and test theirs as well. You will be using your spade for years and years so choose wisely. If there is more than one person digging then you *might* want to buy a spade each, especially if there is a great disparity in size between the two of you, for example.

What is the difference between a spade and a shovel? Well they used to say in Nottingham that a true Northerner was someone who called a spade a bloody shovel (wonder what Alan Titchmarsh thinks about that!?). A shovel is usually used for scooping up loose material, such as coal, corn or dry earth. It usually has raised edges to help keep whatever you are shifting on the blade – sort of a spade with wings.

Note that when you start digging you may get blisters from prolonged spells (sometimes even short spells) if you have nice delicate hands from working in an office – gloves can help. If not, then I recommend blister plasters.

Large fork In some cases, where the ground is stony or when you are turning piles of plant material, a fork is better than a spade. It is similar in dimensions to a spade, but has four tines, or prongs, instead of a blade. Forks are also useful for turning heavy or wet ground over as the tines can slide in more easily than a blade. Care should be taken not to try to lift too much with each action, as the fork tends to lift bigger loads than a spade.

Forks usually come as a standard size, but there are others: a little border fork – not a lot of use on an allotment – might be the thing for those finding a large fork difficult to manage, or for smaller beds. You can also buy a potato fork with flattened ties, but I don't think that it is really value-added. I use my ordinary fork – you just have to be careful when digging up the spuds. A fork is useful when lifting clumps of weeds as you can give them a good shake (like a dog 'towsing' a rat) to get off the valuable top soil, in which the weed will be rooted and which you want to keep, before you chuck it in the weed basket/pile.

Go through the same testing method as for spades. A fork can also be used for bashing clods down, and for spiking ground over in autumn if you do that sort of thing. Note that when we started we bought an inexpensive own-brand fork from a garden centre chain. It seemed to be right for the job. Then in June it just gave up the ghost. The metal where it joined the shaft sheared away and the fork lay on the ground whimpering! We replaced it with a Spear and Jackson fork that was much more expensive – but came with a ten-year guarantee. Be warned!

Hand fork This is great for weeding and taking plants out generally. Also for digging small holes when the ground is hard and a trowel won't penetrate. You can also get them with a very long handle which can save you bending down too much. We have several. Giving children their own fork (and trowel) is a great idea as they then have their own tools which they want to use.

Trowel Get only the very best. They get a lot of use and need to be robust. We went to help my youngest daughter's godmother and her husband landscape their garden in early 2007 and, although we were only digging holes in top soil through cuts in a membrane, we broke three trowels. The best was a twenty-year-old trowel that we borrowed from one of their neighbours – which we returned undamaged in any way! Also available in longer-handled versions.

Rakes They always remind me of Tom and Jerry cartoons, but we hardly ever use ours. Sometimes for preparing a seed bed, but apart from that it doesn't really add much value. It can be used to smooth mulches out where there are no plants. They are usually 12 inches-wide (30 cm) and useful for spacing out plants. After a bed has been dug and left over winter to be weathered, it can be raked over to smooth it out.

Composting bin(s) See Composting, Part III.

Watering can(s) You will need at least two of these, as you will be doing a lot of watering and, if you are on your own, it reduces trips by half by taking both at the same time. It is useful to have different-sized roses to go over the end. If you want to water in nematodes to kill slugs for example, then you need a slightly larger rose, and smaller or finer ones are useful for watering seeds.

We bought a very robust metal can. We already had a plastic one and we bought the two girls their own pink-coloured, strong metal watering cans so they could feel that they had their own tools. They very proudly wrote their names on them and always use them. We also gave them a 'junior' trowel, fork and hand cultivator each, but they were plastic and, quite frankly, useless on anything but fine topsoil.

Propagating/gardener's knife Indispensable for a variety of jobs, from cutting asparagus, cutting string, chopping shoots and possibly even for propagating. It is always in my gardening gilet pocket.

(Dutch) Hoe For taking out small weeds from between your lines of vegetables. Just leave them lying in the sun which will kill them. Note that large weeds should be pulled out and thrown away, otherwise they will grow again.

Secateurs For cutting back growth or cutting off snaking branches up to about $^3/_4$ inch (2 cm) thick; anything larger than that will break the secateurs and is dangerous. Above that size, use loppers. We have several pairs of secateurs. They are in use all year round. Get a good-quality set. Cheap ones will just break and they may injure you in the process and you will have to buy another set. It is a false economy.

Do not buy 'hammer and anvil' secateurs, where the blade comes down on the lower part. Buy 'bypass' secateurs where the blades pass each other like scissors. I have found the former to be useless and very aggravating.

Thick gloves Essential to protect your hands from sharp, nasty, pointy things, although I find that they reduce the sensitivity by a huge amount and often take them off for general work. They are very useful when pulling up large roots as they do increase the grip. Everyone needs their own pair. After our first year mine were worn out inside.

Tub-trug type things for putting weeds in as you pull them out. They are robust, cheap (about a fiver) and come on a great range of vibrant colours. They seem to breed on the site and each time we go more people have them. Great for carrying other things as well.

Plant ties For tying up delicate climbers until they have established themselves around the support. Use a loose figure-of-eight so that they have room to expand. Anchor the tie to something or it will just slip down! They can be bought in a bunch of separate strips or as a reel. Also useful for tying poles together and baubles onto wires to scare birds, etc.

Tough bags For putting weeds and debris in. You will need more than you realise as you hack through your plot.

Poles/sticks For plants to climb up and for support. A traditional way is to create wigwams of 6 foot poles, or long inverted 'V's with a pole across them to hold them together. Shorter poles are useful for marking plants on the ground – put something over the top to protect eyes.

Non-essential but nice to have tools

Carrying sheet Great for laying out and putting rubbish on for disposal. Can be used for laying compost on when you turn it – if you prefer that to using the ground, which I do. Don't buy one – use an old bed-sheet. Useful for moving rooted trees and shrubs as it keeps the soil in.

Riddles *or* sieves, to give them their more prosaic name. I do prefer riddle – with all its connotations. When preparing seed beds you need to make the soil smooth to give them the best start and riddling is the best way. We have two: a coarse one (yes, yes); and a fine one for secondary riddling. My children hate riddling as it is hard work; but there is no finer way of getting stone, debris and weeds out of soil that you have dug over.

It can hurt your back, so be careful how you stand when riddling! And take breaks. The soil afterwards is wonderful – weeds think that it is their birthday!

Scythe These are remarkably effective at clearing large swathes of plants, and the side-to-side swishing movement that you make is very appealing. Carrying one while wearing a cloak always gets you a seat on a bus or train!

Draw hoe Not strictly necessary, but I prefer it for drawing seed lines, and it does the job just as well as the more usual Dutch hoe.

Dibber Very useful for planting larger bulbs and plants, such as leeks. Don't buy one. You can use old spade or four candles. In Scotland I believe it is called a 'dibble'. We inherited ours with the second part of the plot – and very useful it is – but it didn't quite balance out the gift of convolvulus though!

Trug These are the traditional way of harvesting crops. Using a trug makes you feel that you are harvesting crops *properly*. I bought Catherine a lovely wicker traditional trug from the Sir Harold Hillier Gardens (well worth a visit if you are in Hants) and everyone comments on it. Produce arranged in it looks great at our open days. It is also useful for ferrying light things to and from the allotment.

Kneeler To save your knees, although I don't use one (yet!). Kneeling is more comfortable than bending or squatting. Ours has handles to help you get up after a long session if necessary, and doubles as a seat when inverted. Useful for the slightly infirm. My children fight to use it.

Fold-away chairs Very useful for taking a break and having lunch. They are very cheap at about £5. We keep ours in the tool store. We also use them during committee meetings.

Loppers Brilliant for taking down branches, big weeds and unwanted shrubs that are too big for the secateurs. The leverage is wonderful. Don't try to use them on branches thicker than about $1\frac{1}{2}$ inches to 2 inches or you will do yourself and the loppers a mischief. Use a saw!

Saws You probably have some of these around the house. Useful for cutting branches and, for the DIY-minded, making useful items such as sheds, cold frames and compost bins.

Adze A sort of cross between a spade and a pickaxe. Not really necessary but useful if you inherit one.

Mallet For hitting wood. It does less damage to wood than a hammer, eg when putting in pegs for raised beds or for putting in poles. I don't have one. I place a piece of wood on top of what I want to hit and use my hammer – works almost as well if you are careful.

Strimmer The mechanical way of cutting weeds and long grass. We have two strimmers for the use of allotment holders on site – and have more trouble over them than anything else. Either they claim that they don't work, or they can't access them. Sometimes they claim that there is no petrol or that the 'twine' is broken, etc, etc. Enough to make you sharpen the scythe ...

Sledgehammer Not necessary very often, but great for smashing things down, and wonderful for getting rid of tension. If you don't have one, someone else will, so borrow it – don't buy one especially. We do have one of these: now who complained about the strimmer?

Wheelbarrow Absolutely necessary for moving things about. Most sites have communal wheelbarrows, which might be a bit ropey but will probably do the job tolerably well. If not, then buy your own. You will use it all the time for moving soil, sand, manure, rubbish, flagstones for paths, etc.

Water butt If you have the space you may want to consider one of these. By collecting rainwater you will be following the rules of organic gardening and will have a supply of water at hand.

Other items you may need

String/twine For tying things.

Plant labels So you know what you planted where. Be warned that the so-called waterproof or indelible ink pens that you can buy are neither when exposed to sun, wind, moon and rain. We had a lot of white plant labels sticking up out of the ground and in pots next to plants – so we had to guess what they were!

Scissors For cutting string, etc, I use my knife.

Pencils/pens/paper For mapping out the plot and drawing your plan.

Tape measure To get the dimensions. We just bring the one I use from home. Make sure it is a long one. A six foot tailor's tape is of no use on a 100 foot plot!

Sturdy sticks For use as supports for fleeces and netting.

Sickle For cutting down tall weeds and grasses. Not necessary, but if you have one they do the job very effectively. They can also be used to harvest all those cereal crops that you grow.

Shears For cutting grass and young shrub/hedge growth. Not really necessary on an allotment.

Hammers Occasionally useful, especially if you are doing a spot of DIY. Bring from home. Don't buy especially – borrow if you don't have one.

Screwdrivers As for hammers. Useful for putting screws into poles to string wires across for growing rasberries.

Drill For making holes to put screws in, to make it easier to screw them in.

Camera Essential for keeping a record of your progress. Unless you take regular snaps then you will forget what it was like, and how much work you have done. It is also good to have snaps of your crops to remind you of your achievements.

Water and cups We keep large bottles in the store with cups. On hot days, or after a heavy session, you really appreciate a cup of water.

Scarecrows I am not sure whether they really do scare crows away, I have always thought that crows are far too clever to be fooled by straw on a pole inside old clothes. But scarecrows are great fun to make with your children, a great talking point, and really make a plot look 'farmed'.

We talked about making one for ages – but we only really got down to it for a school open day where the allotment society had a stall.

We had a Name the Scarecrow competition, a Draw the Scarecrow competition and a Find the Golden Pumpkin on the map of the allotment that the stupid scarecrow, who has no brain, had lost. Plus the Scarecrow's Bran Tub where children got little packets of sweets and seeds or other presents, and the Scarecrow's green fact sheets on recycling and food.

Great fun and it raised:

- awareness of the allotment society;
- awareness of green issues;
- money for the school; and
- money for us.

A definite thumbs up all round (but not from the scarecrow who doesn't have any!).

See How to build a scarecrow.

Clothing

What the well-dressed man or woman about the allotment should wear: Trinny and Susannah eat your hearts out!

The clothes you wear should be driven by two criteria:

- what is comfortable when you are working on the allotment; and
- what you need to protect you while you do the job.

The clothes will of course vary with the seasons. While a pair of shorts and a T-shirt may be fine in the heat of a scorching August day, they might be less appropriate in January (unless you are a very hardy annual!).

Before you go to the allotment, take a moment to consider the factors that will determine what you need to wear:

- what you are going to do;
- how you are going to get to the allotment; and
- what the weather will be like.

What you intend to do is a key driver. If you are going to harvest crops like lettuce or leeks and do a little gentle weeding, then clearly heavy-duty protection is not necessary. If, however, you are going to attempt to cut a swathe through the thick jungle that is heavily infested with two-inch brambles, nettles and thistles, and which may conceal who knows what within its spiky embrace, then clearly stout boots, tough trousers, a protective coat or jacket and gloves will be the order of the day. You mustn't mind if they get ripped or snagged – because that will happen!

The weather is also crucial. Dressing for the probable (and often variable) climatic conditions is a good idea. There is nothing worse than having to work in soaking, cold T-shirts and shorts after a freezing downpour and then realising that you still have to cycle the four miles home. Likewise, wearing a heavy Barbour, cords and thick socks under boots when the sun is at its zenith and pouring out rays to heat the air up to 35°C will cause you to resemble one of your wilting shoots in no time at all.

Footwear

The right footwear is critical. You cannot carry out heavy digging in wet conditions in a pair of ballet pumps. I usually wear either heavy boots or wellies if it is very wet. On dryer days (old) deck shoes are fine – even if digging. You should consider the level of protection that you may need.

If climbing up ladders – say to lop branches – then boots will feel more comfortable on the rungs if you are standing for any length of time, as they support the instep of your foot.

When dealing with sharp things, stout boots will also protect your feet. Thorns are very good at penetrating even leather.

Keep a large plastic bag in the boot of your car for when you drive and it is wet. Wellies can make a lot of mess – especially four pairs!

(9)

Sheds and Tool Stores

With all the tools that you now have, you will need somewhere to store them, plus all the other paraphernalia that you will acquire: pots, potting compost, fertiliser, slug traps, beer and so on.

Sheds

What is an allotment without a shed? Alan Titchmarsh – for many the modern guru of all things gardeny – waxes lyrical about them, and with good reason. But in fact the majority of allotments that I have visited do not have sheds. Whether this is because they are not deemed necessary or, as on our site, they are prohibited under the terms of the lease (except for a communal large shed hard up against a north-easterly facing hedge where it casts no shade) I am not sure.

I do know, however, that, if we were allowed one, I would get one like a shot.

If you have one then I believe that you are very fortunate: and if they are allowed and you haven't got one, then get one now!

A shed:

- is great for storing everything that you need *in situ*;

- can be a place of sanctuary on cold wet days;

- is a place where you can keep a table and chairs, barbecue, charcoal, etc;

- is good for keeping your plot tidy;

- can serve as a potting shed;

- is a warm dry, snug place for a cup of tea;

- is where you can plan your plot planting and survey your domain;

- can serve as a propagator, hot house, etc;

- can be used to harden off plants prior to planting them out;

- offers a cool place of shade on hot days, where you can seek refuge with cold beers or a chilled glass of wine or two – and then cycle back home wobbly;

- also sometimes provides refuge for creatures. There will always be spiders, woodlice and so on lurking in corners or dark nooks and crannies: but if you are lucky butterflies may hibernate inside, and on occasions birds may nest. Just be aware of that before you lock it up and go away for weeks on end for the summer holidays;

- can be used to support climbing plants such as vines or melons – or flowers such as clematis and honeysuckle. These also soften the harsh and sometimes stark outlines, making it blend in with the rest of the site. Remember a doctor can bury his mistakes – an architect can only advise his clients to grow climbing plants.

You can spend what you like on sheds. Some have the most amazing things in them – almost like small homes! Or you could make one, if you are DIY-minded (I am not). Historically on allotments they were built out of recycled materials – and there is a great tradition of building them from packing cases, pallets, old windows and all sorts of 'stuff'.

Of course, whenever someone says that they are 'going to build a shed' I am always reminded of the sinister chap in Harold Pinter's play *The Caretaker* – but I am sure there is no one like that on your allotment (or maybe there is!).

Tool stores

We are, however, very fortunately allowed a tool store, as long as it isn't over a yard (metre) high. These are a godsend. When we first came to our allotment we had to bring our tools with us every time as there was no store – or at least not one that we wanted to use. I did smash up a very old, weather-beaten collection of bits of wood and felt, that might – with a bit of imagination – once have been a tool store, or just a strange box (possibly belonging to the caretaker).

Having to bring tools with us each time was a crashing bore as it took ages to load and unload the car and carry them all through our (terraced) house. So we resolved to buy a tool store – not quite the Pinteresque shed, but necessary! After that we could cycle more frequently – all part of the master plan, you see.

Tool stores come in all shapes and sizes, and can be made from wood, plastic and even metal. There is a surprising price variation, but around £100 is probably the maximum you need to spend on one that is about 6 feet by 3 feet by 3 feet and good quality. We looked at several and in the end bought a plastic one that seemed right for us. It had two doors that opened outwards and a roof that lifted up.

We had to put it together ourselves, of course, and wasn't that fun? The instructions purported to be in about twenty languages – but I think that they had been written by Martians, and had lost a bit in translation. It took two of us (grown-ups) about three hours to do it – two strong children would probably have managed it better! Everything kept moving against us; the bits that were meant to slot easily in place didn't and a piece broke off (not too serious, luckily) as we struggled with it all.

It was also an absolutely bitterly cold January day, with soft, gentle, freezing rain falling down as we assembled it. Dealing with small screws when your fingers are numb and you are kneeling inside a 3 foot by 3 foot shed trying to hold a screwdriver, a door and a frame, while your wife holds the roof up to stop it dropping on your head is a pleasure that is best avoided. Memo – pick a dry day!

When we had finished it looked OK – but it was a slight rhomboid shape, so needed a slight nudge to close properly – pathetic really. It has proved to be thoroughly disappointing in terms of quality, but it serves its purpose of storing everything. In fact, we now have so much we need a second one (definitely Pinter!).

Key tool store points

- Make sure it opens out at the front rather than having top access – it is a lot easier to get things in and out.

- Make sure it has shelves inside for storing things such as gloves, plant labels, twine and so on.

- Ensure that the ground is flat underneath it. We were lucky that there was a concrete path at the back of our plot which we could use – and even then it wasn't 'true'.

- If your site is open to 'visitors' then make sure the store is very robust and lockable. The replacement value of all your tools may run to hundreds of pounds, to say nothing of the aggravation if you lose them in the middle of a critical period.

- Keep it tidy (famous last words!). You will always find that the thing you want is at the back and if it is just a mess (where you have thrown everything in at the end of a tiring day before you go home) you *will* get irritated when seeking it.

- Get a child to help you put it together!

- Place it at the end of the plot – ideally away from the path – but that will, of course, depend on your own particular site. Ours is tucked away up at the top end well away from anything else.

- Don't forget to check for weeds from time to time, particularly perennial ones trying to sneak in behind it.

10

Organic Principles

Organic gardening for us isn't about being 'worthy'. We do have a dish-washer and we don't knit yoghurt or wear open-toed sandals and raffia-spun cardigans! Nor is it about making life harder for ourselves. It is, rather, about wanting to work with nature, instead of nuking every other living thing in sight to ensure that our few chosen plants survive. I have never used a pesticide or herbicide in all my years of gardening. I have never seen the need. I may have been lucky but – apart from the odd attack of blackfly on beans – I have never suffered anything like a biblical plague of locusts.

Too often the techniques developed for mass production have been applied to allotments and the garden. The indiscriminate use of chemicals is a prime example of this, whether as herbicides, pesticides or fertilisers. In my view they are unnecessary and do not work properly, storing up issues that come back to bite you (or your crops) later on.

I suppose that my experience has been that if you grow things in balance then they stay in balance. I have never grown large aggregations of crops of the same sort – as farmers are wont to do of course – and so I have never suffered the pest issue of similar sizes. It is only natural that large amounts of food (whether crops or prey) will attract large numbers of pests or predators (see graph for relationship between them – indicative data only).

crops/pests relationship

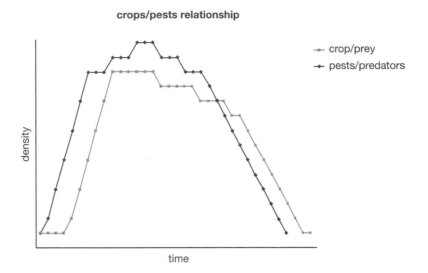

There is a time lag of course as they feed and then decrease as the food supply dwindles.

Breaking up large groupings with other crops helps enormously, as pests that thrive on one crop don't necessarily like others. Intercropping and companion planting are good techniques for this.

What does organic mean?

An important element is bio-diversity. This term describes the many types of organisms such as animals, plants and micro-organisms living in habitats or eco-systems. Well-managed soil contains an incredible number (bio-diversity) of organisms that are essential for the health of the soil and the eco-system. A teaspoon of good, healthy soil will contain more organisms than the population of the human race.

There are a number of bodies that promote organic principles. They have useful websites and publish good books to help you grow organically.

Bio-diversity

Bio-diversity encompasses the whole variety of life on Earth. It includes all species of plants and animals, but also their genetic variation, and the complex eco-systems of which they are part. It is not restricted to rare or threatened species but includes the whole of the natural world from the commonplace to the critically endangered.

The world is losing bio-diversity at an ever-increasing rate as a result of human activity. In the UK we have lost over 100 species during the last century, with many more species and habitats in danger of disappearing, especially at the local level. On a world scale the rate of loss is now recognised to be a cause for serious concern, requiring concerted international action to prevent continued loss of bio-diversity.

Source: DEFRA

The Soil Association

The Soil Association is a body that seeks to promote sensible, organic and healthy farming and gardening practices.

It was only founded as recently as 1946, which is when pesticide use had really started to take hold, driven by the need to grow food during the Second World War to feed the nation. A far-sighted group of farmers, scientists and nutritionists were concerned about the potential negative effects of intensive farming practices on plant, animal, human and environmental health.

The catalyst was the publication of *The Living Soil* by Lady Eve Balfour in 1943. The book presented the case for an alternative, sustainable approach to agriculture that has since become known as organic farming.

In the ensuing years the organisation has developed organic standards and now works with consumers, farmers, growers, processors, retailers and policy makers.

A quote from the Soil Association website:

But at its heart our mission remains the same – to create an informed body of public opinion about these links and to promote organic agriculture as a sustainable alternative to intensive farming methods.

Today the Soil Association is the UK's leading organic organisation, with over 180 staff based in our Bristol headquarters, in regional centres and working as certification inspectors across the country. The Soil Association's director is Patrick Holden, who reports to the Council of Trustees.

You might expect something so vital to be organised and supported by the government. But in fact the Soil Association is a charity, reliant on donations and on the support of its members and the public to carry out its work.

Since 1946 we have been working to raise awareness about the positive health and environmental benefits of organic food and farming and supporting farmers in producing natural food consumers can trust ...

Garden Organic – formerly the Henry Doubleday Research Association (HDRA)

This is the premier organic society in the UK – if not the world. Below are extracts from its website.

- Garden Organic is the working name of the Henry Doubleday Research Association (HDRA). We are a registered charity, and Europe's largest organic membership organisation. We are dedicated to researching and promoting organic gardening, farming and food.

- Our Research and Development Section is working to improve commercial organic growing in Britain.

- Our Information and Education Section provides advice to its over 30,500 members and regularly helps the media, industry and statutory bodies. Garden Organic staff write books and articles for the national press, and appear regularly on television and radio.

- Our Sustainable Waste Management team promote home composting through Master Composter schemes and research related to home composting. Find out about Master Composter schemes in your area on our dedicated website www.homecomposting.org.uk.

- Our three organic display gardens at Ryton near Coventry, Yalding near Maidstone, and Audley End near Saffron Walden, are open to the public and attract thousands of visitors each year. We also have food, gardening and gift shops at our three sites, selling one of the best ranges of quality organic products in the UK, and we have restaurants at Ryton and Yalding.

- Our Heritage Seed Library saves hundreds of old and unusual vegetable varieties for posterity, also distributing them to its members. Anyone can join.

- Our International Programme carries out research and advisory work with organisations across the tropics to develop and promote organic practices of benefit to small-scale farmers. Our Overseas Organic Support Group helps to fund this work.

- We work with Chase Organics Ltd to produce *The Organic Gardening Catalogue*, offering, by mail order, the very best selection of organic products in the country. We also run The Organic Wine Club in association with Vinceremos Wines. Catalogues are available on request.

- We hold National Potato Days, kindly sponsored by Waitrose, National Organic Gardening Weekends and dozens of other events.

- At time of writing, Garden Organic with its associated trading company Organic Enterprises Ltd, has over 150 members of staff, who continually strive to promote excellence in all things organic.

The history of HDRA

The Henry Doubleday Research Association (HDRA) began in 1954 as a result of the inspiration and initiative of one man, Lawrence Hills. As an horticulturalist he had a keen interest in organic growing, but he earned his living as a freelance journalist writing for *The Observer, Punch* and *The Countryman*. Whilst researching a book called *Russian Comfrey*, he discovered that the plant grown widely in Britain today was introduced in the nineteenth century by a Quaker smallholder named Henry Doubleday.

When Doubleday came across comfrey he was so intrigued by its possibilities as a useful crop that he devoted the rest of his life to popularising it. Hills took up his crusade and before long requests were coming from far and wide for plants and additional information.

Eventually Hills was able to raise £300 to rent an acre of land at Bocking, near Braintree in Essex, and he began to experiment with comfrey. By 1958 the enterprise had reached a point where it had to become official or be dropped altogether, so he decided to set up a charitable research association to study the uses of comfrey and – more significantly – to improve ways of growing plants organically. He named the association after his pioneering Victorian mentor.

Basic tenets of organic gardening

The basic rule of organic gardening is simply this:

Look after the soil and it will look after you.

The key factors are:

- Manage the whole **area** organically – not just the fruit and vegetables.
- Make the area 'wildlife friendly', encouraging natural creatures to control pests.
- Learn to distinguish pests from predators.
- Play to your soil's strengths, capitalising on its particular characteristics.
- Make soil care a priority.
- Make compost and leafmould to feed the soil.
- Reuse and recycle, to cut down the use of finite resources and reduce disposal problems.
- Use organically grown seeds as far as possible.
- Consider the environmental implications when choosing materials for hard landscaping, fencing, soil improvement and so forth.
- Collect rainwater, and reduce the need for watering by improving the soil and growing appropriate plants.
- Make local sources your first choice.

- Control weeds without herbicides.

- Avoid the use of preservative-treated wood.

Stop using slug pellets! They kill the creatures that eat them and have dele-terious effects on the food chain.

Recycling

Although this book is not specifically about the environment and green issues, it is not possible to ignore this aspect of having an allotment, and nor should it be ignored. For many people having good fresh meat and veg, produced naturally is important, and therefore following many of the green paths is equally important to them.

Recycling is an idea which is becoming increasingly relevant to our lives. Politicians of every hue are now on the 'green bandwagon' and if this improves the environment and the planet it is no bad thing. Legislation is being passed virtually every month to try to improve the environment, reduce usage and wastage and reduce landfills. EU legislation will punish local authorities for overuse of landfills, so they will start putting greater pressure on households to be greener. So stay ahead of the game.

Recycling has, however, always formed an important aspect of allotment life. Many of the things built or put together on allotments (compost bins, sheds, cold frames, greenhouses and so on) were often made of reused materials as people couldn't afford anything else – and it is a great tradi-tion. The 'new' philosophy of recycling merely builds on this and meshes in well with organic growing.

As a consumer you can also exercise pressure. Retailers respond to people power much faster than to other forms, so by following green ways you can make them change too.

The Four Rs
A basic recycling philosophy can be summed up using the Four Rs, in descending order:

Refuse – to accept anything that is not bio degradable or cannot be recycled;
Reduce – where this is not possible reduce the non-biodegradable things that you do have to buy/use;
Reuse – whatever you can;
Recycle – whatever is left.

In this way you can ensure that whatever you do on your allotment also helps the environment.

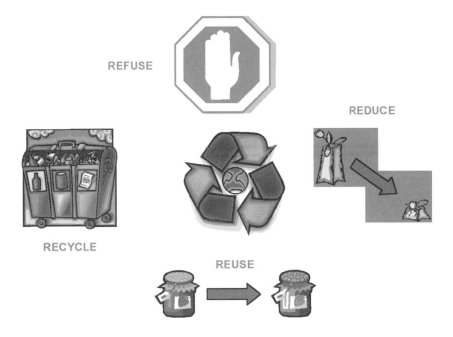

Most councils now provide separate recycling bins to collect key items; and for many domestic households the recycling process involves putting:

- glass in the glass bin;

- paper in the paper recycling bags;

- plastic bottles and cans in the relevant bin; and

- garden cuttings and other items in the 'green' bin.

For those with allotments, however, there are many other useful ideas that can be adopted:

- Using opaque plastic bottles to place on top of sticks to avoid injury.

- Using clear plastic bottles as mini-cloches to protect plants from predatory insects and molluscs, as well as providing a nice warm environment during the early months of the year.

- Using household scraps of vegetables and fruit in your composter.

- Putting cut flowers and hedge clippings in the compost bin helps to add body.

- Egg boxes are perfect for adding body to compost, and they are also ideal for 'chitting' potatoes (see Part III).

- Compost crushed egg shells, loo-rolls and other cardboard items.

Other ideas include:

- Using old car tyres, stacked up and filled with compost for growing potatoes.

- Pizza boxes broken up and added to compost or used in 'trenches'.

- Newspaper crumpled up and added to 'greens' also assists in the composting process.

- Paper and envelopes can be used as scrap paper for making notes.

- Cardboard, newspaper and bubble wrap can be used as packing materials.

- Old CDs can be hung on string from poles and by reflecting the sun act as bird-scarers. Silver multi-faced Christmas baubles can also be used in this way.

- Use old clothes and wood to make a scarecrow.

- Jars and jam pots can be used as small containers to store odds and ends. We use ours for home-made jam, jelly and chutney, etc and to store freshly picked lavender until it is made into lavender bags.

- Plastic bags (where you are forced to have them) can be reused in shops, and used as bin bags around the house and for ferrying items – such as kitchen compost to the plot.

- Paper bags can be composted. I always take a paper bag where there is a choice.

- Used wood can be used as firewood and the ash sprinkled on the soil to add more goodness (eg potash).

- Where it is possible, having your milk delivered in 100 per cent recyclable glass bottles is better than the plastic containers that supermarkets favour.

For further tips, go to www.recycling-guide.org.uk

Since having an allotment our household waste bin is only about two-fifths full.

Some interesting facts and figures
Source: recycling-guide

- UK households produced 30.5 million tonnes of waste in 2003/04, of which only 17% was collected for recycling (source: defra.gov.uk). There is still a great deal of waste which could be recycled that ends up in landfill sites which is harmful to the environment.

- One recycled tin can would save enough energy to power a television for 3 hours.

- One recycled glass bottle would save enough energy to power a computer for 25 minutes.

- One recycled plastic bottle would save enough energy to power a 60 Watt light bulb for 3 hours.

- 70% less energy is required to recycle paper compared with making it from raw materials.

- Up to 60% of the rubbish that ends up in the dustbin could be recycled.

- The unreleased energy contained in the average dustbin each year could power a television for 5,000 hours.

- The largest lake in Britain would be filled with the UK's output of rubbish in only 8 months.

- On average, 16% of the money spent on a product pays for the packaging, which ultimately ends up as rubbish.

- As much as 50% of waste in the average dustbin could be composted.

- Up to 80% of a vehicle can be recycled.

- 9 out of 10 people would recycle more if it were made easier.

Aluminium

- 24 million tonnes of aluminium is produced annually, 51,000 tonnes of which ends up as packaging in the UK.

- If all cans in the UK were recycled, we would need 14 million fewer dustbins.

- £36,000,000 worth of aluminium is thrown away each year.

- Aluminium cans can be recycled and ready to use in just 6 weeks.

Glass

- Each UK family uses an average of 500 glass bottles and jars annually.

- The largest glass furnace produces over 1 million glass bottles and jars *per day*.

- *Glass is 100% recyclable* and can be used again and again.

- Glass that is thrown away and ends up in landfills will **never decompose**.

Paper

- Recycled paper produces 73% less air pollution than if it was made from raw materials.

- 12.5 million tonnes of paper and cardboard are used annually in the UK.

- The average person in the UK gets through 38kg of newspapers per year, much of which is unwanted rubbish to many consumers anyway (colour supplements, 'knowledge', career guides, special reports and so on) and gets junked unopened and unread. You can see them lying on seats in stations or left on trains and buses.

- It takes 24 trees to make 1 ton of newspaper.

Plastic

- 275,000 tonnes of plastic are used each year in the UK – about 15 million bottles per day.

- Most families throw away about 40kg of plastic per year, which could otherwise be recycled.

- The use of plastic in Western Europe is growing about 4% each year.

- Plastic can take up to 500 years to decompose.

Recycling and organic growing are inextricably mixed.

Part II

Know Your Onions – The Plants

Introduction

Part II is about crops: those that are grown on allotments – but indeed could be grown anywhere – and some less common types. I will consider the main categories of produce and the most common plants in each – vegetables, fruit, and herbs – as well as a little on trees, shrubs and flowers.

Each category is split into the main families or groups within them (eg brassica in vegetables, or currants in fruit). I will set out the main characteristics, features and issues. Note that there are hundreds of types of plants in each category. Space does not permit me to discuss them all, so I have concentrated on those that are more frequently grown and a few 'interesting' ones.

Crops are grouped in 'families' for the scientific purpose of understanding them and because they share characteristics. I have also followed this grouping into families for several reasons:

- Knowing the family characteristics will help you to identify types of plant – and the implications that arise from being members of that family (eg the pea family members all have flowers with five petals and produce leguminous pods – hence the old name leguminosa).

- There is a propensity for some pests to attack a particular family, eg cabbage white butterfly for brassicas; carrot fly for roots – it's a Darwinian world down in the top soil!

- Diseases have also adapted to families – eg clubroot for brassicas, blight for tomatoes and potatoes – and they have devastating consequences if not dealt with or controlled.

- Families generally (but not always) share the same likes and dislikes (eg acid, alkaline, wet, dry and so on) and this can be of help in deciding where and when to plant them, and how to nurture them.

- Pests have adapted to their prey. Understanding which plants belong to which family helps enormously when planning crop rotations to minimise diseases and for soil preparation, eg liming for brassicas, manuring for potatoes.

There are around 250,000 families of flowering plants and some of the largest include:

English name	Latin name	Members	Examples
Daisy	Compositiae	25,000	Lettuce, aster
Orchid	Orchidaceae	18,000	Orchids
Pea	Leguminosae	17,000	Peas, broad beans
Grass	Graminae	9,000	Maize, wheat, rye

There are some surprises. I didn't know until I looked into it that asters are lettuces. And how many of you knew that potatoes and tomatoes are not only related to each other but also to deadly nightshade (Bella Donna from the Italian for 'Beautiful Lady') – not many!

(11)
About Our Crops

This book is about getting, starting and managing an allotment. It is not a botany or science book. Nevertheless it is easier to maximise your output from your effort and investment that you put into your allotment if you have at least a basic understanding of how plants grow, so you can use that knowledge to your and their advantage.

Knowing that plants need heat to germinate helps you understand that planting them outside when it is freezing will not work. I will therefore go over some of the relevant aspects of the plant life cycle that have helped me to grow things more successfully.

Understanding the key things that are important to plants will help you in giving them:

- the best start that you can, and then;
- the right environment to ensure that they flourish afterwards.

It is a bit like raising children really except plants don't bring home 'unsuitable' boys!

Optimisation

There is nothing more disappointing than crop failure, so ensuring that growing conditions are the best for each particular plant will help. Optimisation sadly, however, does not guarantee that you will succeed.

In our first year our initial attempt at sowing parsnips scored a spectacular 100 per cent failure rate and the carrots next door had 97 per cent failure – but the turnips in the other half of the row had a 97 per cent success rate. All are root crops, all sown in the same area – I had even specially prepared the soil by adding sand because root crops like it. It is a mystery to me even now as to why it happened. One of our neighbours only three plots away had similar failure with parsnips – which are notoriously difficult to germinate anyway – but her carrots were fantastic.

Perhaps it wasn't warm enough when we planted – I don't know. So we laboriously grubbed the rows up and started again – and failed almost as badly the second time!

Even when you plant seeds and they germinate and seem to be growing well, you can still fail from variables that you can't control – such as the weather and pests – which destroyed our sweetcorn and squashes between them.

Which variety?

There are many varieties of crops; far more than you will ever see in the shops. Modern agri-businesses have progressively bred and selected those strains that meet their requirements. They want plants that can be grown in huge swathes, but which are resistant to the diseases that are more likely to attack such large aggregations of crops. They like uniform-sized crops that mature altogether to facilitate harvest, and which will meet their transport needs, eg by ripening in transit. Furthermore, because of this selection, other beneficial characteristics have sometimes been lost on the way – flavour, texture and taste to name but three.

As a result many excellent varieties of crop have fallen out of favour and are no longer grown, because they do not meet these needs. These old varieties are called Heritage plants and you can still get hold of some of them. By and large they give better (or more interesting) results for the smaller-scale allotment gardener and I would urge you to try them. For example, you can get blue and red potatoes as well as the more common white ones – and that can make a fabulous presentation.

Heritage plants

Organic gardening is founded in bio-diversity. The more variations there are the better. This makes for a more interesting world as well as stronger living organisms as differences are cross-bred and successful characteristics come to the fore. You see this in animal breeds. Often pure-bred dogs can demonstrate very strange tendencies as the diversity has been bred out of them. My uncle had a pure-bred Labrador that just went berserk one day and destroyed his sitting room. It is called inbreeding and is generally recognised as a bad thing, often leading to deformities and even sterility. Anyone who has seen the film 'Deliverance' will have noticed this.

Heritage plants retain many of those characteristics, or genes, that would otherwise be lost. By growing them you reintroduce them and allow them to be reabsorbed into other plants.

By growing unusual or less common varieties you usually get plants that:

- have much better flavour;

- have not been bred for agri-business needs and, therefore, fit in with what you need, ie the plants mature or ripen at different times so that you can harvest those that you need as and when, progressively over the season, rather than in one go;

- often have unusual shapes, which makes them really fun to grow and eat. We don't really need carrots that are all the same shape and size – you cut them up to cook them anyway.

Where our plants come from

Surprisingly, many of the familiar plants that we grow in our allotments and gardens are not indigenous. This shouldn't be too surprising as many thousands of years ago the UK didn't exist per se and was just part of a massive arctic tundra stretching right across northern Europe, where little or nothing grew. As the ice age ended and the ice gradually receded – taking the very cold weather with it – so plants started moving back and colonising what eventually became our islands, when the continent of Europe was cut off by the rising sea, which broke through to give us the North Sea and the English Channel.

The plants that initially grew in the UK – or the British Isles – after the ice age were few and far between and also pretty poor in terms of quality, eg what we would regard as a 'fat' vegetable now didn't exist then. Wild cabbage is a very straggly plant with not much nutritional value in it, and probably lettuce in its original state wouldn't have merited a passing glance. It is selective breeding that has made it a more satisfying food, and there is nothing wrong in that.

The newcomers

Since then plants have been introduced regularly to the UK by successive waves of invaders, by intrepid explorers and also by innovative gardeners and growers. The table below gives some examples of this (note the date of introduction is in many cases not known with any certainty).

UK plant timeline

- Post ice-age — brassicas, broad beans.

- Celtic — cabbage, onion, seakale.

- Roman — carrots, peas, vines, Good King Henry.

- Saxon — hops, herbs, leeks.

- Norman — herbs, garlic.

- Medieval — broccoli, beetroot, spinach, celery.

- Elizabethan — potatoes, Jerusalem artichoke, tomatoes, french beans, endive, chicory.

- Victorian — turnip, runner beans, Brussels sprouts.

What is surprising is not so much when the vegetables were introduced – but where they came from originally. Our diet would be very thin in terms of choice and nutrition were it not for these immigrants. One plant of course stands head and shoulders above the rest – the potato, the mainstay of most food production on allotments and in gardens. What would we do without it? No chips, roast, jacket, boiled, mashed or new potatoes, and no waffles or crisps! What did we do before? Well ... we struggled to feed ourselves.

A staggering proportion of the everyday crops that we now grow come from the Americas – potato, tomato, sweetcorn, French bean (so-called as the Huguenots introduced them) runner bean, sweet potato, aubergine, pumpkin, squash, melon and surprisingly the Jerusalem artichoke. One estimate is that 40 per cent of the crops now grown were originally from the Americas, having been developed by the Mayas, Incas, Aztecs and others. Despite their unimaginably barbaric, blood thirsty ways, they knew their onions!

Global food

And it is not just the Americas – peaches come from China, okra from Africa, spinach from Persia, cucumber from India, swedes not surprisingly from Sweden (a turnip-cross) and guess where Brussels sprouts came from?

Cauliflowers came from the eastern part of the Mediterranean or Arabia, and from the same family many cabbages were cultivated in Germany where their word for it is variously kohl or kraut. Broccoli is from Italy, as is rocket. Mizuna is from Japan (and means juicy), as are mibuna greens. Pak choi is Chinese in origin, and onions came originally from Asia or Egypt (mentioned in the Old Testament) along with garlic and lentils.

Aubergines are from India and were originally called egg-plants as the first cultivars were white and egg-shaped. The darker varieties came later. It is thought that lettuce came from the Caucasus. Its name is from the French for milk, *lait*, as the leaves gave out a milky white liquid.

Our allotments are truly a reflection of our exploration of the world and the global diversity of plants.

Understanding the terms for what we eat

At this point it is worth clarifying some terms. We all talk about fruit and vegetables, but in science they do not have the same meaning – if at all. Vegetable is not a scientific description. We use it to describe some of our food. We also use fruit mainly to describe those things that we regard as not for eating with the main course of a meal but at other times or as puddings. It tends to mean sweeter foods.

A fruit in biology, however, has a specific meaning (see below). The parts of the plant that we eat include the following – and we sometimes eat more than one part of a plant (eg Hamburg parsley where the tops and roots are eaten):

Roots Usually the long taproot of a plant, eg carrots, parsnips, swede, turnips.

Stems The part of the plant above ground and below the flowers, asparagus, celery, kohlrabi, celeriac, cardoons.

Flowers Cauliflower, broccoli, globe artichoke – and flowers from flowers.

Seeds Pine nuts, pumpkin seeds, peanuts, peas, broad beans, runner beans, French beans. In some cases (eg mangetout) you can eat the pods as well.

Tubers The part of a plant that grows underground but isn't the root, eg potatoes, Jerusalam artichokes, yams.

Leaves Cabbage, lettuce, spinach, and of course many flower and herb leaves – nasturtiums, borage, parsley, dill, mint, etc.

Bulbs Layered fleshy parts of the plant below the stem and above the roots, eg onions, garlic, leeks, fennel.

Fruit The part of a plant that holds the seeds (see below), eg tomato, berries, apple, pear, peach, pumpkin, squash, melon, aubergine, pepper.

Plant types

There are many plants in the world (around 290,000) and the plant kingdom comprises of four main types:

- Mosses and worts (24,000).
- Ferns and horsetails (12,000).
- Conifers (600).
- Flowering plants.

The first three groups do not produce flowers and most of our food comes from the latter, flowering category, which has over 250,000 members. There are, however, some crops from the others (eg the conifer group gives us pine nuts, eaten raw or used in pesto, and juniper berries, used for flavouring gin).

A bit more botany. The flowering plants are divided into two main subgroups:

- Those where the first thing to appear above ground is a single leaf (scientific name **monocot**: mono = one; cot = leaf), which includes all grasses such as corn/wheat, rice, maize, oats and barley, as well as others such as dates, bananas and onions (about 40,000).

- Those where two leaves push through (**dicots**) – all the rest (210,000).

You can see the difference if you grow them from seed.

Fungi

A word on fungi. Edible fungi are usually referred to as mushrooms and they are neither animal nor vegetable and have a separate classification that also includes yeast. The others are often called toadstools. Note they are often very poisonous indeed. Never eat fungi unless you are sure what it is. Growing mushrooms usually requires different approaches and techniques from other plants, but is similar to one of the management techniques used by many senior personnel to manage their staff – keep them in the dark and feed them on . . . well you get the idea!

Lichens are 'partnerships' between algae and fungi. On the monoliths at Stonehenge there are some that are over 5,000 years old! This makes lichen one of the longest-living organisms on the planet.

(12)

The Life Cycle of a Plant

Note: If you have a degree in Botany (and what self-respecting allotment holder doesn't?) then you can probably skip this chapter!

The life cycle of a plant (focusing on those that give us our food) involves the following stages:

- Pollination.

- Fertilisation.

- Fruit setting and seed development.

- Seed dispersal.

- Germination.

- Growth.

Then it starts again.

Our actions as food producers on our allotments can affect each of these stages, and our outputs are dependent on the successful completion of each stage, so an understanding of each is very helpful.

Pollination

Plants have two important parts that are engaged in pollination – the 'male' part called the **anther**, and the 'female' part called the **stigma** (note the sexist naming). Pollen is transferred from the anther to the stigma by a variety of processes in order to fertilise it. These include:

- Wind.

- Insects.

- Self-pollination.

- Water.

- Other animals.

Wind Those plants that are pollinated by wind are easily distinguished from those using insects because, as they do not have to attract insects, they have not developed all the interesting characteristics of insect-pollinated flowers (see table). They are often dull to look at or to smell, by comparison with those that rely on insects. Grasses, cereals and many trees are wind-pollinated.

Pollination

Insect attracting	Wind – no need to attract insects
<ul><li>Smaller amounts of pollen – more efficient usage than with wind pollination.</li><li>Brightly coloured petals.</li><li>Often scented, usually contain nectar.</li><li>Pollen often sticky.</li><li>Anthers and stigmas protected inside flower – to brush against insects.</li><li>Stigma has a sticky coating so pollen sticks to it.</li></ul>	<ul><li>Pollen produced in great quantities – shotgun approach as most is wasted.</li><li>Small petals, often dull-coloured with no scent or nectar.</li><li>Pollen very light and smooth – to travel as far as possible and easily on the wind.</li><li>Anthers dangle outside – to release pollen.</li><li>Stigmas hang outside and are feathery or like a net – to catch pollen.</li></ul>

It is a wasteful process in terms of the amounts of pollen produced to the actual seed that 'takes' or germinates, but it is still nonetheless efficient when measured by plant success. More effort is put into producing great quantities of pollen for blowing in the wind (as Bob would say), rather than interesting things (nectar, smell, colours) to attract insects, and which we enjoy so much. The reproductive parts are outside to release the pollen and to catch it as it floats by or falls down. Some species have male and female trees, eg holly.

Examples of wind-pollinated plants include sweetcorn, wheat and beetroot.

It is the vast amounts of pollen produced by these plants that cause hay fever for some people.

Insects Many plants have developed an extremely successful and mutually beneficial relationship (symbiosis) with insects (bees, moths, butterflies, beetles, etc) that carry out the pollination for them.

The plant secretes nectar to attract the insects and this is also usually prettily coloured and sweetly smelling. The insects benefit by getting nectar as food, and the plant benefits by being fertilised. We benefit from this working relationship as we can enjoy the beautiful colours and smells, as well as eating the produce that results and – if you like it – the honey made by bees.

Bees

The most useful insect in the UK for pollination is considered to be the bee, which of course uses the nectar not only as food but also to make honey. A bee's favourite colour is blue, so old-fashioned geraniums, lavender and cornflowers are excellent for attracting bees into your allotment.

If you can, keep bees somewhere on the site –
it will greatly enhance pollination.

The insects are attracted to the flowers and, in order to get at the nectar, they enter the flowers. As they do so they brush against the anthers which are covered in pollen. The pollen sticks to them – either because it is sticky or 'hooked' – and then, after they have sipped the nectar, they fly off and go to another flower. It may be on the same plant or another one. When they enter another flower, then this time the pollen they collected from the last flower rubs off onto the stigma and they collect another load of pollen for the next flower; and so on.

Note that the pollen must come from the same species or the fertilisation will not work, generally speaking – although cross-fertilisation does presumably take place sometimes to provide a cross-breed.

Those plants that rely on moths often have rather pale-coloured petals that show up better at night – and smell nice then as well. At dusk, if you are lucky, you may see the humming-bird moth. This a large moth that hovers, just like a humming bird does, as it takes nectar and pollinates plants. We have one that visits our fuschias.

Examples of insect-pollinated plants are cabbage, courgette, leek, peas (what would our gardens and allotments be like without peas and sweet-peas?), pumpkins and squashes, runner beans and sunflowers. Apples usually need pollen from two other cultivars (types of apple) for real success.

Self-pollination Some plants do not need outside agencies – they are self-pollinating. Examples include lettuce, tomatoes (in the UK, but in its natural habitat it uses bees), French beans and many soft fruits.

Water Some plants produce pollen which floats on water to other plants, eg ribbonwort, but there are not many of these.

Other animals Some flowers are pollinated by other animals, eg humming birds and bats. The process is broadly similar to that for insect pollination.

Pollen

We think of pollen as yellow, but it can be white, black, orange or purple, and it comes in all shapes and sizes. You can apparently identify a plant from the colour and shape of the pollen, presumably with a magnifying glass or microscope – should you wish to!

Fertilisation

Once pollination has taken place and the pollen is on the stigma, the pollen grain 'comes alive' and sends out a tube which grows down to the ovule. Male nuclei travel down it to join with the female cell and transfer genetic material to fertilise it. You can tell when fertilisation has taken place as the plant sheds its petals. They have served their purpose and it does not want to support them, as that would take energy from the next phase – fruiting.

It will not shed all its petals, however, just because one 'flower' has been fertilised. It will support both fruit and flowers at the same time, in order to set more fruit (see photo below). To create larger fruit, pinch out flower buds from a plant, so that it puts effort into the fruit already 'set'.

Fruit setting and seed development

Once fertilisation has taken place, the plant gets cracking on producing its fruit. A fruit, however, is not what you and I might call a fruit – and includes many things that we call vegetables. The word vegetable has *no definition whatsoever* in botany and is just a culinary term for those plant things that we eat as an accompaniment to, say, meat or fish. A fruit is not a vegetable to us and vice versa – that is broadly how we define them.

What is a fruit?

In biological terms, however, a fruit is the thing produced by a plant that contains its seeds, and includes berries, pumpkins, chestnuts, pea pods, pears, apples and cherries, as well as sycamore, plane, lime and ash 'helicopters'.

The honesty flowers in dry arrangements are in fact the fruits: the papery thin silvery circles contain the seeds.

Seeds are usually contained inside a fruit, but can be outside, eg strawberries. They can be separate fruits, eg apples, lemons, or grouped together, eg raspberries, blackberries.

They are divided into two main types: fleshy fruits and dry fruits.

Fleshy fruits are those we most associate with the term 'fruits', eg luscious to eat.

Dry fruits are those we usually class as nuts or legumes (beans and peas).

A **berry** is a fleshy fruit without a stone but which usually has lots of seeds. Examples are kiwi, banana, currant, pepper, coffee and tomato as well as those with 'berry' in their name.

A **drupe** is a fleshy fruit with a single stone – the seed – and includes plum, cherry, coconut, damson, sloe and olive.

Fruits such as apples and pears are called **pomes** (from the word for apple). They have thin coverings, concealing the flesh, and the seeds are inside chambers in the centre of the fruits.

Just to confuse you, **hesperidiums** are berries with thick rinds, eg oranges, limes, lemons, grapefruits.

Further confusion comes from the fact that the strawberry in biological terms is a 'false fruit' as the seeds are on the outside!

Fruits may contain:

- one seed – many nuts, plums, olives;

- a couple of seeds – grapes, sweet chestnuts;

- several seeds – lemons, apples, pea and bean pods, berries, peanuts, honesty;

- sometimes a great many seeds indeed – pumpkins, melons, tomatoes, squashes.

The **fruits** can vary in size from very small – the individual parts of a blackberry – to the biggest in the world – a pumpkin – which can weigh in at 220 lb (100 kg) or more! Note that the UK record is a staggering (literally if you are carrying it) hernia inducing 900 lbs!

The **seeds** also vary in size, from those which you can hardly see to that of the coco de mer which can be up to 45 lb (20kgs). A bowl full of these would do serious damage to your sideboard.

The largest seed in the UK is probably the conker, the seed of the horse chestnut.

There are lot of very confusing names for different fruits – drupes (eg plum), achenes (eg sunflower, nut), as well as samaras, lomentums, siliques, dehiscent, even indehiscent – that expose themselves all the time – but I won't go into those.

They come in all sorts of different shapes – pips, flat, round - and the seed containers vary enormously.

Types of seed container

There are many different seed containers, including:

Fruit Apples, oranges, strawberries, tomatoes, squash, pumpkins, melons.
Nuts Acorn, chestnut, hazel, peanut.

Pods Beans, peas, laburnum.

Flowers Sunflowers, carrots.

Stem pots Poppy, onions.

Helicopters Lime, ash, plane, sycamore.

Once the plant has produced its fruits with its seeds – which will eventually, it hopes, grow into new plants – it needs to get them into the best places to take root and grow. They need to be dispersed far and wide in order to achieve their goal of total world domination – or it seems that way with the billions of seeds produced by some plants!

Seed dispersal

One of the reasons for producing seeds is to ensure that bio-diversity is encouraged and cross-pollination takes place. This makes plants (and indeed anything) stronger. One of the ways of ensuring this is to get the seeds that are produced to travel as far as possible away from the parent (and 'siblings'). This is called **seed dispersal**. It also reduces competition locally for food, water, light, etc and reduces the incidence of a disease in one area wiping out all the plants.

The commonest methods of seed dispersal are:

Natural – using natural events

- **Wind** The seeds are very dry and light and can be blown a surprisingly long way. In some areas the plants have adapted to mature just when the windy season arrives. Typically thousands of seeds are produced to ensure success. The most successful trees in the world (pines) use this method, producing millions of seeds from their pine cones. Others include dandelion 'clocks', cornflower, honesty, the carrot family and several other trees.

  Some such as the sycamore, plane and ash have extensions which act as parachutes or wings to catch the wind and you can often see them spinning gracefully around (helicopters or 'helitocktocks' as my daughters used to call them when they were little). Thistledown produced by cardoons is also wind-dispersed, and these and other down-producing plants yield the 'fairies' that float like gossamer and which children love to chase.

Poppies have a curious bulbous head, just below the flower, with holes in it. As the wind blows it from side to side the seeds spill out. You can see this on a windy day if you are lucky; and it is one of nature's great sights. If you have a video camera, film it and then play it back in slow-motion to get the full and fantastic effect.

- **Explosions** Some plants have special seed cases which – as they dry out and are knocked – shatter or explode, scattering the seeds over a wide area. Good examples of this are the legumes (peas, broad beans), laburnum, lupins, broom, euphorbia, gorse and geraniums. When harvesting peas it is not unusual to see pods at the mangetout stage, edible pea stage and also at the dried-up, waiting-to-explode stage, on the same plant.

- **Water** Some plants live by the sea or streams and produce seeds that are waterproof and spread that way. They can travel many – in fact thousands – of miles. The best-known example to most of us is the coconut. Willows can often be found by streams in the UK, and their seeds are waterproof so that they can float gently down on the water until they come to rest on a bank, germinate and take root. You can often chart the course of a stream or small river from a distance by the willows along its banks.

- **Catapults** Ferns use water in a different way. They are curled up when in a dry state and when water is absorbed, eg after rain, their fronds unroll, throwing out seeds like a catapult.

- **Rock and roll** Seeds are encased in coverings that are rocked out of a tree by wind or animals (or boys conkering) and when they land they burst open and the seed rolls along the ground (conkers, acorns), eventually taking root.

- **Fire** Some plants have adapted to their circumstances to such a great extent that they can only spread their seeds after a fire (some like it hot!!). The seeds and roots are fire-resistant, but the fire triggers their dispersal and afterwards they spring up with plenty of nutrients (ash) to help.

Animal mechanisms – plants and animals have often developed a complex symbiosis for distribution.

- **Fruits of the forest.** Many plants that we enjoy eating didn't develop their flesh and taste for us (difficult to believe, isn't it, as we regard ourselves as the centre of the world). They were developed to encourage birds and other animals such as monkeys – and even fish (there is a fruit-eating piranha in the River Amazon) – to eat them, which is why they are nice and juicy and packed full of goodness. The fruit, however, contains seeds with indigestible coats. This usually allows the seeds to pass through the animal undamaged – often miles away from the parent and wrapped in a good dollop of fertiliser (dung).

Humans often don't eat the seeds (eg apples and pears) and throw them away with, for example, the cores – which also served to distribute them at first. Now they go into a bin (or composter if you are an allotment holder) so it is no longer symbiotic – we are parasites! Many of the fruits that are poisonous to us are not to animals, and they eat them and disperse them in the same way.

- **Hitchhikers** eg goose grass, burdock. The fruits have hooks which grab onto the fur of passing animals and are usually only detached some time later – again a long way away from their starting point. A great game that children have always played is picking chickweed and put it on each other's or parents' backs. It clings tenaciously until taken off. You often see these hitchhikers in sheep wool – teasing is the process of getting rid of them. In olden times thistles were used for this, hence their other name – teazles.

Next time you go for a walk through undergrowth you may find a plant or seed clinging onto your sock. Legend has it that this type of dispersal was the original inspiration for Velcro – and you can see how that would make sense.

- **Couriers** Several animals take seeds (sometimes accidentally) and put them elsewhere, eg mistletoe seeds are very sticky and get stuck on the beaks of birds such as the missel thrush. The birds wipe them off on trees, where they stick and the seed grows and the plant – which is a parasite – is nicely *in situ* until cut off by a druid or a barrow-boy at Christmas. Many animals, eg squirrels, collect nuts and bury them; forgetting where they put them. The seeds then germinate and grow.

Germination

A seed is one of nature's true miracles. From a small – sometimes almost too small to be seen – seed an often massive plant will grow. It is a powerhouse waiting for the right moment and, when conditions are just right, from within the seed the plant will burst out and force its way through the soil and into the light of day. From a cucumber seed half an inch big, you can grow plants 21 feet (7m) long or more. From a tiny grape pip you can grow vines that just spread and spread unless pruned hard every year.

Germination is the process whereby the seed takes root, thrusts its little nose out into the world, and then tries to grow into a big strong plant. Like all life, a plant's time is fraught with obstacles, barriers and things that will try to kill it or eat it. There is nothing that many predators like better than a succulent, young seedling. With unerring accuracy they zero in on your prized or favourite plants, leaving the weeds standing and untouched.

Some germination times (under the right conditions).

One week or less	One to two weeks	Up to a month	Over one month
Squashes	Cabbages	Rocket	Parsnips
Melons	Beans	Parsley	
Pumpkins	Runner beans	Celery	
	Radishes		
	Turnips		
	Melons		
	Tomatoes		

The process whereby a seed is transformed from a usually dried out bit of its mother into a fully fledged member of the plant kingdom is called *germination*. During germination, the young plant emerges from its protective seed coat, ie it grows.

To happen, the process requires:

- Water (moisture).
- Food (held in the seed, initially).
- Warmth.

Some plants perversely require exposure to cold before they germinate – typically those known as hardy (which means that they are tough and can stand the cold!). Seeds grow into plants in two directions at once, up and down and, incidentally, spreading out as well in middle age.

The main steps in this process are:

- Moisture absorption by the seed.

- Root production.

- Shoot production and growth.

- Surface breakthrough and 'real' leaf production.

Moisture absorption

The seed absorbs moisture, which starts the process off by allowing the food reserves of the seed to become available, and softens the hard coating to allow the relevant bits to emerge.

Some seeds are extremely hard and folklore says that you need to 'nick' them to allow them to take in water to get them going. Others swear by rubbing the seeds gently between sandpaper to roughen up the coating. Legend has it that Victorian gardeners used to carry pea seeds around in their waistcoat pocket for months until they had been roughened up!

I have never found any of the above necessary. As long as there is sufficient moisture and warmth, seeds usually manage to absorb water.

Component parts of a seed

Germination varies considerably from plant to plant (see table). There are three main parts to a seed inside the outer covering:

- The embryonic root.

- The embryonic shoot.

- The embryonic leaves.

Root production

A seed first produces a root called a radicle (but not on the left), which grows down towards gravity, no matter which way round you have placed the seed. This is called **geotropism**, meaning 'movement towards the pull of gravity' (Greek *Ge* for *earth* and *tropis* for movement).

The seed will also produce root hairs and further roots which will anchor it within the ground. These will in due course allow it to take in water and – through it – the dissolved food (nutrients) that it will need to grow (see Roots below). The embryonic shot is called a **plumule**.

Shoot production and growth

Next the seed produces a shoot which is called the **hypocotyl**. This develops from the plumule, and it is protected by two false, quasi- or proto-leaves called cotyledons as it pushes through the soil to get to the surface. Sometimes (squashes, for example) the seed cover stays over the plumule as well for extra protection, and you can see it clinging onto one of the leaves after it has broken the surface.

Note that some plants only produce one leaf, such as grasses, some have a lot more – pines can have up to eight – and some have none – these are called **acotyledons**.

The plumule grows away from gravity – no matter which way up you place the seed (anti-geotropism or geo-phobism).

The seed contains enough food for the plumule to reach the surface – provided it isn't too deep – in a fantastic burst of energy.

In-depth analysis

As a general rule, seeds should not be planted at a depth of more than one and a half times their size. If you do they will use up their food supply before they get to the surface and will die. The plant cannot make any more food until it reaches the light.

This is a common cause of crop failure when growing from seed. It is a fine balance – not too deep, or it won't make it – nor too shallow, or it will get dug up and eaten, dessicated by the sun, or killed by frost. It is a miracle that any plant makes it: and of course many do not.

Certification

When you buy a packet of seeds and it says that the seeds have been certified, it doesn't mean that they are mad, but they can be maddening when you are trying to get them to grow! It means that they have been tested for the *probable percentage* that will germinate in the right (optimum) conditions (called viability). Most seed packets will state that the seeds have been tested in accordance with the relevant regulations. It doesn't usually state what the percentage viability is, however, so you can't audit it for accuracy. Note, however, that the optimum conditions rarely exist outside the testing laboratory!

Most seeds sold commercially have a viability close to 100 per cent; but some are not so easy to grow. Carrots only have a viability of about 65 per cent; and it has proved impossible to give anything to parsnips because their germination is so unpredictable – as I know only too well.

F1 hybrids

Note that F1 hybrids are specially produced from crossing two plants to give a definite output and they are more expensive than non-F1 seeds (F1 stands for 'first generation'). For the allotment gardener these are less satisfactory, as they have a tendency to mature all at the same time (unless you engage in a spot of succession sowing), giving you gluts (nasty!).

You should also note that subsequent seeds from an F1 hybrid will not grow 'true'. That is, they will revert to the characteristics of a parent, rather than those of the F1 cross you bought last year. If you don't mind what the result looks like then use the seeds, but if you particularly wish to have that F1 hybrid; you need to buy the F1 seeds every year.

Surface breakthrough and 'real' leaf production

Finally the seedling pushes its shoot through the soil's surface and can start to use the sun's energy to make its own food from the nutrients that the root hairs have taken up using the oxygen from the air. This is called **photosynthesis** (Greek *synthesis* for 'making' *photon* for 'from the light'). Many people think that it is only leaves that can photosynthesise, but in fact any green part of a plant can make food (carbohydrates) from carbon dioxide and water using energy from sunlight. This is effected by the chlorophyll (Greek again meaning 'green leaf') within the green parts.

Obstruction!

The above is what happens in good fine soil. If, however, the shoot encounters a large stone or another type of obstruction, eg a membrane or a thick mulch, then it will not be able to go through and will try to go round it. Whether it succeeds or not depends on how far it has to go/grow before exhausting the food supply and getting into the light. This is the logic behind using membranes and mulches to keep weeds down: it denies them access to the light for photosynthesis.

Plants are, despite this, incredibly tough, and filled with a dynamism and determination to 'see the light'! If you have ever seen a tiny plant pushing through the asphalt on the pavement and looked at how much it displaces to get to the air and light, then you will understand this.

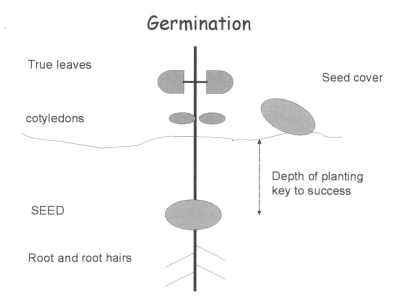

Germination

True leaves

Seed cover

cotyledons

Depth of planting
key to success

SEED

Root and root hairs

The cotyledons open up on contact with the light, splitting the seed cover open, and then turn green to start the process of converting nutrients to energy using photosynthesis.

True leaves

Next the first true leaves appear above the cotyledons. These allow the plant to use the sun's energy, make more roots, strengthen the stem, grow more leaves, etc. At this stage it is usual to transplant the seedlings out if you have not grown them *in situ*. Where they are sown *in situ* then, after the true leaves have appeared, they should be 'thinned out' to reduce competition for resources and ensure fewer but healthier, stronger and better yielding plants.

After this we are back to the beginning of the life cycle and the plant will, with a following wind and at the right time, start to produce flowers for pollination and then fruit – which in many cases is what you want to harvest.

Other ways of reproducing

While most plants produce seeds, others have ancillary methods of reproducing themselves. These are:

- **Suckers** These are shoots that grow up from the ground but are attached to the roots of the plant. They often grow more vigorously than the parent and often root if they fall over and touch down. For control it is best to cut them off below ground. You can use them to propagate by staking them until they have rooted and then severing them (see Runners also).

- **Bulbs** These are condensed shoots. In winter the stalk dies back and the roots shrivel as it sucks the goodness back. It then stays quiescent until spring. It is a store of food and allows growth to take place in the following season. It consists of a modified shoot in the centre protected by overlapping layers (quasi-leaves) and roots growing at the base. You set them in the ground and away they go. Examples include onions, garlic, and of course daffodils, tulips and snowdrops. They produce seeds as well.

- **Corms** are similar (eg crocus) but are condensed stems. A bud sits on the top and roots appear from underneath.

- **Runners (stolons)** are long horizontal shoots that grow along the ground producing roots and growth at the nodes or tip. Examples of these are strawberries and currants, as well as the creeping buttercup. They can be many feet long!

- **Rhizomes** are stems that grow horizontally underground, for example mint, iris and the dandelion. They can spread very fast. Mint is very hard to control because of this. The best way is to sink a bottomless container in the ground and plant the mint inside it, then chop round it to keep the growth down.

- **Tubers** are swollen stems, the best known being the potato. Buds appear all over it, called 'eyes'. For the best results rub out all except one, or cut the tuber into sections each with an 'eye'. A tuber can also be a swollen root, eg dahlias.

- **Clones/daughters** Some plants produce little versions of themselves and when they touch down they produce roots and a new plant is born. These can be taken off and replanted to give you free plants. One of the most common is the spider plant.

Roots

A few words on roots. The word is from Anglo-Saxon and is related to *wyrt* or *wort*, meaning plant. The political word 'radical' is from the Latin for root – *radix* – and was a term for those who wanted to tear up the system by its roots, which is the same root (groan) as the name for the initial root from a seed – radicle.

The two major functions of roots are:

- To take in food by absorbing water in which nutrients are dissolved.

- To anchor the plant in the ground.

They often function in the storage of food – and it is often this part that we eat (parsnips, beetroots, carrots). Some other items that come from roots include liquorice, ginger, ginseng, angelica, and of course the mandrake root, which is famous in legend.

Osmosis

Plants take in water through the root hairs on the outside of the root. These are very delicate and it is for this reason that you never pull a plant that you want to keep or transplant by the root, as it breaks the hairs off. These hairs only live for a few days and as the root grows it keeps sending out new ones.

The process by which the plant absorbs water is osmosis. You can see the effects of this if you walk in wet conditions in leather shoes – the soles absorb the water and your feet get wet. If you leave a towel with its edge just in water, then the water will creep up it until it is all wet. You can also cause osmosis by cutting off the bottom of a potato, scooping out the centre and standing it in a bowl of water. Next morning it will contain water as it has been absorbed.

Types of roots

The first root to emerge is called the **primary root** and it is the radicle of the seedling. As the plant grows it can often send out new root shots sideways. These are called lateral roots.

There are two main types of root system:

- The **taproot** system's first (primary) root is the main root, often with much smaller roots running off from it. These roots can often penetrate very deep indeed. They can also be the devil to pull out as they can anchor a plant extremely well. Dandelions are a good example of one of these (as are parsnips and carrots). As well as anchorage, they have a major food-storage function.

- Lots of roots with no dominant root, called **diffuse** roots. They spread out and primarily absorb nutrients and give anchorage. They are often much more shallow than taproots and store little food.

Other types of roots

Aerial roots The roots are above the plant and can be seen, eg Swiss cheese plants/ or ivy, where they arc used to anchor the plant to walls.

Propagative These are roots that form on the side of the plant's roots and then grow up and out to make suckers, which form new plants.

Cluster roots Very densely packed roots that do not go very far. This means that they do not anchor the plant very well. Peas and beans have roots like these.

Mycelium Some fungi have a curious root that is a network of fibres. It grows outwards from the centre and the fruiting buds – mushrooms or toadstools – grow on the edge. That is why you see 'fairy rings' in wood-land where the mycelium has spread outwards to form a circle.

Parasitic roots Roots of parasitic plants that take in food directly from other plants (for example, mistletoe) are called haustorial (from Latin for water-drawer, as in a well).

Root facts

Tree roots can often be as deep as the tree is high. Think about this before trying to pull a large plant, shrub, bush or tree out.

As the roots grow longer they often get thicker as well. This is called secondary growth. In this case they usually develop hard woody external coverings which act as a very strong tree structure or tree architecture. You can often see this where rain or river water has eroded soil, and what look like underground branches (but are in fact roots) are visible – and easy to trip over!

Most roots lie relatively close to the surface so that they can easily pick up air and water from top-soil. After storms you can sometimes see trees that have been blown over, and the roots are most commonly of the diffuse sort, rather than tap roots. That is why they blew over – the roots do not go that deep and the tops of the trees act as sails to catch the full force of the wind.

In Victorian times, placing a paving stone below trees was a technique used to limit root growth.

Bonsai trees are bred small by keeping the roots very small.

Root benefits

The roots of trees and other plants often help in binding soil together. In many areas (Easter Island, for example) where all trees were cut down, the soil was eroded by wind and rain and the land became uncultivable. This is still happening in many parts of the world today, especially in rainforests, with devastating effects on wildlife.

Plants from the legume family – beans, peas and so on – have special nodules that absorb nitrogen and then fix it in the soil, thus improving it. Many green manure crops (clover, alfalfa, trefoil, lupin) are grown with this purpose in mind.

Plant Families

Why learn about plant families?

There are several reasons for this. It is not a way of showing off, but practical and helpful in maximising outputs from your allotment. Plant families often share characteristics, likes, dislikes and diseases and pests. This knowledge is important when considering rotations to reduce the incidence of diseases, and for feeding and general care.

It can help you to identify a new plant. If your unknown plant demonstrates characteristics of a family grouping then this can help when trying to identify it. Are those seedlings carrots, beetroots or others – including weeds?

If you decide to collect your own seeds (a very good idea) then knowing the plant family will help you if you are unfamiliar with the plants in question. For example:

- Peas and beans hold their seeds in the pods, which hang down and which we eat of course.

- Brassica seed containers look like those from honesty – seeds contained within two very thin membranes.

- Mint, a member of the nettle family, doesn't have seed pods.

● Poppies have a seed pod at the top of the stalk that is blown in the wind, sending out the seeds in fine streams.

Seed size

Sometimes knowing about plant families allows you to tell how big the seeds will be. The seed-bearing fruits of cucurbitaceae are berries (tomatoes) or large fleshy fruits (melons, squashes, gourds and pumpkins) and have lots of big seeds inside the fruit.

The seeds from the carrot family are tiny and come from the flowers.

But the key factor about knowing the plant families is so that you can understand which plants are in which family and will therefore share the same characteristics in terms of what and how to feed or augment them, eg brassicas and lime. It is also to ensure that you don't follow one member of a family – say cabbage – with another, for example sprouts or cauliflower, so disease doesn't build up and pests don't hang around, knowing that there will be a supply of their favourite plants.

Knowing the unlikely members of the same family will also enable you to avoid following cabbages with turnip which, although grown as a 'root' crop, is, in fact, a member of the brassica family, as its name – *brassica rapa* – tells you. It is also related to the swede – *brassica napus*.

In the following pages I will look at the key items:

● Characteristics.

● How to grow and when to plant.

● Issues.

● Harvesting.

I have collated all the plants into three categories:

● Vegetables.

● Fruit.

● Grasses.

As vegetables are mostly what are grown in allotments, I have given the major vegetable families a chapter each. Then there is one chapter on fruit and others for herbs and grasses.

The main families of vegetables are:

- Brassica (cabbages, cauliflowers, turnips).

- Cucurbits (squashes, cucumbers, pumpkins).

- Alliaiacae (onions, leeks).

- Solanacae (tomatoes/potatoes).

- Asters (lettuce).

- Legumes (peas, beans).

- Apiaiacae (celery, carrots, parsnips).

- Chenopodiaceae (beetroot, chard, spinach).

Many writers lump all root crops together, but they are from different families and therefore it is important to remember this when planning crop rotation. Thus, swedes, radish and turnip are all dealt with under Brassica as that is the family to which they belong.

(14)

Brassica – The Cabbage Family

This family has been one of the mainstays of European vegetable gardening for centuries. They are tough plants and have adapted to our northern winters. It is a large family and includes cabbages, turnips, sprouts, kale, broccoli, calabrese, purple sprouting, swedes and cauliflowers. There are also several important or well-known non-vegetable plants such as oil-seed rape – which forms those hideous yellow swathes that are such blots on the landscape and that smell that makes you gag – and flowers such as wallflowers, which can be found in millions of UK gardens, alyssum with its pretty white flowers often planted with lobelia (blue) and salvias (red) for a (patriotic) colourful display; and honesty, so beloved of dry decorations. Brassicas can be found pretty much all over the world, although most species live in the northern temperate region.

Which part of the brassica do we eat?

We eat every bit – depending on the plant. These plants are grown for their leaves, buds, roots, stems and even shoots. This family is a classic example of selective breeding over time, and its members have been bred to emphasise the parts that we want to eat:

- Large, fleshy roots in turnips or swedes.

- Large leaves for cabbages and kale.

- Large flower buds for cauliflower, calabrese and broccoli.

It is the flowers which give this plant family its original name of Cruciferae. They are made up of four petals in a cross shape (cruciform).

We love these plants and gardeners grow many of them, often and in profusion. Unfortunately others love them too, such as pigeons, rabbits, caterpillars and slugs/snails, who will feast on them well – even if the plants are protected.

Soil conditions for growing brassicas

Typically brassicas like soil that is moisture-retentive, but firm and rich in nitrogen. They are usually put in to follow legumes. They also like alkaline soil and liming is necessary on acid soils during the previous autumn.

Some are very rapid growers, such as rocket (hence its name) and radish. Others take a very long time and are sown for harvesting the following season.

Brassicas can be easily grown from seed *in situ* or raised in seed beds or propagators and planted out later on. This can be especially useful for the slower-growing members; allowing you to catch-crop (see page 141) in the ground until you are ready to plant the main brassicas out.

The brasicas covered in this chapter are:

- Cabbage.
- Brussels sprouts.
- Swedes.
- Broccoli/calabrese/purple sprouting.
- Cauliflower.
- Kale.

- Turnips.
- Kohlrabi.
- Rocket.
- Radish.
- Cress.
- Mustard.

Cabbage

Characteristics

This is a case where a lot of effort has been put into breeding plants that are available in slightly different forms virtually all year round. There are several types – savoy, red, green and white – which can be planted to mature at different times of the year.

How to grow and when to plant

Cabbage can be sown all year round to provide a staple crop depending on type.

Annual cabbage cycle

	J	F	M	A	M	J	J	A	S	O	N	D
Winter												
Sow					✓	✓	✓					
Plant out						✓	✓	✓				
Harvest	✓	✓	✓							✓	✓	✓
Spring												
Sow							✓	✓	✓			
Plant out								✓	✓	✓		
Harvest			✓	✓	✓	✓						
Summer												
Sow		✓	✓	✓	✓	✓						
Plant out				✓	✓	✓	✓					
Harvest						✓	✓	✓	✓	✓		
Autumn												
Sow			✓	✓	✓							
Plant out					✓	✓	✓					
Harvest								✓	✓	✓	✓	

We grow red cabbage for autumn and winter. It goes well with meat when cooked with apples and is a traditional accompaniment to Christmas turkey for us.

Spring cabbages grow over winter ready for harvesting early next year (but need to be planted when it is still warmish, eg late September). You can sow them *in situ*; or propagate them in seed trays and then plant out. This reduces their exposure to predators and the vagaries of winter while they are still young and tender plants.

Choose the hardy varieties that are frost-resistant for spring and winter crops.

If possible, sow a few at a time to avoid gluts, and provide nice, healthy plants for eating throughout the year.

Sow spring cabbages about 1 foot (30 cm) apart, and summer and winter cabbages between 14 and 18 inches (35 and 50 cm), with rows about 1 foot (30 cm) apart.

The soil must be firm to stop 'wobble'. In autumn, earth the stems up to offer further protection against wind.

In dry times a loose mulch of straw helps.

Keep weeds down to avoid competition, but hoe very carefully so as not to damage the stems. Note that this is difficult if you cover the plot in netting. We do and therefore have to pull the weeds out by hand through or under the netting. This is a back-breaking and laborious experience, but necessary to keep butterflies and other pests off.

Issues

- Clubroot – typical cabbage issue. Rotation and liming help to reduce this.

- Cabbage white butterfly – lays eggs which become caterpillars that munch away happily on your plants. Netting the plants to keep butterflies away is a good solution.

- Cabbage root fly – a nuisance. See Pests.

- Rot – can be an issue. Take off dead leaves and burn them. Do not compost.

- Acidity – make sure the soil is limed. A pH of 6–7.5 is best (see Clubroot above).

- Water – regular water gives the best growth, but do not over-water. In normal conditions (reasonable dry summers) one good watering a week is sufficient. If the ground is very dry, do not drench it as this may cause the 'heads' to split. Water a little every day for a week until it is moist again.

Harvesting

Depending on the type you plant and when, cabbages can be harvested all year round.

Spring cabbage from March to June.

Summer cabbage from June to October.

Autumn cabbage from July to October.

Winter cabbage from October to March.

Cut off the plants close to the ground with a sharp knife. If you cut an X in the remaining stump you may get a second crop of mini-cabbages (this hasn't worked for me yet!).

Store in a cool shed or in a refrigerator (two weeks or so), but it is best to leave them *in situ* wherever possible. Those that are prone to damage by frost should, of course, be harvested before it arrives.

Cabbage can be eaten raw, both in salads and as coleslaw (Dutch *koolsla* for cabbage salad), or cooked, which is how we usually eat it (boiled, braised or steamed), and it can even be made into soups which can be frozen and stored.

Cabbage is very good for you. It contains vitamin C and antioxidants. Some varieties can be stir-fried and of course some can be pickled. Many people do not like cabbage as they (as I did) have memories of over-cooked, tasteless, green stuff from school. Cooked properly, however, it is delicious – as I keep telling my children, who of course get it at school and turn their noses up at it at home!

Brussels sprouts

Characteristics

We don't normally grow these as nobody likes them very much, but for next year we have decided to give them a go. They are in essence miniature cabbages that grow in profusion on a long stem about 1 yard (1 metre) high.

It is a hardy winter crop – hence its association with Christmas in the depths of winter – and a touch of frost improves the flavour. It has a long growth season (seed to crop is five or six months) but repays with a long cropping period.

How to grow and when to plant

Sprouts can be sown from April onwards until July. They require plenty of sun and protection from wind, as they are top-heavy when in bud and can be blown over. Consider protecting them with wind breaks if that is an issue. They are best raised in seed propagators/beds and then transplanted. Seedlings appear in about a week.

Plant them 1 foot (30 cm) apart with the same distance between rows. They like pH around 7.0. They like rich moist soil which must be firmed around them for stability. Make sure that they are planted deeply with the lowest leaves touching the surface to help avoid root fly.

Issues

- Top-heavy in winds – earth up soil to protect them. On very windy sites, stake them for extra protection.
- Cabbage white butterfly – see Cabbages.
- Clubroot – see Cabbages.

Harvesting

Don't let the sprouts get bigger than 1–1$\frac{1}{2}$ inches (2cm) in diameter before harvesting them. Pick only those you need. Cut them off with a sharp knife, starting at the bottom with the more mature ones and leaving the younger ones for next time. Take a few from each plant. They are very hardy and will be fine on the stem over winter.

If you cut the top 6 inches (15 cm) of the stem off, all the sprouts will mature at the same time about six weeks later – which is useful if you are mass catering at Christmas and want to serve this traditional vegetable. You can freeze them.

When all the sprouts have been collected the leafy tops can be used as cabbage.

In Victorian times the stems were 'cured' and used as walking sticks!

Swedes

Characteristics

Latin name: *napo brassica* (from *napus* meaning 'turnip')

Also called the yellow turnip and in the USA a rutabaga. It is a cross between turnip and cabbage. It is said to have been grown in Sweden, where its the name is rotabagge. In the USA it is also called Swedish turnip. In Scotland it is also sometimes called a 'neep', from the Anglo-Saxon *naep* for turnip, in turn derived from the Latin word, and, confusingly, a turnip is called a swede! In northern England it is also called a 'snadgy' which I think is a great name!

The swede is hardier than the turnip – due to its cabbage crossing no doubt – and so is a good winter crop. It is also much larger than a turnip and is generally thought to taste sweeter. It can be purple, brown or green in colour, with yellow flesh inside.

How to grow and when to plant

Swedes need a long growing season (six months or so) so sow them in spring/early summer for autumn and winter. They enjoy cool damp conditions and need rich soil. They can be propagated or sown *in situ*, under mesh to protect them from pests. Sow seeds no more than $^3/_4$ inc (2 cm) deep, in rows about 18 inches (45 cm) wide for larger types, slightly less for smaller ones, and then to 6–8 inches (15–20 cm) apart.

Keep them well watered, but do not over-water. They like a soil pH of 6.0 to 6.5.

Give a light dressing of fertiliser before planting. Swedes like to follow on from crops that had plenty of organic matter (potatoes or squashes).

Issues

- Lack of water will cause Swedes to bolt; or if watered after a dry spell they will split.

- Slugs and snails love them!

- Clubroot – See Cabbages.

- Cabbage white butterfly – see Cabbages.

- Cabbage root fly – see Pests.

Harvesting

Swedes are hardy and a touch of frost improves the flavour, but they can be difficult to get out of frozen ground. If it is very wet in winter then lift them or they will become prone to rot. They tend to become a bit woody by the new year if left in the ground. Store them in boxes in layers of sand.

Broccoli/calabrese/purple sprouting

Characteristics

This is one of the favourite vegetables in our family. We eat it every week and the girls have always loved it – contrary to what many adults expect from children. It is very easy to grow – but also all too easily eaten by pests. Broccoli, calabrese (named after the Calabria region in Italy where it came from) and purple sprouting are all variations on a theme. It is a cut-and-come-again vegetable and will keep producing new buds or curds for some time.

How to grow and when to plant

You can either sow from seed *in situ* or buy plug plants. Broccoli will grow in just about any soil but prefers heavy soil that is tending towards clay (ie ideal on our allotment). Make sure that the soil is very firm and compacted because broccoli grows best in that medium. If sown under cover, sow in early spring for planting out in June or July.

Use a dibber to make holes 2 foot (60 cm) apart and the same distance between rows. The transplants are best puddled in, as for leeks.

Broccoli is best grown on soil that was enriched the previous year and with a pH of around 6.5.

Issues

- The young plants must be covered to protect them from the usual depredations from a whole array of pests – cabbage white butterflies, pigeons, caterpillars, etc.

- The plants are prone to suffer in high wind so consider a wind break or staking them (or both).

Harvesting

Depending on which variety you choose, harvesting can take place all year round. Pick the main head first, to allow the others to develop. Pick every few days.

Broccoli is a bad storer so eat it at once. It might store in a refrigerator for a few days, but soon goes yellow and nasty!

Cauliflower

Characteristics

One of the mainstays of Sunday lunches when I was a child at home. With a roast, gravy and served with onion sauce it epitomises Sundays at home for me.

Note that cauliflower is a difficult plant to grow. In poor soil or bad conditions it will still grow, but the curds will not be up to much. The later maturing varieties are easier. We didn't grow these in our first year, deciding to wait until we had established our plot, and tried easier plants first.

How to grow and when to plant

Cauliflower is best sown under cover for transplanting out. They need to be kept at 80 °F while germinating for the best results.

As soon as they have five leaves you can transplant them out – usually in June. They like a rich soil with a pH of at least 6.5. If necessary, add manure well before planting out. A mulch will also help to conserve the moisture. Cauliflowers are a pretty large plant, so plan for them to be in rows 2 feet (60cm) wide with the same space between plants. Use dibbers and puddle them in as for leeks.

Issues

- Cabbage white butterfly – see Cabbages.

- In colder periods cover the plants with fleecy protection. In fact it is best to plant winter varieties in a sheltered spot.

- The heads (curds) need protection from cold and sun so tie the leaves around them. Some varieties have now been bred so that the leaves curl around them and protect them – amazing!

- Copper rings can keep slugs away and other types of collars may prevent root fly. These involve an initial high outlay – but people swear by them. We shall be investing in some next year.

Harvesting

Cauliflowers can be harvested virtually all year round if you have succession sown with the right types for the time of year. From sowing to cropping is about four months. Winter varieties stay in the ground longer – up to nine months!

They will keep for a week or so – longer in a refrigerator. If you have a dark, cool shed they will keep for up to three weeks – spray with water occasionally to keep them cool. Yellow/brown curds are a sign that they are past their best – similarly if the head has opened up.

Kale

Characteristics

From the German for cabbage – *kohl* – kale is a very hardy plant (*brassica oleracea*). It is also known as borecole and curly kale. It is yet another example of selective brassica breeding, this time for its leaves. It is full of vitamins, resistant to the typical brassica diseases and pests, and will grow in just about any soil. Curiously though, you very rarely see it growing. This is because it is associated with bitter-tasting leaves. There are two reasons for this: the leaves are best when very young and tender – not when older when they are indeed horrible; and the older varieties were more bitter than the newer 'sweeter'-tasting varieties which have done much to improve kale's reputation.

Kale is a winter vegetable – yet another of the 'hungry time' plants. It is better after the frost, so January onwards.

How to grow and when to plant

Station sow outside in late May or early June 1 foot (30 cm) apart and slightly wider between rows three or four seeds to a station and then thin. Germination is around a week and a half, and they only require 45 °F.

Issues

- Too much water. If this is a problem, dig in lots of organic matter before planting to help drainage.

- Really hard frost will kill kale so if that is forecast then cover it with fleece. However, normal frost makes kale thrive!

Harvesting

Use only the newer leaves in the centre of the crown. Leave the rest – they are not worth it.

Turnips

Characteristics

Although thought of as a root, turnip is a brassica (*brassica rapa*). It has also suffered from the school dinner syndrome: but home-grown and – perhaps more importantly – home-cooked – they are delicious. I sneaked them into my children's food by using them in a vegetable roast with potatoes and parsnips, carrots and onions, without telling them.

You can also eat the young tops as leafy vegetables.

We were far more successful with these than the other root crops!

How to grow and when to plant

Turnips share characteristics with swedes, which is not surprising. They prefer a light soil. If you have clay (as we do) then dig in lots of organic manure to help it. They prefer a pH of at least 6.0.

Sow them *in situ* in shallow rows, covering them with a fine layer of soil. They take just over a week to germinate. They need 42 °F (5 °C) for germination, so in the south of the UK you might be able to sow in late February.

When they are about 1 inch (3 cm) high, thin to about 3 inches (8 cm) apart. Leave 1 foot (30 cm) between rows. Water well and weed regularly. Hoe carefully between the rows.

Issues

- Slugs and snails – use organic repellent.

- Drought conditions produce hard little wooden balls which are indigestible, so water little and often. Too much water by contrast after a dry spell will cause them to split. Mulching to conserve water is a good idea, especially if you are away for extended periods in the summer.

- Canker can be an issue especially if the plants are damaged.

- Cabbage white butterfly – see Cabbages.

- Cabbage root fly – see Pests.

Harvesting

You can harvest them from five to six weeks after planting for earlies; and later for the main crop, winter roots – up to late December or early January. A hard frost will kill the plants so harvest before then and store the roots in shallow boxes with sand.

If you keep cutting the tops they will grow again and make a useful early spring green.

Kohlrabi

Characteristics

Kohlrabi is German for cabbage-turnip (not to be confused with swede, which in Swedish is *rutabaga* – turnip-cabbage!) and looks like a monster from outer space. Despite its fearsome looks it has a delicate flavour.

It sits above the ground so soil does not need to be dug that deeply.

We didn't grow these in our first year but decided to give them a go later on precisely because they look so weird.

How to grow and when to plant

This plant prefers warm and sheltered spots but not too hot. It needs water to make the stem swell.

It can be planted from March until August and will be ready in about six to eight weeks.

Sow the seeds about $^3/_4$ inch (2 cm) deep in rows about 1 foot (30 cm) apart.

Sow them a few at a time every few weeks or so to ensure a good supply. If left too long they go 'woody'.

When the seedlings are through, thin out to one every 6 inches (15 cm). Mulching will help in dry periods. Take off any leaves that are discoloured as well as any side shoots, so as to concentrate the effort into the stem.

The green types are usually sown as earlies and the purple types for later on in the year.

Issues

- Water is a prerequisite, so water often and heavily (except in deluges). The flavour is better when they grow quickly.

- If your soil is poor try using a liquid feed, rich in nitrogen.

- Clubroot – see Cabbages.

- Cabbage white butterfly – see Cabbages.

Harvesting

Pick when tennis ball-sized and check regularly to ensure they do not grow too big and woody.

Kahlrabi does not store very well, but will keep for a couple of weeks in a refrigerator.

It can be eaten raw or cooked.

You can also cook the leaves, as for spinach.

Make sure that you will eat what you sow or it will go to waste very quickly.

Rocket

Characteristics

Not as everyone thinks a lettuce, but a member of the brassica family (*eruca vesicaria*). The trendy vegetable of the chattering classes of Highgate and Islington (where they all think it is a lettuce as well) is also called rucola and arugula.

Rocket is a great catch-crop as it needs only three weeks – hence its UK name. It can be grown most of the year because, being a brassica, it is very hardy and adapted to our northern climes.

How to grow and when to plant

Rocket must be the easiest plant to grow. It likes any soil and partial shade, and needs moisture. The flavour changes as the weather warms up and it becomes more peppery. Use finely raked soil for sowing.

Sow it every two weeks for continuous crops from early March (when it is warm enough outside) or alternatively sow under cover and transplant out.

As autumn approaches, cover it with a fleece to protect it.

Issues

- Hot weather will cause rocket to bolt, so grow it next to taller plants (eg sweetcorn) for shade.

- Water is crucial to keep it tasty rather than hot tasting.

- Clubroot – see Cabbages.

- Cabbage white butterfly – see Cabbages.

- Cabbage root fly – see Pests.

Harvesting

Take the leaves when they are about 3 to 4 inches (7 to 10 cm) long. Cut them about 1inch above ground level and new leaves will sprout.

If they are large taste them, as larger leaves tend to be more peppery.

Wash the leaves well. Rocket does not store for more than a couple of days so only pick what you wish to use.

Let some plants flower and harvest the seeds. You can eat the flowers too, apparently.

Radish

Characteristics

Another surprising member of the brassica family (*raphanus sativus*) which loves our cooler climate and grows very quickly – three weeks. A good thing for children to do is to trace out their name, plant the seeds and in a few weeks their name will be picked out in radishes.

Some radishes are round globes, but others such as French breakfast or Daikon are long like thick fingers. They can be white, red, pink or black in colour. Some can be hot – very hot indeed!

Radishes are also useful for sowing with other plants that are slower (eg parsnips) to mark the line and also provide a catch-crop.

How to grow and when to plant

Radishes germinate in only one or two days, so if you want to see early success this is the crop for you.

Sow in early spring *in situ* and if you want lots all year round keep sowing every two weeks. You can sow them anywhere! They prefer a pH of 6.5–7.5.

Sow winter varieties later on: they can be left longer in the ground for harvesting as you wish.

Issues

- Lack of water results in little red balls of wood, which might be useful for snooker but no good for eating; keep them well watered at all times and do not let them get too big.

Harvesting

Take them when they are about 1 inch (2.5 cm) in diameter – all at once per sowing.

Let one or two of them go to seed and you will get masses for next year.

The immature seed pods can also be eaten.

Cress

We all remember growing this as children in weird animal shapes – but I don't know anybody that grows it on the site. It is one of those garnishes that everybody leaves behind on their plates. It only takes about a week to grow, but why bother? We don't. A fun thing to do in school, or with your children; but not a lot of value to my mind. It is often linked with mustard.

Mustard

Used for making mustard of course, but on an allotment it has a special use as a green manure. Sow it thickly to suppress weeds and then dig it in later on. *Brassica hirta* is the edible mustard. *Sinapis alba* is the green manure.

How to grow and when to plant

Sow it after you have harvested a main crop and leave it to grow. Best early spring. It takes about six weeks before it is ready to dig in. You then need to leave it about the same time to let it decompose

For the edible crop it takes about three weeks to grow. You can also make soup from it and if you know how – mustard.

15

Legumes – The Pea and Bean Family

This is a large family. There are over 17,000 species throughout the world. It includes many well-known vegetables such as broad beans, runner beans and peas, and some interesting plants like mimosa and cassia. There are also green manure and fodder crops such as clover or lucerne and lots of weeds – the vetches and trefoils. Some climb, some grow along the ground and some are trees.

Many legumes are what is known as 'nitrogen fixers' – that is, they take nitrogen from the air and store it in their root nodules. They therefore manage very well in poor soil. When they have finished flowering and producing fruits, this nitrogen is left in the ground and enriches it for others.

It is the seed pods that give this family its name. The pod may contain just one or several seeds, and they are usually large, and sometimes brightly coloured. The main vegetables that we grow usually have several seeds within the pod. The coat of the individual seed is often watertight. They usually germinate quickly given the right amount of water to penetrate the hard coating.

The familiar produce such as beans, peas and lentils are also known as pulses – from the Latin for bean porridge – and they have long been a staple food for humans. They can be eaten fresh from the pod, cooked in any number of ways and dried. Dried pulses make excellent nourishing soup. Where would we be on long cold winter nights without London Particular, split pea soup or bacon, tomato and lentil soup?

Legumes are packed full of protein and preserve very well – dried, frozen or made into soup and frozen.

Peas

Characteristics

Green fat pods hanging down symbolise these easy-to-grow vegetables. There are many varieties – early peas, late peas, mangetout, sugar-snaps. With these latter two you eat the pods as well (hence the name – from French meaning 'eat everything'). They are reputed to be the oldest culti-vated plants in the world. Seeds have been found in dwellings from the early bronze age.

Do not forget either their cousin the sweet pea – we grow it for its lovely flowers and rich fragrance.

By nature the pea is a climber and so it needs good support. You can, how-ever, buy dwarf varieties that do not require a trellis or stakes, but we grow original climbing varieties. Most peas that are harvested and that we buy are frozen or canned, but taking a pod off the plant, breaking it open and eating the peas fresh cannot be beaten. They have a nutty flavour that is lost during the preserving process. One of the issues with gathering peas is that often more get eaten than harvested.

They do take up a lot of space relative to the harvest – but what sort of allotment doesn't grow peas?

How to grow and when to plant

Peas can be planted outside from March. It is best if you have the space to sow them in batches every four weeks or so to provide several crops. We intended to do that in our first year – but forgot to put our second crop in. They like good rich moisture-retentive soil. They need plenty of water, as this is what makes the peas fat.

Germination is tricky. They need warmth to germinate and March weather can be unpredictable. A good trick is to sow them indoors and then plant them out. Carol Klein in her series *Grow your Own Veg* recommends using roof guttering and then sliding them into position when they have germinated.

You can use the root trainers that were developed for sweet peas and this allows good root growth as well. We just sow *in situ*.

Transplant them when they are about 4 inches (10 cm) tall and can be handled.

If sowing *in situ*, sow them about 2 inches (5 cm) deep, about 6 inches (15cm) apart, in two rows about 1 foot (30 cm) apart. Use crossed bamboo pole stakes for support, as with runner beans. This supports the plants and ensures that air circulates. If it turns cold after sowing *in situ* then cover the ground with fleece or cloches for extra heat.

Some recommend hoeing around the plants, but to be honest we didn't and it didn't matter very much (we pulled the weeds out though).

Dwarf peas are usually planted in blocks to give each other mutual support. You can also use pea sticks – which are just short sticks. Don't forget to place something over the ends to save your eyes from being poked out!

Issues

- Mice love peas. So do birds and they will dig them up – although we didn't have any trouble in our first year. Cover the pea seeds with spiky branches or cover in netting or fleece.

- Water is key – check every week for moisture. Mulching can help.

- Pea moth – see Pests.

Harvesting

Keep harvesting so that the plant continues to produce more. Take all pods that are ready – even if you are late with the picking – then you will get fresh ones developing.

If harvesting as mangetout, then you need to catch them just as the peas are visible in the pod. If you miss this (all too easy for busy people) just use them as normal peas (mangepeas as one of our friends called them).

After harvest, do not pull the plants up but cut them off at ground level. This leaves the roots in to fix the nitrogen for next season.

Storing isn't really an issue as we eat all we produce – and so will you probably.

Runner beans

Characteristics

Another foreign plant that has been adopted everywhere, the runner bean is originally from Central America (Mexico) and used to warmer climes than chilly Britain. It was introduced by John Tradescant (of *Tradescantia* fame) in the seventeenth century and has become a firm favourite. It was originally cultivated for its beautiful flowers – until the beans were found to be edible in the eighteenth century.

Although they are perennials in their native lands, because the frost kills them in the UK we grow runner beans as annuals. They will produce a tuber (like potatoes) which would hibernate in the soil during the non-growing season in Mexico – but this isn't really practicable in the UK due to the cold. They are very vigorous growers; often reaching 8 feet (2.4 m) or more. The crop is amazing and it keeps cropping until the first frosts. We had so many beans that at one stage we had to give them away and we only planted a relatively small area of the plot with them.

How to grow and when to plant

They are very, very easy to grow. They will grow anywhere, but heavy clay (like ours) will reap the benefits of having been dug over to aid drainage and having lots of organic manure dug in first.

Dig out two small trenches 2 inches (5 cm) deep and 2 feet (60 cm) apart. Construct a long bamboo cane pyramid ('A' frame) with 8 foot (2.4 m) tall canes, set about 8 inches (20 cm) apart on both sides and add a cross piece (or two). Anchor it very securely in the soil. Then sow two seeds at the bottom of every cane.

You can also create a wigwam by placing canes around a 1 yard (1 m) diameter circle about 6 inches (15 cm) apart and tying them at the top.

As the plants grow they will wind round the canes – but giving them a hand if they get a bit lost is a good idea, so tie them on gently. Watch out for convolvulus – it will also grow up the canes and strangle the beans given half a chance.

When the plants have reached the top of the cane, pinch out the shoots to encourage them to put their effort into flowers and beans.

3 sisters – or 2 $\frac{1}{2}$ really!

We sowed squashes, courgettes and pumpkins underneath the plants in the cool, and to suppress weeds. We had the main bean site with cucurbits underneath, and an experimental '3 sisters' site with sweetcorn, beans and cucurbits. To be honest this gave us mixed success, as slugs ate the squashes – but not the weeds under the main bean crop.

On the other site the courgettes flourished under the sweetcorn, but the beans in that grouping didn't. Later on the squirrels destroyed the sweet-corn – but we did get lots of tasty courgettes!

Issues

- Runner beans need plenty of water, so do not let them dry out. Water makes the beans fat! In really hot times, a mulch can help. We used straw, which also helps keep slugs away from the cucurbits.

- Aphids are a nuisance, but let the ladybirds take care of them. Or you can spray the plants with dilute soap solution.

Harvesting

Pick as soon as the beans are ready (about 6 inches or 15 cm long) and keep picking. They will keep producing. Do not let them get too long or they go hard and nasty – like they used to be at school!

Take off all long, old pods to encourage the development of young, tender, new ones. When we find tough pods, we open them, take out the beans for next year, then compost the hard skins.

If you take the beans off a little late and they have started to go a bit tough, use a potato peeler to take off the nasty edges on both sides.

Note that some people suffer a rash from the hairs on the plant. If you do, wear gloves and long sleeves when harvesting.

French beans

Characteristics

These are very similar to runner beans. They were brought to Britain by the Huguenots, who were French Protestants betrayed and expelled by Louis XVI. They are smaller than runner beans, and for some people have a better flavour. The plants grow in the same manner to runner beans, being vigorous climbers. They can be harvested when young and eaten whole, or left to turn into flageolet beans and ultimately into haricot beans. In China, as a result of this they are called sandomame – the 'three times bean'. They are also called string beans, Kenyan beans, Borlotti beans (popular in Italy) or kidney beans.

They come in several colours – red, blue, yellow, striped and the more familiar green. Next year we are going to go for blue and yellow to brighten up dinner times. There are two types – climbing and dwarf or bush – with the difference self-evident. Climbers tend to be less prone to disease as the air can circulate better, but dwarf plants are usually 18 inches (45 cm) tall and easier to grow under cover. This is important if your site is cold for much of the year – as French beans love warmth (being originally from Central and South America).

Climbers give a better yield and crop continuously, whereas dwarves mature all at once over a short period, so it is best to succession sow dwarf varieties over a few weeks to ensure a constant supply.

How to grow and when to plant

French beans need a warm sunny site that is sheltered. For that reason it may be easier for you to grow runner beans depending on your circumstances. They also like very rich soil, so it is best to dig out a trench and fill it with organic matter before sowing.

If your site is cold and/or exposed to wind and driving rain, go for dwarf varieties which you can protect more easily. They like a pH of around 7.0.

Sow *in situ* when the temperature has warmed up – late May onwards; although you can grow the climbers under cover and transplant them out in summer. Warm the soil up for them by covering it before sowing or transplanting. Harden the plantlets off first before placing them in their final site.

For sowing *in situ*, plant the beans 2 inches (5 cm) deep, about 8 inches (20 cm) apart in rows. They are tricky to germinate so expect around 25 per cent losses. You can always plant a few extra elsewhere to plug gaps. Place climbers in rows 2 feet (60 cm) apart and give them stout support with canes as for runner beans. They will grow up to 8 feet (2.4 m) like runner beans. You can also train them up arches, wigwams and along fences. Their flowers are very pretty as well.

With dwarf varieties, earth them up to the bottom layer of leaves for extra support.

Issues

- Cold will kill French beans. If there is a sudden cold snap then you must cover them up.

- Birds, slugs and mice (the usual suspects) will also eat young seedlings, so protection is a good idea.

- Wind and hard rain will damage them, so ensure that they are sheltered.

- A mulch is a very good idea as they need lots of water – but only after the flowers have appeared or you will get too many leaves.

- Aphids of course are a problem.

Harvesting

Keep picking and they will keep producing. They should snap easily and not be stringy.

To get haricot beans, leave them on the plant for a few weeks longer. Harvest the dwarf varieties in the order that you sowed them.

Climbers will crop for the whole summer. If you can see the beans bulging out then they have passed the French bean stage and are well on their way to becoming haricots.

Flageolets sit in between these stages when the beans are quite small – tricky to spot!

Broad beans

Characteristics

This was our first successful crop. We had lashings of beans which went down very well. We then left the roots in to fix the nitrogen. The beans are found in pods wrapped in a lovely velvety blanket to keep them nice and warm. They like cool conditions so are perfect for our climate.

If you are starting out on your allotment, then broad beans are a must to grow – they are so easy you can virtually guarantee success. Don't worry if you think that you don't like broad beans – I never did until we grew them. Cooked properly they are wonderful. We are going to grow a lot more next year.

Broad beans are one of the oldest-known crops – being mentioned in the Bible and having been found from Neolithic times! Before potatoes they were one of the staple crops for humans in Britain and elsewhere and until relatively recently were the most widely grown bean in the country. In Ancient Rome they were used for voting in the Senate – black meant *non* (no) the whiter beans *ita vero* (yes). Interestingly, the Spanish 'swapped' broad beans, for runner beans, introducing them to South and Central America.

Steal a march on nature. Sow your broad beans in October/November so they crop earlier the following year.

How to grow and when to plant

One of the curious things about broad beans is that successive sowings often catch up with earlier sowings – even if months apart. They like heavy soil so are perfect for our allotment – but will grow anywhere, being hardy. If possible the soil should be pH neutral.

Dig in plenty of organic matter before sowing. They have very large beans that are easy to plant directly into the soil. Sow them in rows 18 inches (45 cm) apart, 2 inches (5 cm) deep, with 6 inches (15 cm) between seeds in late March or April. You can also plant a crop in October for early cropping next year. They reach maturity in about $2\frac{1}{2}$ months. Support the plants with stakes and string. Winter sowings do not need organic matter dug in. Broad beans ideally like sunny sheltered spots, but are hardy and can be grown anywhere.

Issues

- Aphids (blackfly) are attracted to broad beans. Pinching out the growing tips after the pods start to appear can help avoid this.

- Pigeons and mice will try to eat the seeds or seedlings, so protect them with sharp pointy things laid over the seeds, or netting when they are a little larger.

- The pods get heavy and can break the stems, so ensure that the support is adequate. We use the same arrangement as for runner beans.

- Once the beans are growing, water well. Mulching also helps.

- Spots on the leaves – 'Chocolate spot' can occur if it is very wet and humid early on and 'Rust' may appear if it is dry. They are not usually very serious.

Harvesting

Broad beans are the first bean to mature and if you sowed over winter you can start picking them in June. Pick the bottom beans first as they are the most mature, but don't let any get too big. Gently twist them off or use secateurs.

Once you have finished harvesting, do not pull the plants up. Cut them down and leave the roots to set nitrogen. Compost the rest.

For storing, you can dry them, or blanche them and freeze them.

Clover

This is only really grown as a green manure. It is a nitrogen fixer and puts back goodness into the soil (see Green Manures). Sow after you have harvested a crop and leave to over-winter then dig in in early spring.

It grows very fast and you can also eat the young shoots in salads.

16

Solanaceae – Tomato and Potato Family

When we planted tomatoes my younger daughter remarked with remarkable innocent insight that they looked rather like potato plants. How right she was!

This family is probably the most widely and intensely grown plant family in the UK, if not the whole world. There are about 2,500 species, including some of the best-known and well-loved – tomatoes and potatoes – as well as aubergines and peppers (hot and sweet). Several herbs and flowers are members, including petunias, and it includes the cape gooseberry and the shoo-fly plant. The flowers usually have five petals in several shapes. The fruit is usually a berry with lots of seeds.

A lot of the plants are climbers, ramblers or spreaders and they usually give immense yields.

Its members represent one of the real benefits of globalisation and shared produce knowledge.

The family, however, has many plants with alkaloids and accordingly also contains some not-so-nice plants, such as deadly nightshade (*belladonna*), henbane and thorn apple, as well as tobacco (*nicotiana*). So when Stan

Freiberg, the US comedian, in one of his famous sketches talked about Walter Raleigh – 'Nutty Walt' (who is credited with bringing the potato to Britain) – putting a potato in a pipe and smoking it, he was not so far wide of the mark!

Fateful plants

The Belladonna family is called atropa after Atropos, the Greek Fate who cut the chords of life. The poison produced is called atropine.

When tomatoes and potatoes were first introduced they suffered from the link with deadly nightshade and were viewed with deep suspicion. They were grown for their foliage and pretty-coloured fruit, but not eaten.

The family perversely enough, takes its name from that deadly nightshade – solanum.

Another famous member of the family is the **mandrake**, a plant to which all sorts of magical qualities have been attributed over the years in legend and history. It is mentioned several times by Shakespeare and is mentioned by John Donne, *inter alia*, in one of his famous poems ('… get with child a mandrake root'). It is also believed to be the plant referred to in the Song of Songs in the Bible. One of the qualities was that its roots were shaped rather like a human being and that its shriek would kill you if you lifted it from the ground (as seen in *Harry Potter*). It was also reputed to be an aid to conception. The Arabic name for it was Djinn's eggs (Devil's eggs). Every part of the plant is poisonous!

Tomato

Characteristics

Also known as *pomo d'oro* and *pomme d'amour* (love apple) because it was commonly believed to have aphrodisiac properties – alas unproven! The tomato was reputedly developed by Aztecs, in what is now Mexico, and the name comes from the Aztec word *tomatl*, although it is believed to be native to the mountains of Peru (as are potatoes).

Tomatoes are very popular and grown by many people who do not grow any other vegetables (eg my mother). You will often see growbags on patios and sunny paths around houses with tomato plants poking up. I don't like raw tomatoes but like them cooked (in common with many people). As they are banned on our site because of blight, we grow a few in hanging baskets or growbags on our patio. Although technically a berry (fruit), the tomato is not as sweet as other fruit and is therefore classed as a vegetable for culinary purposes.

Huge amounts of tomatoes are produced globally. In 2005 China produced 31.2 million tonnes, the USA 11 million, Turkey 9.7 million, and Egypt and India some 7.5 million tonnes each. I don't know how many tomatoes make up a tonne – but I imagine it is quite a lot!

There are hundreds of types of cultivars. We think of tomatoes as red – but they can also be yellow, orange, white, purple and striped. They come in all shapes and sizes – tiny cherry, long plum, massive beefsteak and the more usual spherical ones. The plum varieties are those used in sauces and Italian cooking.

How to grow and when to plant

The seeds of a tomato are abundant in the fruit and incredibly resilient. They grow on sewage farms, having passed unaltered through the human digestive system. They are very easy to grow, taking only a couple of months from sowing to harvest (with a following wind). They need sunshine to optimise growth. They are often grown in greenhouses or on sunny patios where they can bask in the sunshine reflected off walls.

Some, eg tumbling Toms, can be grown in hanging baskets and window boxes where they cascade over the sides.

Tomatoes like very rich soil, so often are grown in growbags. If grown in soil they like lots of compost well dug in. All tomatoes need lots of goodness, moisture, light and sun. The better the shelter, the better and earlier the crop. Many people build greenhouses and suchlike on allotments just to grow tomatoes.

Sow the seeds in a seed tray and keep it warm but dark. When shoots emerge, move them into a warm but well-lit place to grow on. Transplant them into 3 inch (9 cm) pots when they can be handled easily. Plant them out when they are around 8 inches (20 cm) tall. Keep the plants about 18 inches (45 cm) apart. Make sure there is no danger of frost, as this will kill them immediately. If planting them out, harden them off in a cold frame or unheated greenhouse for a few days.

Tomatoes are easy to germinate so don't sow too many. (If you do, you can sell them at your open days as they are always popular.)

Each tomato plant needs about 4 pints (2 litres) of water every day!

Keep them moist but do not over-water. Make sure that they are fed regularly. In early spring using heated water (at about 75°F) can help. When growing outside, a mulch helps conserve moisture and prevent disease spores from splashing up from the soil as you water.

Types
There are two main types of plant:

- Indeterminate – long climbing type that produces lots of side shoots and is usually trained up a support. Easier to think of it as a vine!
- Determinate – forms a dense bush.

Vine As the name suggests, they hang like grapes. These need support to ensure that they do not collapse under their weight. Usually best grown in greenhouses. You need to snap off the side shoots to concentrate the growth on the main stem and fruits. This also helps to ensure air circulates and there will be less chance of disease. Indeterminate.

Cherry Tiny sweet tomatoes. Indeterminate.

Plum Sometimes also called pear tomatoes. They are more elongated than usual tomatoes and very juicy. Indeterminate.

Bush Determinate. They grow about 1 yard (1 m) tall. Do not prune them. Often grown outdoors.

Beefsteak Huge fruits up to 2.2 lb (1 kg).

Issues

- The main issue is blight. This affects the whole plant and spreads like wildfire. The leaves, stem and then the fruit go black and die. There is little that you can do except cremate the affected plants. Tomatoes are still banned on our site because of tomato blight.

- Never grow them in the same site as the previous year – rotate them to minimise pests and blight. In many cases, growbags are recommended even on allotment sites to reduce blight.

- Aphids and white fly are pests.

Harvesting

As the fruits ripen, pick them off. If left too long they will split and rot. Cut the stalk leaving a little attached to the fruit. Green fruits can be left to ripen in a cool dark place under layers of newspaper. Never multi-stack them; only single layers. Check frequently for ripe or diseased fruits and remove them.

Towards the end of the season you can chop around the plant to sever the roots. This makes the plant ripen the fruit more quickly so you can beat the frosts. If mild frost is forecast, cover them in fleece to protect them. When it is time for hard frosts, uproot the plant and hang it upside down in a cool but frost-free place. The fruits will continue to ripen. The fruits do not keep very long once ripe, so use them or freeze them. You can make chutney with green tomatoes of course. Ripe fruits don't last very well and putting them in a refrigerator ruins the flavour (if you do keep them there, let them stand for a while outside to regain taste.) Tomatoes can be made into sauces, bottled, frozen or turned into chutney.

Potato

Characteristics

Reputedly named after an American Indian/Peruvian princess and brought to Britain by Walter Raleigh, the potato is called the 'earth-apple' in many other countries (France *pomme de terre*; Holland *aardappel*, Germany *kartoffeln*). Originally from the highlands of Peru, it has been grown everywhere: but cool mountains are still best for growing the seed potatoes, and much of the UK's are grown in the Highlands of Scotland, where its original cool conditions are replicated.

The salvation of Europe in the eighteenth century, with its immense yields the potato quickly replaced all other vegetables to become the main source of food. The dependence became too great, however, and when blight hit the crops it caused massive famine in the nineteenth century, which devastated many areas and caused the mass migrations from Scotland and Ireland to the USA and other parts of the British Empire. One of the reasons the blight spread so quickly was the custom of using the previous year's potatoes and swapping them with others.

There are hundreds of varieties – both for new/earlies and main crops. They are very easy to grow and give excellent yields. Digging up the first potatoes of the year is always a great moment. As you put in the fork and lever the soil up, seeing the new yellow potatoes contrasting with the dark earth, almost shining out, is wonderful. Children love to collect potatoes.

How to grow and when to plant

Potatoes are not hardy and frost kills them, but they grow so vigorously that it is very easy to get several crops even in our cooler northern climes.

Cropping

Potatoes are grouped according to their season of harvest:

- Earlies.
- Second earlies.
- Main crop: often divided again into early and late maincrop.

I find this confusing and unhelpful as it is quite a pain to plant four different types of potatoes on an allotment. I just think of them as two types – earlies and main crops.

In general, early varieties are lower yielding but need less space, and as they mature earlier they miss many of the diseases that affect the later potatoes (eg blight).

Chitting

I hadn't realised until writing this book that, although I had grown thousands of potatoes, I had never seen a potato seed – and indeed still haven't. You don't grow potatoes from seed – you grow them by buying seed potatoes, small tubers that will grow into the plant. Having got them, the best thing to do is to leave them in the light to start sprouting. This is called chitting and it gives them a really good head start. I have been unable to find a definition of this strange word. I believe it is of fourteenth century origin meaning 'young thing' (as in chit of a girl).

You do not have to do this, but if you merely plant the seed potatoes in the ground the crop will neither be as heavy nor as soon – so it is really essential for earlies. What you are trying to do is extend the growing season. The best thing to do is to stand the seed potatoes upright (with the eyes at the top) in an egg box. These are ideal in shape and size. From Christmas start saving egg boxes! Place them in a cool room with plenty of light and very soon you will see white tendrils sprouting forth. I always rub out the other eyes so that there is only one sturdy main shoot. You can cut the potatoes up to give more, but this can lead to disease.

Examine the potatoes carefully and discard any that are shrivelled or damaged.

There are over a hundred types of potatoes and they come in many colours – white, yellow red and even blue. Next year we are going to try the blue ones for interest at the dinner table! Choose potatoes carefully. Some are best for mashing, others for roasting, and yet more best for frying.

Planting

I always double dig the ground, putting in plenty of organic matter. Earlies can be planted mid-March to early April, depending on how far north you live and of course the weather conditions. After chitting earlies should be planted in rows about 2 feet (60 cm) wide with 1 foot (30 cm) between tubers.

The main crop is usually planted in the first half of April, or by late April if you live further north in the UK. Once again, the actual time will depend on the weather (it is very hard to plant them if the ground is frozen!). Main crops need more space than earlies, as they will be bigger plants: so increase the row width to about $2\frac{1}{2}$ feet (75 cm) and space the potatoes out by $1\frac{1}{2}$ to 2 feet (45–60 cm).

Plant them about 6 inches (15 cm) deep, but do not plant them if weather is very wet.

One of the side benefits of growing potatoes is that they 'clean' the soil. As the plants grow, you should earth up the soil around them. This is to ensure that the tubers stay away from the light and do not turn green. Green potatoes are inedible and in fact highly toxic (containing cyanide/prussic acid). Green potatoes look very like mandrake tubers!

As you do this, take out weeds and ensure that they do not grow to compete with the potatoes. Keep earthing the plants up until the foliage is touching across the rows.

Water

Potatoes need regular water to grow, so this is essential in dry periods. Mulching with straw or grass helps to conserve moisture, but grass has a propensity to set seed and grow so be careful with it. Plenty of water (but not too much) early on will give better yields.

Issues

- Potatoes can suffer from a number of pests and diseases, the worst of which is blight (see Issues, Part III), which is prevalent in warm, wet summers. In addition, they are prone to attacks by slugs (what isn't?), wireworms, cutworms and scab. Scab is not so serious – it just affects the look of the potatoes by forming scabs on the surface which disappear when peeling. It can be sorted by ensuring that the soil pH is around 5.5.

● Holes in the potatoes are usually caused by soil-living slugs, cutworms or wireworms. Digging over in winter helps reduce this. One of the issues with the no-dig philosophy is that the soil isn't turned over and therefore many pests are not exposed to their predators and stay snug in the soil until they can eat your crops.

● Another major issue – fortunately rare in the UK – is the Colorado beetle, which devastates crops. There is a statutory duty to report the presence of this pest to the authorities and it is a criminal offence not to do so.

Potato tips

Rotation is critical with potatoes as pests build up. Never save potatoes from the previous year – the incidence of disease will be very high. Always buy certified seed potatoes only. Do not use shop-bought potatoes as they are often treated with all sorts of sprays and will probably not sprout, are probably inorganic, and will not be certified as disease-free for seeding.

Harvesting

Early varieties can be harvested from June, or just after the plants have flowered. We leave them in the ground until we need them, taking some every week.

Main crops can be left until autumn but they will be more prone to blight and slugs and other pests. Harvest on a dry day; rub off the soil and let them dry out for a while. They can be stored in paper or hessian stacks (to keep the light out) in a cool place away from water or damp. Potatoes can also be stored in a clamp (see Part III Chapter 32 – Enjoying the Fruits of your Labour). Discard any damaged or diseased potatoes – **do not compost them**.

As the weather gets warm in spring, the potatoes will start to shrivel and sprout, so finish them up before that.

Aubergine

Also called the egg plant and, still called that in the USA, because the first cultivars were white and egg-shaped and sized. Now the long purple type is more familiar. Aubergines contain nicotine but in much lower quantities than tobacco. They are used in that Greek favourite – moussaka. Called melanzana in Spanish (I once ordered it as a starter in Spain, thinking it was melon and was deeply shocked at what arrived!), its Latin name is *solanum melongena* – hence the confusion!

Characteristics

Aubergines come in all shapes and sizes, from black, through purple and green to white. They are heat-lovers and therefore difficult to grow outdoors in the UK, being subtropical in origin (Asia and India).

How to grow and when to plant

Aubergines need a lot of sunshine and warmth. They take about six months to reach maturity, and are therefore best sown indoors for transplant out when it becomes warmer – more so the further north you are.

Even then, best results are from indoor growth. They can be grown in a very sheltered and sunny spot, but will not grow below about 70°F (20°C) which is not a common temperature in the UK for very long. They like a neutral soil pH.

Aubergines need to be sown (and will only germinate) in soil which is at least 70°F – hence the need to sow indoors. They take about two weeks to germinate. When they are through and can be handled (when the first true leaves appear) prick them out into medium-sized pots and keep them at a constant 65°F.

If you are going to plant them outside, then warming the soil is essential, ie lay a black plastic sheet over it. Plant them out only when the flowers appear. When they are about, 1 foot (30 cm) high, then pinch out the tips to encourage stronger growth.

Water them with tepid water and keep covered for a couple of weeks as they acclimatise. Keep fruits down to four or five for larger produce. Feed fortnightly with a fertiliser high in potash after the fruits set. Pinch out any side shoots. If necessary, the plants can be staked or tied to a trellis.

Issues
- Mainly susceptibility to cold – not recommended for open sites.
- Aphids may affect them and, in greenhouses, red spider mites.

Harvesting
Harvest when the fruits are at the optimum size – 6 inches (15 cm) for most cultivars – and before they become dull. They will start to become tough to eat and bitter if that happens. Wear gloves when dealing with them – they have sharp spines. They will last a few days in the refrigerator and can be frozen or turned into chutney.

Note: Only grow as many as you will use. It might be a good idea to succession-sow plants so that you get a few each month, unless you use them all the time – otherwise they will be wasted.

Peppers

Characteristics

There are two types of pepper – hot (chilli) and sweet (bell). There are several terms for these types both used interchangeably. I use pepper for sweet and chilli for the hotter types. Others call them capsicums, chiles, chilis, peppers, chilli peppers, bell peppers, etc. Capsicum is from the Latin word for 'bite' reflecting the heat within many.

Peppers need a lot more warmth than tomatoes, so are often grown in greenhouses or on window ledges. The hotter the sun; and the more of it, the hotter the chilli. They are almost all green at first, developing their different colours later. Ripe peppers are usually red, green, yellow or orange – even purple – and come in all shapes and sizes – long, thin, short, fat, plump and round. They always look very interesting in supermarkets where they are displayed altogether.

Heat

Capsaicin, a bitter alkaloid, gives the heat in chilli peppers. The heat of a pepper is measured using the Scoville index. This measures how much sugar water solution would be required to negate the heat (also now called 'piquancy'). A spoon of chilli that had a rating of 100 would need to be mixed with 100 spoonfuls of sugared water to negate the heat. The index was developed by an American chemist, Wilbur Scoville, in 1902. It was originally based on a tasting panel – nowadays it is analysed by computer.

To give an idea of the range:

- a sweet pepper is usually rated zero;

- banana peppers are between 100 and 500;

- Cayenne pepper is 30,000 to 60,000;

- Thai peppers are about 150,000;

- and habanero peppers are rated at 200,000 plus – that is hot, hot, hot!

When dealing with hot chillis, such as these latter two, it is best to wear protective glasses, as getting juice in your eyes – or even rubbing your hands across your face – is painful. Some are used to manufacture pepper spray (which has a rating of 2,000,000 plus).

According to *The Times* (1 April 2006), however, the hottest chilli in the world is not Mexican, and neither from the USA nor India, but in fact British – the Dorset Naga (Hindi for snake). It is claimed that this variety, grown from a plant bought from a Bangladeshi shop in Bournemouth and cultivated in poly tunnels, has a Scoville rating of 900,000, which could kill from several paces! (I note that date is April Fool's Day, so I have just a nagging, or nagaing, doubt about the veracity of this article!)

How to grow and when to plant

Heat is the essential ingredient for these plants. You can buy plants and seeds. They are also easily raised from seeds you can take from peppers/chillis you have bought. We have done so successfully with both sweet peppers and hot chillis; however, in 2007 the virtual absence of sunshine meant that yields were very poor and the high rainfall rotted many. They are best grown in growbags on patios or next to walls that will reflect the heat back, or in greenhouses/poly tunnels to preserve the warmth as they require around 21°C for success.

Sow the seed in late winter indoors. It takes about 30 days to germinate and six months of growing. Plant out when it is warm in a very sunny spot or into larger pots in greenhouses. Pinch out the top shoots when the plants are say 10 inches (25 cm) tall to encourage bushiness rather than tall straggly plants that may become top-heavy and break with the weight of fruit. Alternatively, you can stake them.

Issues

- The main issue is a lack of sun. Aphids and red spider mites in greenhouses can be discouraged by spraying with a fine mist of water to increase humidity.

- Avoid rot through over-watering.

Harvesting

Once the fruit has set the plant will not produce any more, so keep picking them to encourage growth. Sweet peppers can be picked when green but starting to change colour, and will ripen off the bough. The longer you leave them on the plant, however, the sweeter they will become. They will last for several weeks in a refrigerator and they can easily be frozen. Cut them off – never pull as you may break the branches. Leave hot chillis on the plant to ripen. When harvesting hot chillis, wear gloves and protective glasses.

Harvest them all before the frost arrives. Hot chilli plants can be uprooted at the end of the season and, if left to hang upside down indoors; the fruits will continue to ripen.

(17)

Alliaceae – The Onion Family

All of these plants have a characteristic strong smell and feature in cooking throughout the world. Many recipes start off by browning onions before adding in many other ingredients.

Many can be eaten raw in salads (onions and spring onions) or with other things, eg cheese and onion sandwiches (that really clears the sinus!). They are used in salsa, in many Indian curries and other Asian foods, and many other recipes. Pickled onions are a standard accompaniment to many foods in the UK and supermarkets sell special pickling vinegar just for that.

Garlic has gone from being synonymous with 'Johnny foreigner' to a staple in British food.

Leeks have a much more delicate flavour and are a fantastic accompaniment to ham when they are cooked in a cheese or mustard sauce.

Competitions are often held for the biggest onion or leek on allotments and passions can run high!

Onions

Characteristics

Onions have long been recognised as food – the pyramids were built on garlic and onions (along with lentils and a few other things such as barley beer). Eating onions has, like garlic, been shown to lower cholesterol levels and blood pressure. Clever people are said to know their onions! World annual production is something in the region of 50 million tonnes – that's a lot of onions!

Sliced onions can irritate the eyes. The onion contains sulphur and when it gets in the eyes it mixes with tears and forms dilute sulphuric acid which causes the eye to sting. The eye produces more tears to flush it away and that is why some people cry over spilt (sorry, sliced) onions. It is the slicing that causes the gases to be released. Cutting them under running water or washing them first helps.

Just about every allotment grows onions – they are quite easy and deliver the goods.

Them what 'as the biggest feet grows the best onions, tha knows!

How to grow and when to plant

Although they can be grown from seed, which is easy to harvest, onions are more commonly grown from 'sets'. These are onion bulbs which are put out in the ground in spring or in late autumn for an early crop. They are very hardy indeed.

Onions like rich, sunny, well-drained soil. Dig in the organic matter well before you put them in (autumn the year before is best) to let it be absorbed into the soil. As sets are already partly grown, they develop rapidly and soon are pushing through.

Order sets from seed and plant firms and they will arrive just when you need to plant them in early March. Plant them 6 inches (15 cm) apart in rows 1 foot (30 cm) apart with just the tips showing.

The soil should be firmed down well. They say that those with the biggest feet get the best onions as they tread the soil down more firmly. Cover them with sharp pointy things to keep scavengers off. Water them lightly, keeping the foliage dry to avoid rot.

As the onions grow you can ease the soil away gently so that the bulb 'sits' on the surface. We didn't do this as ours pushed themselves out – but keep an eye on them and do it if necessary.

Onions have shallow roots so weeding between the rows is necessary to minimise competition.

They grow in the cool part of the year and in summer the plants start pulling goodness back from the leaves and roots ready to over-winter, and this is what makes the bulb swell (just like any other, of course).

Issues

- Onion fly – see Pests. Those planted from sets are much less likely to be affected.

- White rot – bulbs get fluffy white growth and the foliage goes yellow and wilts – burn them and do not use that area for onions for at least three years.

- Bolting – caused by the weather.

- Eelworms – see Pests.

- Rotating crops deals with many diseases.

Harvesting

You can take onions out whenever you want to – the longer you leave them the bigger they are. They are finally ready when the foliage goes yellowy and papery and flops. Allow them to dry very well before storing them – ideally on wire mesh to let the air circulate. If it is dry, we lift them and leave them on the surface while we work on the allotment, taking them home after. Use any that are damaged straight away. If any have very thick necks (like rugby players) then use those also. Tie the long tops together and hang them up in a cool dry place in a traditional 'rope', or put them on wooden trays.

Leeks

Characteristics

The national vegetable of my home country, Wales, where it is called *cenhinen*. Interestingly, the other symbol of Wales, the daffodil, is called *cenhenin Bedr* or *Pedr* – St Peter's leek!

The Welsh reputedly wore leeks when led by St David to distinguish themselves from Saxons (Sassnaeg) at a battle. Hence that well-known Welsh proverb, *Gwisg cenhinen yn dy gap a gwisgi hi yn dy galon* (Wear a leek in your cap but also in your heart).

The name probably comes from a word meaning scales used to describe the layers in bulbs. Shakespeare has Fluellen force the braggart Pistol to eat a leek raw in *Henry V*.

The leek is also called a scallion in some parts of the UK, named after Ascalon, a port in Palestine from where they were presumably imported. This cousin of the onion has many of the same characteristics, but with slight variations – layered skin, but whiter and much longer, like a fat, long spring onion.

Leeks are very hardy biennials. They are grown as annuals and are so tough they will withstand just about any weather. Due to their root system they are very good for the soil as well.

How to grow and when to plant

Leeks are rarely grown from seed but usually bought as young seedlings for planting. They like a neutral pH and will grow anywhere. Prepare the bed earlier in the season by digging organic matter in, and then plant in March.

Leeks are not planted like any other crops. Make a series of holes using a dibber (see Tools) about 6 inches (15 cm) deep, 6 inches apart, in rows 6 inches (30 cm) wide. Place the plants in and pour water into the holes. This is called 'puddling-in'. We stagger the plants in alternate rows as well.

Then just leave them and the soil builds up and blanches them. Great!

If you want even longer leeks then you can earth them up. We don't bother – we like low-maintenance plants!

Water frequently when the weather is dry – every ten days or so in normal times. We also mulch with straw, but do not let the leeks get very wet or stand in water or they will rot.

Issues
- Few, luckily. Leek rust sometimes appears in damp weather. Use varieties that are resistant and if you are unlucky to be affected, throw the rusty leeks away.

Harvesting
You can usually start harvesting in September. They will be useable right over winter and, depending on how many you sow and the vagaries of the weather, they may last up until April. Leave them in the ground until you want them – dead easy.

Garlic

Characteristics
'O tempora! o mores!' – how times have changed. In my parents' days garlic was hardly ever eaten outside of a small number of restaurants being seen as foreign and therefore under suspicion (even though it is native to the UK).

Fortunately our tastes and prejudices have changed and now it is found in many households.

It is a powerful anti-bacterial and was much used to treat wounds by rubbing on them and has long been seen as medicinal and beneficial.

In legend it keeps vampires away – it's probably the smell.

Plant garlic on the shortest day – harvest on the longest day.

Garlic needs lots of sun. In 2007 we lost our entire crop, which had been jogging along nicely, due to two weeks of persistent miserable weather.

How to grow and when to plant

Garlic is planted out in autumn for over-wintering and harvesting from early summer through until Christmas. An old adage says, 'Plant on the shortest day – harvest on the longest day' (winter solstice and summer solstice) to get the best of the sun.

Garlic needs a sunny site that is well-drained. If the soil is heavy then dig organic matter into it – possibly some sand as well for drainage.

Garlic comes as bulbs, which you split apart and plant as individual cloves. Push them gently into the soft soil until their tips are just below the ground or just showing, about 4 inches (10 cm) apart; in rows 1 foot (30 cm) apart. Gently firm them in.

Like onions garlic has shallow roots so you must keep the weeds down. It does not need much watering unless it is very dry. When the bulbs are large, do not water as it might cause them to rot (so will lots of rain!).

For a second crop you can plant in spring to mature in autumn.

Issues

- Animals will try to eat the bulbs so a covering of sharp pointy things will keep them off.

- White rot – see Onions.

- Weeds – mulching helps.

Harvesting

Those planted in the previous autumn will be ready in late spring/early summer. As the foliage dies back and becomes yellowy, check the bulbs for size. Harvest when they have become bulbs. Use a small fork. Spread them out to dry in the right conditions (ie not in the rain or on wet soil). Remove the soil and trim the tops and roots.

When they are dry, the outer skins form a tight seal to protect the insides. They should be stored in the dark at temperatures between 0°C and 5°C.

Shallots

Characteristics

Quite different from its close cousin the onion, the shallot – although grown from a bulb – multiplies as it grows and you get a cluster of bulbs, each usually with two cloves.

Note that if you grow from seed you only get one bulb.

Shallots are milder than onions – often described as apple-flavoured – with a lingering gentle, onion after-taste.

The name is a variation on scallion. They were brought back by Crusaders and originally called eschallots, a corruption of the name of the port in Palestine called Ascalon.

They come in all shapes and sizes: globe, long, flattened and shaped like spindles. They can be white, purple, yellow, orange and brown.

How to grow and when to plant

You can either plant in late autumn for an early crop the following year, or in February or March for a late crop that year. Plant the sets in rows as for onions with the tip just showing.

Issues

- See Onions.

Harvesting

Store as for onions after drying – they will last up to a year in the right conditions.

Chives

How to grow and when to plant

Basically you put chives in and they get on with it. Once in, you need do little except chop off the stalks when you need them.

In autumn you can lift and divide. They are hardy and will die down in autumn and regrow in spring.

Mark where you have put them, so that you don't dig them up accidentally.

We do nothing to ours, except water in dry spells, and they have always been there for us.

See Herbs for more details.

(18)

Apiaceae – The Celery Family

Formerly knkow as umbelliferae, there are more than 2,850 members of this family, found mainly in temperate regions. Some well-known members are carrot, parsnip, celery, fennel and angelica, along with weeds such as cow parsley and hogweed. Some are poisonous, notably hemlock, as Socrates found out – no more carrot juice for me, thanks. The Romans introduced carrots to the UK and considered that they grew best here in all the empire.

Apiaceae, or root vegetables, are a wonderful roast accompaniment to roast meats for a traditional dinner or lunch.

Carrots

Characteristics

This versatile crop can be eaten raw, boiled, steamed or roasted. It also makes wonderful soups, eg carrot and coriander. Sliced and mixed with other vegetables, carrots are a major component of crudités with dips.

Carrots are all-year-round crops, although primarily for winter, as the plant is storing up goodness for next year's growth.

We have had poor success with carrots so far – even after making the soil sandy – but we shall persevere as they are among our favourite vegetables. It is claimed that they were originally purple and the Dutch bred the orange version to match their national colour – but I am not sure if I believe that. Purple, red and yellow carrots are available but somehow they just don't look right!

How to grow and when to plant

Carrots need sunny, well-drained soil – but are tricky to germinate. They like deep well-worked soil. If this is an issue for you, then grow the shorter rounder varieties. If you need to add organic matter, do it well in advance (up to a year is generally good), so that the carrots don't react and fork from too much richness.

If your soil is really heavy, you could use a raised bed, but you will still need to rotate your crops so it might be too much effort.

Sow in rows in well-prepared ground, thinly. Carrot seeds are very small and blow away easily, so take care.

Sow them as soon as the soil is warm enough – March if you are lucky. Raising in trays and transplanting doesn't really work as it inhibits root development, but you could use root trainers and then transplant outside.

Carrots should germinate in about twenty days or so.

Try to sow them thinly as it is the pulling out and bruising of plants that attracts the carrot fly. Thinning in the evening is best, as the flies have less time before dark to find them. You want them about 6 inches (15 cm) apart to maximise growth.

Weeding is critical to reduce competition for resources. Carrots need the right amount of water – too little and they will not grow properly, too much after a dry spell and they will split as the roots are unable to cope with the sudden excess. Water in moderation. Mulching also helps.

Issues

- Largely trouble-free – if you can get them to grow!

- Carrot fly – Sowing an early crop misses their attentions. Grow later ones under fleece and take care when thinning. Throw the thinnings into the compost bin or eat them if they are large enough. Never leave them lying around, as they will attract the fly. Intercropping with onions is supposed to help, as it confuses the flies (in theory). Barriers help, as does growing in containers above the flies' flight path. See Pests.

Harvesting

Carrots can be pulled when young or left to grow into larger specimens. You can leave them in the ground, but they will rot in very wet conditions.

To store, lift them when ready and place them in shallow trays in sand in cool conditions.

Parsnips

Characteristics

My favourite roast vegetable. Parsnips have a much nicer taste than potatoes or carrots. They go so well with roast that we have them in season every week. Curiously, although my father-in-law was an excellent gardener he never grew them and my wife had never had them until she met me.

How to grow and when to plant

This is another plant that is tricky to grow. It is a slow germinator, needing around three weeks, and you will need to sow lots of seeds as many won't make it. Once established and growing, however, they are pretty trouble-free. They are immensely hardy biennials and the bit we eat is the root that stores the goodness for the following year's growth. Dig the ground over very deeply before planting to loosen it. Double digging is best. If adding organic matter, then dig it over the autumn before you intend to plant.

Sow the seeds (which are very light so do it on a still day) thickly in rows. It is best to wait until May when the ground is much warmer as this helps them to germinate. When they come through, thin as necessary to leave them about 6 inches (15 cm) apart. Rows should be about 1 foot (30 cm) wide. Stagger the plants if you can.

Always use new seeds each year as they do not keep. You can buy them or harvest your own from those you've left in the ground to flower the following year. Weed frequently and a mulch helps. They do not need much watering, except in drought conditions. If the foliage wilts, then water little and often.

Issues

- Largely trouble-free.

- Parsnips like sunny sites and sandy soil, so a lack of these will impair their growth.

- Carrot fly – see Pests.

Harvesting

Parsnips will sit happily in the ground and a touch of frost improves the flavour; in fact, the colder the winter the sweeter the parsnips as the cold turns the starch into sugar

Larger, older parsnips develop a woody core. Cut this out and compost it then cook the rest. These are best roasted. They can also be sliced very thinly and make excellent crisps. Store as for carrots. Leave a few to flower next year, as insects love them.

Celery

Characteristics

The crunchy and unique taste of celery is a delight in salads (and – if you can get them – with fresh Waldorfs), with cheese, and as a wonderful thick cream of celery soup. A little salt on a fresh crunchy stick really brings out the flavour. Of course, for those of you dieting, you use more energy eating it than you get back and it provides good roughage.

Celery is a very hardy plant. Its wild version was called 'smallage' in medieval Britain. Its origins lie in the damper regions of southern Europe. It is another example of selective breeding to give the fat juicy crunchable stems that we prize so much today.

Celery is a high-maintenance plant, and for that reason many do not grow it. We didn't either in our first year, deciding that, as it is quite difficult, we would concentrate on other relatively easy plants and then give it a whirl next year. It requires trenching and earthing up to blanch it – or you can cover it with corrugated cardboard and other substitutes.

It is considered to be a semi-aquatic plant by some. Although I wouldn't go that far, it does need lots of water. It can come in surprising colours and there are, apart from the normal green but blanched white varieties, purple, green, pink and red versions. I am convinced that it ought to be a relative of rhubarb which also needs blanching – but not so apparently.

Nowadays with breeding you can get self-blanching varieties, which makes the whole process much easier, although they are not as hardy.

How to grow and when to plant

Celery requires very rich, well-drained soil that is moist (but not waterlogged). It is difficult to grow from seed so plants are recommended, but we are going to try it from seed next year (masochists!).

Celery is grown in trenches which are progressively back-filled with earth to keep the plants white (blanched) as you grow. The soil excavated from the trench needs to be worked before you backfill to ensure that it is friable – this means lots of extra hard work!

Excavate a trench about 1 foot (30 cm) deep and 15 inches (36 cm) wide in early spring. Fork in plenty of organic matter and then replace the soil to just 3 inches (8 cm) short of the top. Let it settle. Put the residual soil (which should be the equivalent of 6 inches (15 cm)) in a neat pile running along the side of the trench.

If growing from seed, use a seed tray and after about three weeks, (when the seedlings have two 'true' leaves), pot them on and harden them off.

Plant the seedlings out when there is no danger of frost, in late May or thereabouts, about 6 inches (15 cm) apart. Water them in and monitor constantly to ensure that they stay moist.

When they are 12 inches (30 cm) high or so, loosely tie up the leaves and start earthing up the soil. Always make sure that the soil is damp when you do this as it helps conserve the moisture – water first if it is not.

Some wrap the plants in cardboard as well as earthing them up – too much work for me though!

Self-blanching

Self-blanching types are not planted in trenches but in blocks. Prepare the ground in the same way as for normal celery, but in a square or rectangle. Plant them out about 1 foot (30 cm) apart. Note that this is easier, but they are not as crisp, nor as hardy. I don't doubt, however, that gradually they will be further improved and will eventually replace blanching types, which will also improve the lot of the gardener! Obviously you don't need to earth up these types, but a mulch helps conserve moisture.

Issues

- The usual suspects –Slugs and snails love celery, like we do.
- Carrot fly – see Carrots.

Harvesting

Normal celery is ready from October. Being frost-hardy, it will last *in situ* all winter. Covering it in straw helps keep frosts off.

Self-blanching celery is ready earlier and will not withstand frosts.

Celery will not store for long so leave it in the ground as long as you can. It can be frozen but must be cooked. Its best to make it into soup which freezes really well.

Celeriac

Characteristics

This close cousin of celery is much easier to grow, requiring no earthing up and looking more like a giant white kohlrabi. It is also called knob celery, celery root and turnip-rooted celery for obvious reasons once you see it. I think it wins the prize for the ugliest vegetable as it looks rather like a troll's head – all knobs and warts.

Celeriac has been bred to provide a huge root for eating. Its name apparently is from the Italian *seleri*, from the Latin *selenon* (after the Moon Goddess, Selene) – probably the same root as celery (pun intended).

Celeriac is a biennial, as is celery, and takes a long time to grow. The root is peeled and the flesh is rather like potato with a faint celery taste. It is low in calories, has no fat and is full of fibre. It is commonly served in France, and it is delicious with a creamy taste.

How to grow and when to plant

This plant, unlike celery, is grown in ordinary soil – untrenched, fertile, well-drained and in a sunny location, with a pH between 6.5 and 7.5.

Sow the seeds in February or March indoors, as they need lots of time to grow. Harden them off first before transplanting. You can also sow outdoors under cover in a shallow trench.

Plant them – or thin them – to 1 foot (30 cm) apart with 18 inches (45 cm) between rows. Do not plant them too deeply as they like to sit on top like onions, rather then in the soil. Trim off any side shoots to concentrate the energy in the main root. Give them a good mulch to keep them moist, and keep them weed-free.

Issues

- Generally trouble-free – another reason to grow celeriac.
- Make sure it has plenty of water or it might split.
- Slugs and snails, of course.

Harvesting

Available from late summer until early spring. Leave it in the ground, covering with straw to protect from hard frosts. Celeriac makes delicious soup and it can be boiled, fried or roasted. The French use it grated for remoulade – a mayonnaise sauce – delicious.

Hamburg parsley

Characteristics

This plant is a dual plant. It is grown for its roots, which are white like parsnips, although thinner, and for its green leafy tops which can be used for parsley flavouring. It takes a long time to mature (seven to eight months) but provides a winter crop.

The roots can be roasted, boiled or mashed – and make good soup. It is very popular in Germany (hence its name) and eastern Europe.

We grew this in our first year and I am ashamed to say that we forgot about it, somehow knocked over the markers and then couldn't find it among the weeds. Eventually we found it and harvested it in the autumn, luckily.

How to grow and when to plant

Sow as for parsnips, in deep, rich soil in late March or early April. As with its relatives, germination is slow and tricky. Sow radishes with it to mark the line. It likes a pH of 6.5 to 7.0.

Thin to about 8 inches (20 cm) when the plants are about 2 inches (5 cm) or so high.

Once established and thinned out, mulch. Cover in straw during winter for frost protection.

Water well.

Issues

- Few.

Harvesting

Autumn and winter. It will store best in the ground.

Parsley

Characteristics

A very friendly lion! See Herbs.

19

Asteraceae – The Lettuce or Daisy Family

This is one of the largest plant families, with over 20,000 species globally. It includes weeds (dandelion and thistle) flowers (aster, daisies, chrysanthemums, sunflowers), and several edible plants (cardoon, chicory, endives, lettuce and artichokes).

It takes its name from the characteristic shape of the flower – a star (from the Latin *astro*) – and the fruits are achenes (dry).

Cardoon

Characteristics

A beast of a plant – they look like triffids or giant thistles. It grows to a massive 7 or 8 feet tall and spreads out with fantastic silver, grey-green foliage. It takes up a huge amount of space for little benefit, in my view. We inherited several (they self-set) but do not grow them deliberately. They provide a monumental backdrop to other plants – but the effort to cook them is simply not worth it in my opinion. Cardoon was very popular with the Victorians and is originally thought to be from North Africa.

How to grow and when to plant

They require no effort at all unless you intend to eat them. Then you need to blanch them. Some writers recommend staking – but those growing on my plot would not be knocked over by a bulldozer.

The heads produce thousands of gossamer-like seeds – fairies – and they self-set everywhere. It is difficult to imagine such a huge plant growing from such an ethereal little thing – but it does. Plant them in pots and they will grow easily. Plant out in rich soil.

You also get off-sets – little plants that grow up from the root. These can be cut off and transplanted.

Alternatively, plant them *in situ* in late spring – sow several seeds and thin later.

To blanch, pull the stems together and tie them up. Wear gloves and thick clothes as they are very sharp. Wrap them up in newspaper or cardboard to block out the light.

Issues

- Absolutely none that I am aware of.

Harvesting

You can harvest cardoons after a month of blanching. Lift with a fork. Cut off the roots and leaves. It is a perennial so in theory you can divide the roots – if you want a flock of triffids! Most treat it as an annual and re-sow the following year.

You get a lot of compostable material from one cardoon!

Chicory

Characteristics

Chicory is known in France as the endive, where the endive is called chicory – just to confuse you! It is a perennial but grown as an annual. I don't grow it or its cousin the endive. The best-known is called Witloof, which is Flemish for 'white loaf'. Rumour has it that it was a Flemish (Belgian) farmer who came home from the wars in the early nineteenth Century and found that his chicory growing in the dark had been blanched and grown fat and sweet. Since then it has became very common to 'force' chicory in the dark like rhubarb to produce the best crop, known as chicons.

Radiccio is a chicory with red leaves ready in autumn.

I always associate chicory with French coffee – which is foul!

How to grow and when to plant

For non-forcing types, grow them in a poly tunnel to assist in development.

Sow radiccio in summer for autumn eating. It germinates easily and grows quickly. Thin it and use the thinnings in salads.

Witloof (forced) is either covered in a bucket, or lifted and stored indoors. To do this, cut the stems down to 2 inches (5 cm), cover them in straw and place a bucket (or forcing jar) on top, then leave them.

To blanch them indoors, lift them, cut off the roots and again trim them down to 2 inches. Put them in dry sand in a dark, cool place. About a month before you want them plant them, in a pot. The plants will grow.

Issues

- Few, but slugs and snails will try to get into the pots and eat them.

Harvesting

Break the chicons off and more should grow afterwards. They are eaten raw in salads – quite bitter – or braised as a side dish to meat, when they are very tasty.

Endive

Characteristics
Closely related to dandelion and chicory, which is why they are bitter. Called chicory in France – we don't quite know why!

New varieties of endive are less bitter and more pleasant in a salad and they can be harvested until late spring the following year. As with chicory, endive requires blanching.

How to grow and when to plant
Sow in rows in late March, $^1/_2$ inch (1 cm) deep and thin to 1 foot (30 cm) when the first true leaves appear. Leave the same distance between rows. Choose a sunny open spot with rich soil. Water them frequently to ensure that they are moist but not waterlogged or standing in a puddle.

Issues
- Slugs and snails.
- Brown rot can occur if you tie them up when wet.

Harvesting
After three months or so and when they are dry, tie the leaves up to keep them off the ground. You can then blanch a few at a time. Cover them with a pot and leave for two to three weeks, when they should be ready. As you harvest one, cover another. Put a small stone between the upturned rim of the pot and the soil for ventilation. Check them every few days – turf out any slugs and snails.

Cut the leaves off at ground level with a sharp knife.

Globe artichoke

Characteristics
Another triffid, like the cardoon, but its little brother, growing only (only!) to about 4 to 5 feet (1.25–1.5 m). Not to be confused with the Jerusalem artichoke, which is grown for its roots. Although very closely related to the

cardoon, it is the heads (calyx) that are eaten. Pull the leaves off and dip them in a delicious hollandaise sauce, or just pure butter. Globe artichoke is a perennial so select a spot and it will stay there for years. However, it is usually replanted after a few years to stop it going woody. It takes its name from the shape of the heads.

The flowers are loved by bees, so if you grow a few plants, leave one or two to flower. You will also get seeds. Legend has it that Catherine de Medici introduced the globe atichoke into France (along with gourmet cooking) when she married Henri II.

How to grow and when to plant

It is very easy to grow. Unusually it reverts to its spindly forbears if grown from seed, so it is usually grown from root propagations or 'off-sets'. You can also buy them in pots ready for planting out. If buying, look for a named variety, or they might be raised from seed and could revert. Plant with at least 1 yard (1 m) between the plants, with the crown just below the surface. Water them in and then mulch them. Give them plenty of water. Cut them down to ground level in winter. In their first year, protect from frost.

Take off-sets from one-third of the plants every year to enable you to replace them every three years. Cut them off below ground level, keeping as much root as possible, and plant them, watering them well. They will wilt but perk up later on (usually!). We have done this and successfully transplanted one from London to my sister-in-law's garden in Hampshire!

Issues
- None really – just herbivores.

Harvesting

When the heads are plump and tender, but still closed, cut the largest ones off first. Take about 6 inches (15 cm) of stem with them. Cook the heads whole.If you are not going to eat it straight away, place the stem in a glass or small vase of water and put it in the fridge (or a very cool room) and it will last for about a week.

Eat the sepals and the braised hearts. The stuff around the heart is called the 'choke' and must be removed before cooking.

Jerusalem artichoke

Characteristics

Another huge perennial plant. It's amazing how many huge plants come from the humble lettuce family! It has nothing to do with Jerusalem, and was originally a native of north-eastern America, where this relative of the sunflower was called, sun root by the native Americans. It was brought to Europe in the seventeenth century.

Its European (English) name comes from the Italian for sunflower – *girasole* – allegedly. It is also called topinambor and recently the Americans have started to call it sunchoke.

It is grown for its roots or tubers which have a very nutty flavour and are similar to potatoes in that they can be roasted, mashed, boiled, chipped, etc. Unlike potatoes, however, they do not store starch but the carbohydrate inulin. This has the unfortunate effect of causing a lot of wind in some people, so beware.

Jerusalem artichoke are invasive and, like potatoes, can grow from a piece of tuber left in the ground. If you do not want them on the same site (which is how they are usually grown) then you must grub up all tubers. They can be quite deep. On new or difficult sites they can be used to break down the soil through the root system.

How to grow and when to plant

The Jerusalem artichoke is originally from the cooler parts of North America, so it is well-adapted to our climate. They can grow anywhere, but for the best results dig in lots of organic matter in clay soil well before you plant them.

Tubers can be bought or anybody who grows artichokes will usually give you one or two.

Plant the tubers where they won't shade any other plants as, given their height (up to 9 feet (3 m)), this will be an issue. Plant them 2 feet (60 cm) apart, with 3 feet (90 cm) between the rows – if you plant that many!

When they are 1 foot (30c m) tall, earth up the roots for stability, but do not feed as that will encourage lots of foliage.

Issues

- The height and foliage usually suppress weeds.

- Few pests, apart from slugs and snails, which will try to eat the tubers.

Harvesting

After the first frosts, cut down the foliage to 6 feet (15 cm) and then harvest as you need. Use the foliage as protection from frost. The roots are best left in the ground. The roots are very knobbly and can be difficult to peel. Newer varieties have been developed to ease this. They are peeled and cooked as for potatoes. They also make great soup.

As Jerusalem artichoke contain inulin, which breaks down into fructose, they are also good for diabetics.

Each plant will give you about a dozen tubers. Keep some (the best) for next year.

Lettuce

Characteristics

Its name means 'milky' as the substance from the broken leaves looks like that, and milk in Romance languages is *lait* or *latte*. Lettuce is originally from the Middle East, and was a rather thin, weedy plant. A few years ago you would only find one or two varieties for a few short weeks of the year. Now there are many more and you can grow it for most of the year.

There are four main types of lettuce: butterhead, crisphead, cos and loose-leaf. The first three are known as hearting types and have densely packed centres. Cos has the distinctive upright leaves, named after the island in Greece where it was developed.

Lettuce is easy to grow but also easy to lose!

How to grow and when to plant

Lettuce prefers loose sandy soil. If your soil is clay, then mix sand in to loosen it. Lettuce prefers to germinate in cooler times – unlike most plants.

You can grow it for spring or summer.

For spring lettuce, sow in autumn $\frac{1}{2}$ inch deep and cover to protect. Sow thickly and then thin when the seedlings are through.

For summer lettuce, sow outdoors *in situ* in late spring/early summer. It will grow surprisingly fast and you can harvest only a few weeks after planting.

Thin all plantings to about 9 inches (22 cm) apart. Rows should be about 1 foot (30 cm) apart.

Lettuce keeps poorly so succession sowing is best. You ideally want a few plants maturing every week (allowing for losses).

Issues

- Slugs and snails love lettuce. So too do aphids, birds and rabbits.

- Lettuce need a constant supply of water. If they do not get it, they go brown and wilt.

- Lettuce do not like strong sun and may bolt.

Harvesting

Cut the heads close to the ground and eat as soon as you can. They do not keep for long.

20

Cucurbitaceae – The Gourd Family

Possibly my favourite group of crops to grow. They are the 100 m sprinters in the race for life. These seeds just want to grow – fast and big. Put them in soil, water them and in a few days their leaves are thrusting through the soil. Their pots always seem to be straining to hold them. They grow at a fantastic rate with good manure underneath them.

Plant them out as soon as you can and give them plenty of room – they will need it. They are all climbers or spreaders and give great ground cover

This family includes cucumbers, courgettes, marrows, melons, squash, pumpkins and gourds. They usually have yellowy/orange trumpet-shaped flowers.

Pumpkins and squashes have long been important food plants in Central and North America, complementing the other local staple foods of maize and beans. Archeologists have found traces of these plants in human habitations going back some 7,000 years in Mexico. The main types include:

Cucumbers – deliciously cool summer vegetable used for sandwiches and familiar in salads and for cold soup.

Marrows – long or rounded fruits of various colours. We are usually familiar with the long green marrows. The immature fruits are eaten as courgettes (zucchini).

Pumpkins – including varieties with some of the largest fruits of the vegetable world.

Winter squashes – highly ornamental, edible fruits that ripen in the autumn, eg Turk's turban, acorn, onion, summer lightning, butternut, web, kabocha, all of which are grown on our allotments. I gave several seeds to the people who have the next-door allotment. Theirs have flourished where as ours have been well and truly munched!

Summer squashes – softer than winter ones and need more care.

Cucumbers

Characteristics

The cucumber (*cucumis sativis*) is a creeping vine that roots in the ground and grows up trellises or other supporting frames, using its thin, spiralling tendrils to anchor it. The plant has large leaves that form a canopy over the fruit. It is an essential ingredient in raita the Indian dish with yoghurt, and the basis of the Spanish cold soup gazpacho. It is also used in Bloody Marys and Pimm's, and makes good hot soup with cream and dill. In fact it's very versatile indeed.

Both my children love cucumber – but it is my youngest daughter's favourite. Whenever we went anywhere when she was very little we would ask for a plate of cucumber. We often got strange looks but they would bring it and she would munch it all. We used to call her the cucumber monster!

The fruit is usually long and cylindrical with tapered ends, and may be as large as 2 feet (60 cm) long and 4 inches (10 cm) in diameter. More usual sizes are about half that. Cucumbers can be round or lemon-shaped, spiky or smooth, white or yellow.

Today, cucumbers are grown almost everywhere and are the fourth most cultivated vegetable crop in the world after tomatoes, brassicas and onions.

There are three general types of cucumber:

- Greenhouse or indoor.

- Outdoor or ridge.

- Pickling cucumbers or gherkins.

How to grow and when to plant

Cucumbers are best grown in a warm, sheltered environment like a greenhouse, but they can also be grown outdoors under cold frames or cloches. They are very tender plants of tropical or subtropical origin and need lots of warmth. There are also bush varieties. If grown up fences or a trellis they look very pretty.

You can sow cucumbers from seed under cover in early spring or outdoors from May onwards. Sow lots of seeds – they are a massive seller at open days. Slugs often eat people's plants so they are often looking for replacements. You can even buy chitted seed, but I don't think that is necessary.

Cucumber has nice large seeds that are easy to handle. Sow three seeds, edgeways up, then thin to the strongest. If growing for transplanting, this can be done after the plants have two or more true leaves.

You can also buy plants. You can grow them in the soil; in growbags – ideal for ramblers; or in very large pots that contain enough food to sustain them. Put them in the sunniest spot. Covering helps enormously. When they reach the top of the support, pinch out the shoots to encourage flowering/fruiting.

In addition to warmth, cucumbers need lots of water. In fact, cucumbers are about 99 per cent water in a green skin! Water little and often.

The climbing versions need to be supported and tied in or the weight of the fruits will bring the plant crashing down around you.

Issues

- Slugs and snails. See Pests.

- Rot and mildew can be an issue if the plants get too wet. Keep them off the ground, and water carefully so as not to get the foliage too wet.

- Poor weather and strong winds will affect the plants so protection is essential – grow them in a sheltered spot.

- Masculine flowers give horrible bitter fruit. Grow all-female cultivars.

Harvesting

They should be ready – with warmth and a following wind – in about three months. The best time to pick them is in the morning before they heat up. Cut them off with a sharp knife when they are about 1 foot (30 cm) long. Take large ones off that are too big (they will be bitter) to encourage others to grow. By taking 'immature' fruits (ie before they reach their full size – but still a foot long!), the plant will keep producing new cucumbers.

Cucumbers don't store at all well but can be pickled. Pickled gherkins are an essential ingredient for pastrami sandwiches in the USA.

Melons

Characteristics

Melons (*cucumis melo*) are sweet edible fruits and are divided into two categories:

- Muskmelon.
- Watermelon.

Melons have been enjoyed for thousands of years in many countries and are thought to have originated in Persia or Armenia, and are reputed to have been grown in the Garden of Eden.

Muskmelon

Muskmelon varieties have either pitted, rough skin, like cantaloupes and Christmas melons, or smooth skin, like honeydew and casaba melons. They come in lots of interesting colours: grey, dark green, yellow, pale green and orange. They have masses of large seeds.

Watermelon

Watermelons were originally from the drier areas of tropical and subtropical Africa. They have been cultivated in the Mediterranean region for over 3,000 years and are now grown throughout the tropics and subtropics. They are very popular in the southern states of the USA and in hot countries generally.

The flesh is over 90 per cent water. It is usually red or yellow, but can be pink, orange or white. Watermelons tend to be less tasty than muskmelons. The most frequently seen watermelon is green or greenish-grey and striped. They have lots of shiny black seeds embedded in the flesh. The flesh of watermelon can range from white or yellow to pink or red and has a drier texture than muskmelon.

How to grow and when to plant

It is advisable to grow muskmelons in our cooler climate and the cantaloupe varieties are best. You can buy plants to get a head start.

Sow them in exactly the same way as for cucumber, but do not put them out until all danger of frost has passed. The secret to ripening melons is lots of warmth. Growing under cover gives best results. Warm the soil before putting the plants out. If you have raised plants indoors, then harden them off as well before setting them in their final site. Do not let more than three or four fruits set or they will be small.

Thin them when they are $1\frac{1}{2}$ inches (4 cm) in diameter. As with cucumbers, melons need plenty of water, little and often. Try to ensure that the remaining fruits are all roughly the same size as they need to ripen together (see harvesting below).

Pinch out the tips of a few leaves after the fruits to encourage more growth.

If they are climbers, then support the fruits with nets or they will break the vines. Some people use string vests, tights or bras! For ground trailers put bricks, flat stones or boards under the fruit to keep them off the ground.

Issues

- Slugs and snails will eat the young plants and other animals will eat the crop – keep the plants covered.

- Aphids, white rot – see Problems.

Harvesting

Melons are ready in early autumn. They smell sweet when ready. Do not water them for a few days before you want them – they will be sweeter as they will concentrate the sugar, and over-watering will cause them to split.

Use at once – melons do not store very long.

Gourds

Characteristics

The gourd family has about 800 species but they are grown mainly for their usefulness as containers rather than as a vegetable. They are not really edible. Gourds is a term that is loosely applied to some, or all, of the fruits from the Cucurbitaceae family, depending on the country. It is a version of cucurbit! While we generally use gourd to mean a hard-shelled squash grown for ornamental or useful purposes, it is often used to mean any member of the cucurbit family.

Gourds are fun for children to grow and they can make things out of them and paint them. But be careful – I remember as a child seeing one in the next-door neighbour's fruit bowl and trying to bite it. I nearly lost my front teeth!

Calabash Although often called a gourd it is not a gourd – it just looks like one. It is, in fact, a very hard-shelled pod of a tree originally from

South America. The pods hang down from the branches and vary greatly in size and shape. They are between 4 and 18 inches long, depending on where and how they grow. When they are dry the shell becomes hard. The flesh is spongy and juicy, with lots of flat, dark brown seeds which are used to make a dish called carabobo. Its name comes from the Arabic *qua'ra yabisha,* meaning 'dry gourd', via the Spanish *calabaza.* The Mexican calabash is often dried and the shells are painted and made into maracas.

Bottle gourds come in all shapes and sizes. When dried, they are used as water bottles, ladles, cups, musical instruments, fish net floats and rafts.

Dishcloth gourd Also called the vegetable sponge. The interior is a loofah, used in baths.

Gourds can be treated as for squashes and pumpkins.

Pumpkins

Characteristics
Not just for Hallowe'en lanterns, these vegetables make fantastic eating when roasted and fabulous soups (see Recipes).

Pumpkins (*cucurbita maxima*) grow over the ground, spreading out as they go. They will elbow other plants aside.

I usually plant seeds in smallish pots, growing them indoors or in shelter during the cooler months and transferring those that are successful – a surprisingly high percentage – to larger pots before planting them out. They are great fun for children to grow as there is something wondrous about pumpkins. Don't plant them out until all the frosts have gone – they will die.

How to grow and when to plant
Pumpkins are very fast germinators – 7–10 days. During this time, the seeds need moisture and warmth. Once they have germinated, the two cotyledons push up – still with the seed cover on them. This falls off later on. The true leaves appear next and then yellow flowers appear in only a few weeks. These are what will turn into the fruit.

Pumpkins need very rich, warm soil, lots of water and a sheltered site. Pumpkins are often planted on a mound of compost or enriched soil. This helps them to drain, but it isn't strictly necessary to have a mound. They will spread out and suppress weeds. They grow well under peas/beans and sweetcorn (see 3 Sisters). It takes them three to four months to grow to maturity and be ready for picking. They are usually harvested in autumn, which of course is when Hallowe'en falls. If you want to grow a very, very big pumpkin, then pinch out all shoots/flowers except one. All the plant's energy will go into making that one as big as it can. Of course, if it gets eaten by pests you have lost it all!

Save the seeds to grow new pumpkins next year. They produce masses. You can also eat pumpkin seeds dried.

Some people use beer to feed pumpkins – but that is expensive unless you can get the drip-tray contents from a local pub.

The fewer the fruits the larger they will be. You should expect between three and five decent-sized fruits from a plant.

Issues

- Slugs and snails – these ate all of our initial crops! Protect the plants well with organic slug repellent. Cover them as well with fleeces in the early stages. This is not so easy when they get very large!
- Aphids.

Harvesting

Pumpkins are ready in autumn. Leave them for a few days to harden off further, but well before any hint of frost. Leave as long a stem as possible. This is where rot starts. When the rind is nice and tough you can keep them in a cool place. They will last a surprisingly long time.

You can eat the flowers fried in batter.

Pumpkins make fantastic soup, can be sliced and roasted, and one of our favourite dishes is chicken in a pumpkin, roasted whole (see Recipes).

Squashes

Characteristics
There are literally hundreds of varieties, split into two main types – winter and summer squashes.

Harvesting our first winter squash was a fantastic experience – we had lost so many to pests that we never thought we would get any. Towards the end of the summer, having planted replacements for many of the casualties, we started to get some real progress. We lost a few more – but the rest soldiered on. I cut the first one on 23 September an Acorn Squash – referring to shape not size, and set it proudly in the kitchen for everybody to see. It was impressive and a very good moment for the family.

Winter squashes
Treat as for pumpkins.

Summer squashes
There are many types of these, including courgettes and marrows. They have much softer skins (rinds) than winter squashes and come in all sorts of sizes, colours and shapes – differentiating is not easy. Courgettes are also called *zucchini* (Italian).

When to grow and how to plant
Summer squashes have lovely big seeds that are full of energy. We had masses of courgettes from just one plant all through the summer. We gave a couple to one of our fellow allotment holders and they had an even bigger crop than we did! They are fantastic crops. If you plant too many plants you will just be giving them away.

They love the sun and need plenty of water. Either sow under cover for transplanting out when it is warm enough (May) or sow *in situ*. Dig a pit and fill it with compost then put the plant or seeds in it (thin to one plant later on) and off they go.

Give them plenty of space.

Issues

● See Pumpkins.

Harvesting

Use a sharp knife to cut courgettes when they are about 4 to 6 inches (10–15 cm) long. The more you take the more the plants will produce. If you leave courgettes too long they become marrows. When harvesting summer squashes it is best to wear gloves, as they are often very spiny, and use secateurs.

Summer squashes do not store for very long. We use courgettes as an aubergine substitute in moussaka. Marrows tend to have no flavour unless stuffed with something like tomatoey mince.

If you go away during the productive times, make sure someone else harvests the squashes for you or you will end up with fewer very large fruits.

(21)

Chenopodiaceae

This group includes leafy and root crops. It includes several well-known crops, such as beetroot, spinach and chard, as well as less familiar Good King Kenry and orache. Its members inspire loathing and loving. How many people really like beetroot and spinach?

The crops are usually included as 'roots' for rotational purposes.

Mangoldwurzel

A short word on the mangoldwurzel or mangelwurzel. Yes it is a real vegetable, which is either white or yellow and can be eaten. I have to say that I have never seen it anywhere, but it is such a great name that I thought I would mention it. It was developed in the eighteenth century in Germany for feeding cattle and pigs. The name comes from the German *Mangel/Mangold* (beet) and *Wurzel* (root).

You can eat it as a root vegetable (boil it and serve like mashed potato with butter) or you can eat the leaves (best lightly steamed or lightly boiled).

Beetroot

Characteristics

Originally developed in the sixteenth century, probably in Italy, beetroot spread to central and eastern Europe where it became a staple food. When I first flew to Poland all I could see growing were beetroots and cabbages. Borscht is a well-known soup made from it. Sometimes it is horrible, at other times it is delightful. Try it with cream and vodka stirred in! Beetroot Latin name is *beta vulgaris* – common beet.

Beetroot is very easy and very fast to grow, and can be round, long and thin, flat and oval. It can be coloured red, purple, white, golden yellow and even striped. The most commonly grown are the globe varieties, which can be eaten as baby beets or left to grow to about tennis ball size. Beetroot is hardy and will do best in with a pH of soil 6.5–7.5.

How to grow and when to plant

Beetroots can be sown over a long period and in fact this is a very good idea so that you get a few every so often. Start in March *in situ*, slightly earlier under cover. Thin the seedlings before planting out. The seeds usually have several seeds within them. Some people soak them before planting for 12 hours or so. Sow them thinly and then cut off the unwanted seedlings that emerge to ground level to leave only one every 4 inches (10 cm) in rows 1 foot (30 cm) apart.

Moisture is critical, so mulch when the plants are about 2 or 3 inches tall.

Weed carefully so as not to damage the roots.

Issues

- Few, but they may bolt if they have insufficient water or the temperature drops. If the latter case looks likely then cover them.

Harvesting

Baby beets can be lifted after six weeks or so, and the full-sized ones after a couple of months. The larger they become the more likely they are to go woody, so golf ball size may be best for earlies, tennis ball for lates. Beetroot can be stored in trays of sand in cool sheds.

Spinach

Characteristics

I loathe it – but Catherine likes it. Originally from the cooler parts of the Middle East – Persia – spinach is well-suited to our climate. The link with strength and hence the invention of the cartoon character Popeye the Sailorman, whose strength increased after eating a can of spinach, allegedly came about after a mistake by a scientist claiming that its iron content was exceptionally high. It was later found to be a misplaced decimal point that had overstated it by ten times! In fact, spinach does have a slightly higher iron content than many other plants, but not a significant level.

Note that New Zealand spinach is an entirely unrelated crop.

How to grow and when to plant

Spinach grows very fast and prefers cool temperatures. It can be sown twice – once in early spring and again in late autumn – either *in situ* or outdoors. Sow and thin out to 6 inches (15 cm) and 1 foot (30 cm) between rows. You can eat the thinnings.

Water well before and after thinning and periodically mulch. You can succession-sow by sowing just as the previous crop comes up.

Issues

- Bolting in heat – water well and mulch to conserve moisture.
- Beet leaf miner.
- Mildew – keep a good space between plants.
- Snails, slug and birds – netting will help.

Harvesting

Harvest spinach from May to September. Start picking when the leaves are 2 inches (5 cm) tall. You can cut the whole plant down to 1 inch (2.5 cm) above ground and it should sprout again.

Chard

Characteristics

Also called seakale beet, silver beet and Swiss chard, chard is grown for its leaves as well as its stems. It comes in a fantastic range of colours and it is worth growing just for the display it makes; and is often used in borders for that very purpose. Its stalks can be yellow, pink, red, white and orange. One of the cultivars is called Bright lights, which sums it up very well. It is hardier (ie more tolerant to heat) than spinach and full of vitamins.

The leaves are used as spinach but the stems are used as a substitute for seakale or even asparagus or steamed like celery. It is very versatile and easy to grow. It is quite salt-tolerant so useful for coastal settings. It prefers a slightly alkaline soil with a pH of 6.7–7.5.

How to grow and when to plant

Chard can be planted outside from late March and if succession-sown will allow you to crop into the late autumn and, if you are lucky, into next summer. It can be sown under cover from February.

We didn't grow it in our first year but we put it on the list for the next year because of its versatility and the fantastic colours.

Station sow about 18 inches (45 cm) apart in rows about 15 inches (36 cm) apart. Typically a few seeds are sown at each station then thinned.

Watering well and mulching help. Chard will withstand a normal winter, but covering will give a better crop yield.

Issues

- Usual herbivores.
- Possibly beet leaf miner – covering early in the season prevents the mother laying eggs.
- May bolt if it gets too dry – but less likely to bolt than spinach.

Harvesting

Pick the outside leaves – this will encourage the inside leaves to grow. If the leaves become coarse, cut the whole plant down to the ground. Don't let them get too long or the flavour deteriorates – no longer than 9 inches (24 cm). Use straight away after cutting with a sharp knife or secateurs: only cut what you want to use. Leave about 2 inches (5 cm). Leaves are good in salad. Steam or stir-fry the stems.

Good King Henry

Characteristics

Introduced by the Roman army, this is a perennial plant used in salads (*chenopodium bonus-henricus*). It is rarely seen in shops as it doesn't keep very long after picking, but is mentioned in *The Herbs*! Its German name is *Fette Henne,* where it was reputedly used for fattening up hens.

The name Good King Henry is thought to have been coined solely to distinguish it from another similar plant called Bad Henry (*malus henricus*) – meaning bad elves (from German) and nothing to with Good King Hal (Henry V) of England. It is also known as English mercury, Lincolnshire spinach, Mercury goosefoot and Fat hen.

It is easy to grow and will grow just about anywhere. It will grow up to 1 yard (1 m) tall. It tastes a little like asparagus.

How to grow and when to plant

Sow in spring thinly and thin further to 15 inches (36 cm) between plants.

Divide it every three years.

Issues

- Few except herbivores.
- Likes plenty of water.

Harvesting

Harvest in the second year. Cut off the flowers in the following spring to encourage the leaves. You can eat the leaves and young shoots.

(22)

Fruit

Most fruits that we grow belong to the rose family – rosaceae. There are some 3,000-odd species in this family, including well-known garden trees and shrubs such as roses, hawthorn, cotoneaster and rowan (mountain ash) as well as many fruits: apple, pear, cherry, plum, peach, raspberry and strawberry. With the possible exception of peaches, they are all well adapted to our climate.

Most allotment holders tend to grow soft fruits such as berries and currants. This is because often trees are prohibited on allotments (as they are on ours), although many allow smaller trees and espaliers.

Raspberries

Characteristics

In the UK we grow the best raspberries in the world. They are hardy plants and will grow in cooler conditions as well as sunny sites. There are many varieties (cultivars) and they can be red or yellow. I prefer the red ones as I think the yellow look under-ripe – but it is your preference. They like acidic soil and, as they have shallow roots, need lots of watering in drought times. They usually follow strawberries to give a long period of berry harvests.

How to grow and when to plant

Raspberries are usually planted in rows and staked. On our allotment we discovered a very unruly and unkempt bed of raspberries. They hadn't been staked or cut down properly. We had already put in two rows of our raspberries, so I just cut these newly discovered plants down. They cropped better than expected – and I think will be even better next year.

Buy what are called 'bare-rooted' plants and put them in the ground in late autumn or early winter. You must never put them where other family members have been (blackberries, strawberries) or disease will build up. **Make sure that they are certified 'virus-free'**.

Choose an area that is sunny and try to place the rows running north to south so they receive full sun. It is the combination of plenty of water and lots of sun that makes big juicy tasty berries.

Weed the area well, put in organic matter and then construct a support. I put in two 6 foot (1.9 m) poles and strung wire at 2 feet (60 cm), 3 feet (90 cm) and 5 feet (150 cm). The raspberries didn't reach the 5-inch wire in the first year – but we are hoping they will next year. Plant the raspberries on the side of the wire support system with about 18 inches (45 cm) between plants.

Raspberries grow from new growth, so cut down the old growth to ground level and tie in the new ones – cutting them off level with the top wire (if they reach it, of course!).

Issues

- Birds will eat them so netting may be required.
- Raspberry beetle – you may get maggots in the fruit from the raspberry beetle. Digging over the soil in winter helps remove this pest. Remove any maggoty fruit and burn.
- Aphids.
- Waterlogged soil will make raspberries susceptible to disease.

Harvesting

Check every few days in season and harvest the raspberries as they come. If you keep taking them, it encourages the others to ripen. Fresh raspberries taste delicious and they also freeze well and make excellent pies, jams and jellies. Plants should last for about ten years before you have to replace them. Note: they are delicious and very few make it back home!!

Blueberries

Characteristics

These cousins of the bilberry thrive in acidic soils. In alkaline they will be very unhappy. They like damp but never waterlogged soil. They are not trained on supports and grow in free-form bushes. They like a sunny position, although we grow ours at the back of our plot where they get some shade, but the soil is slightly more suited to fruit. Always plant two or three as this helps with pollination and fertilisation. You should buy plants that are two or three years old so that you can expect some crop in the first year and they will get a better start. They reach full production at about six years.

In theory you should only use rainwater as tapwater is alkaline – but this is not always practicable – and it is OK because, given our climate, there is enough rainwater to counter the natural alkalinity of the tapwater. Blueberries like soil with a pH of between 4.5 and 6.0 but we haven't done anything special for ours.

Blueberries are very good for you and are considered a 'superfood' with very high levels of antioxidants.

How to grow and when to plant

Plant them in late autumn, leaving 4 to 5 feet between each bush. Firm them in well and water them in. A mulch of pine needles (which are acidic) is a very good idea, we use our Christmas tree. Prune out any stems that are four years old during the winter months to encourage new growth.

Issues

- It is advisable to net the bushes as birds love the berries.

- A bonus is that blueberries do not suffer from many diseases.

Harvesting

When the fruit is that beautiful deep blue, it can be harvested. The berries should be used as soon as possible, but they can be frozen or preserved in jams, jellies, etc. They add a real something to fresh fruit salads and are wonderful in cottage cheese!

Strawberries

Characteristics

I love strawberries. They always remind me of lazy summer days during cricket matches for the school when strawberries and strawberry jam were served at tea. Some start producing fruit in late spring, but most a little later. Wimbledon is synonymous with strawberries.

Allotment strawberries will probably not be as big as commercial strawberries – but they will taste better and you know that they haven't been flown in from Spain.

How to grow and when to plant

Strawberries actually like clay (yes!) but can grow just about anywhere. They are easy to grow and propagate well. We have masses.

They need sun and plenty of water, but not waterlogged soil. They are very hardy, in fact needing winter cold to stimulate flowering. There is a variety known as Alpine with very small but sweet berries which of course started out as a woodland plant in the UK.

Double dig the soil and put in plenty of organic matter. Plant in rows about 18 inches (45 cm) apart with the crown just above soil level, not resting on it. Give them a good mulch. It is traditional – and this is where they get their name from – to put straw under the plants to protect the berries. We also use it for a mulch along with wood chippings.

Make sure that they are certified 'virus-free'.

Strawberries propagate by sending out runners. Either remove them or peg them down in pots. After a couple of months cut the runner and you have your new plant. They sell very well at open days too!

You can cover them in spring with cloches to force an early crop if you wish.

Move the bed every three years. We don't know how old ours is, so in year two we will be setting up a new one.

Issues

- The usual herbivores and slugs will eat the fruit. One of my allotment neighbours thinks that frogs and toads eat them. If that is the case I don't begrudge them a few, as long as they eat slugs and snails as well!
- Net them from the birds.
- Blight and beetles as for raspberries.

Harvesting

Pick strawberries as they ripen – and try not to eat them all straight away. We let the children pick them and they really enjoy it. They don't keep very long – so use them quickly.

Strawberries don't freeze very well, but of course make excellent jam.

After harvesting, cut the foliage back to leave a small stalk. Compost the leaves and the straw.

Do not return them to a site that has had berries for six years.

Currants (ribes)

Characteristics

We tend to use this word to mean three species of plant that are, in fact, not currants at all. The name comes from *reisin de Corauntz*, which referred to small raisins – still called currants – from Corinth in southern Greece. The word was then used, later on by association, to describe the unrelated northern European berries (from the genus *Ribes*) which looked like the Greek currants when they were introduced to Britain in the sixteenth century.

Three types of currants are grown typically on allotments:

- Redcurrants (*ribes rubrum*).

- Whitecurrants (*ribes petrauem*), which are closely related.

- Blackcurrants (*ribes nigrum*).

We don't grow blackcurrants as we don't really eat them, but we grow both red and white ones which we like very much in fruit salad.

Currants are hardy and not too fussy about soil as long as it is acidic and not too heavy. They crop quite heavily when in full production and one plant of each will probably be adequate.

How to grow and when to plant

Manure the site well and set the plants about 4 or 5 feet apart. They are pruned hard each year so will not grow more than this and it promotes good air circulation. They do not like wind or salty air so if these are problems then screening may be necessary. Mulching helps conserve moisture.

The winter chill is very important in producing a good crop. The berries grow on what are called 'strigs' (from the Latin for stalk).

Issues

- They need plenty of water.

- Birds will eat them, so netting is critical.

- They prefer acidic soil, so mulch with pine needles.

Harvesting

In late autumn the berries should have swollen and changed to the correct colour. Pick off the clusters, not the individual berries. You can expect them to crop for twenty years and longer!

Whitecurrants are sweeter than redcurrants and can be eaten without cooking, but redcurrants in full bloom are one of the fantastic sights of late summer/autumn as they cascade down the branches. Redcurrants are best cooked as they can be acidic. They make great pies, jams and jellies.

Pruning

Growth of fruit is from new shoots, so older ones are cut out to encourage new ones called spurs. Side shoots are cut back in summer to about five leaves to encourage fruit growth and improve air circulation – this also helps to keep pests away as they often lurk in the tips of plants. Cut off any suckers.

Note that blackcurrants fruit on shoots that are a year old, while red and white currants fruit on branches that are two years old or more.

Give them a boost feed by using manure every three years or so.

Gooseberries

Characteristics

Another member of the *Ribes* family and possibly the easiest to grow. The general descriptions under currants above apply here. People either love them or hate them. We don't care for them much and so don't grow them at all.

They are slightly more prone to drooping than currants so need some staking or tying up.

Two interesting crosses are the jostaberry, which is a gooseberry/blackcurrant cross and therefore lacks the thorns, with fruit that are similar to blackcurrants but larger, and the Worcestershire berry, which is an even more thorny version of the gooseberry.

How to grow and when to plant

They are grown as bushes and can be white, yellow, the more familiar green, and pink or red. Some are for eating and others for cooking – make sure you buy the right type for your needs. Plant them in full sun, but they will tolerate some shade. Double dig the ground and add organic matter the autumn before planting.

Gooseberries are very hardy and like clay soil. Either plant in late autumn or early spring. Buy 'bare-rooted' plants and make a hole wide enough for them to spread out. They are droopy bushes so prune them to make them grow upright and keep them off the soil which can lead to nasty diseases such as fungal infections, as well as acting as ladders for slugs and snails.

Gooseberries are very prickly so always wear gloves and protective sleeves. Shorts are not a good idea!

Prune each branch to three or four buds only in winter, and take out old stems. In summer cut them back to about six leaves.

Issues

- Birds will eat the berries given half a chance, so net the bushes.
- Aphids – Gooseberry sawfly: keep this at bay by excavating a little of the soil, taking up any mulch around the bush in winter and then burning it. Replace it with new soil.

Harvesting

Take a first 'thinning' crop in late spring/early summer to encourage the remainder to fatten up. Use the thinnings in pies. If gathering for cooking, you can pick them when still hard but starting to colour; for eating, wait until they are fully ready. You usually take them all in one go.

Gooseberries and their pies can be frozen. They also make jams and jellies.

You can transplant very easily by taking cuttings in the autumn.

Blackberries

Characteristics

These very hardy plants are well-established natives and you can see them in every part of the country. They grow well in just about any soil unless it is very wet. They are very useful for giving fruit, but the devil of a nuisance as a perennial weed. When we started sorting out our plot there were literally hundreds of little bramble seedlings everywhere: some with extensive root systems, some just starting out. It required a lot of effort to tame them. I have to say though, they are the easiest fruit to grow.

The main blackberry area consisted of a couple of very well-established plants with stems a couple of inches thick in parts. I cut it back very hard indeed and throughout the year I kept pruning the new growths back. After our bumper crop I gave it another very hard pruning for winter. This removes side shoots that will sap the growth of flowers and ultimately berries on the main stems and keeps it under control, because it is a vigorous grower.

Our blackberries are trained across an arrangement of posts and cross posts, which makes harvesting easier as we can access the fruit from both sides. They also enjoy full sun, which is the best condition for them.

How to grow and when to plant

If starting from scratch, put new canes in the soil between November and March. Either put in posts and wires, or grow the plant against a wall or hedge (the disadvantage there is that it is harder to get to the other side). Give the soil a good feed – best to dig a trench and fill it with compost.

If you have established plants, cut them back very hard in late autumn or early spring and train the main shoots along whatever support you have. On many sites the blackberry plants form a natural arch.

Once established, they don't really need feeding as they generate extensive root systems that quest everywhere for food and water.

If you can, plant them so that they run north to south, then both sides will benefit from a good dose of sunshine. Ours, however, run across our plot roughly west to east and it doesn't seem to affect them. Water is what makes them fat and juicy, so in droughts give them plenty. Mulching helps.

They are ready when the fruit is big, turning from red to black and luscious. Keep picking and it will keep cropping. Cut off any side branches where all the fruit has been picked.

Issues
- If birds are a nuisance then net the plants to keep them off. We didn't find we had any problem with that at all.

Harvesting
Remember to take containers with you to put the blackberries in. We use the lidded salad boxes that come with takeaways: as they are just right for freezing later.

Either use them straight away or freeze them as they start fermenting and deteriorating almost at once – we left a box out and they had mould on them a day later! They are wonderful in blackberry and apple pies/crumbles – one of my favourites on a winter's night with custard. They also make very rich jams and jellies.

Grapes

A quick word on grapes. As the climate changes, so the crops that you can grow change. In medieval times it was very common for grapes to be grown in the UK and wine was made from them. As the climate cooled, vines gradually disappeared. Over the last twenty years or so, as temperatures have warmed up and increasingly hardy vines have been bred, the grape has become commonplace. This, coupled with improved management techniques, has seen a resurgence in the UK wine industry and increasingly good, drinkable wine. One of my friends has a vineyard in the south of England and the white wine is very good indeed. We don't yet see the very rich reds – as we don't yet get the warmth of the sun that Mediterranean countries receive – but I am sure they will come.

We can't all grow grapes that will make good eating or good wine. But we have grown one for many years and they provide excellent foliage and fence/wall covering. Each year I cut it back to a small stub and every year it grows with a vigour that even surpasses the squashes and pumpkins. We don't 'farm' it for grapes – although we get plenty of very small ones (even after culling they are not big enough for eating) – but they are great plants and make our patio look very continental in summer and autumn.

Grapes are not really a crop for allotments – but why not give them a go if you have the space? We found one growing on our allotment. We left it in the first year to see what happened, but it wasn't very well so we took it out.

A warm, south-facing wall where the roots can be kept cool is ideal.

Grapes can be kept for a surprisingly long time given the right storage conditions and methodologies. If you do manage to grow large grapes, then when harvesting leave the stem on both sides of the bunch, leaving the stem as long as possible on one side. If you place the long stem in a bottle of water, laid flat on its side, then the grapes will absorb the water and keep for a surprising time. You need cool, dark storage conditions as well, and need to top up the bottle with tepid water.

23

Perennial Crops

These are those crops that are raised in permanent beds. They include asparagus, rhubarb, Jerusalem and globe artichokes, cardoons and horse-radish. Artichokes and cardoons have been dealt with in their family chapter and few people grow horseradish, so I have just dealt with rhubarb and asparagus here.

Rhubarb

Characteristics

This is another example of the confusion between fruit and vegetable. Most people believe that it is a fruit, but in fact rhubarb is a vegetable, grown for its pinky-coloured stems – not its fruit, nor its leaves which are highly toxic as they contain oxalic acid! It is thought to have come originally from places like Siberia, which with its swings of temperature between plus 40°C and minus 40°C makes for intensely hardy plants.

Rubarb is from the same family as buckwheat, sorrel and knotweed and is a perennial. It is grown on the same (permanent) site each year. It is naturally a very tart plant that makes you pull a face when you eat it unsweetened – and was traditionally cooked with masses of sugar to counteract that taste. For this reason it didn't really become popular until sugar was readily available in the sixteenth century.

In the UK a major site is the rhubarb triangle of Wakefield, Leeds and Morley, due to the soil being particularly good. Rhubarb is a plant that inspires hot passions. People either love it or detest it. I personally fall into the latter camp, but our friends bite our hands off when we offer the produce to them. It always sells well at open days.

Blanching
Rhubarb needs cold to optimise its growth, and is blanched usually.

According to Peter Thoday in *The Victorian Kitchen Garden* this was discovered accidentally. Some workmen were digging or excavating a trench and rather carelessly threw the soil over some rhubarb plants that were growing nearby. When they came to put the soil back, and uncovered the plant, it was found that the blanching had improved the sweetness immeasurably and this is what has been done ever since.

How to grow and when to plant
As a very hardy plant, rhubarb can grow just about anywhere but it prefers a neutral soil with sun. Ours grows on the edge of our allotment in full sun. The soil needs to be well-drained.

Rhubarb is usually planted by using dormant crowns. You don't really need more than two or three plants even if you like it.

Dig the ground over and put in plenty of organic matter. Plant the crowns out in late autumn with 1 yard (1 m) between the plants and place them just below the surface. Don't harvest it in the first year, but do take off the flowers. Mulch in the autumn, after taking all the foliage off.

Forcing
This produces earlier and more tender (sweeter) stems by increasing the temperature. In winter, cover the plant with a large pot or bucket (or special rhubarb forcer) full of straw. It can be further assisted by piling hot manure over the pot to increase the temperature. This forces the shoots to grow earlier and also blanches them at the same time by excluding light. Once shoots have appeared, keep inspecting them and harvest as required. It is best to force different plants each year.

Issues

- Having evolved to cope with the hideous conditions in places like Siberia, rhubarb is usually trouble-free, but it might get crown rot. There is no cure – burn the plant and plant another one, elsewhere.

- It is a good idea to split the plant every few years to encourage new growth, otherwise it will only last about ten years. Dig it up in late summer and chop it into a couple of pieces with a spade, making sure each has root and a bud. Then replant them – or give them to someone else.

Harvesting

Usually one of the first crops of the year. Rhubarb can be harvested until summer. Do not cut the stalks – twist them off, taking only about half and leaving the rest.

Although the leaves are poisonous to eat they are quite safe to compost as the poison breaks down easily, and one plant produces a lot of leaves.

Rhubarb can be chopped up and frozen very easily. Some people add chopped cicely leaves to the rhubarb when cooking it as this reduces the need for sugar. Do not eat it raw!

Asparagus

Characteristics

This plant which is prized for its succulent stems requires some effort for a short crop in late spring early summer. But if you like asparagus – as we do – it is well worth the effort, especially if you can devote a permanent site to the crop.

How to grow and when to plant

Asparagus will grow in most soil, provided it is well-drained. If your soil is heavy, you should consider creating a raised bed. Asparagus prefers a soil pH of 6.5–7.5.

The effort comes in the preparation. It is best to double dig and fork in plenty of organic matter. We also riddled the soil to get rid of the weeds – and my goodness weren't there hundreds. It took ages.

You can grow asparagus from seed, but germination is tricky and unreliable, so it is more usual to buy crowns – plants that are already one year old.

Sow the seeds in February for transplanting in early summer. For crowns, plant in March or April. Male plants are used as they are more reliable and do not set seed.

As the bed is permanent – twenty years or so – make it a good one. The traditional bed is about 5 feet wide, with three ridges about 18 to 24 inches (45–60 cm) apart. Raise up the soil to ensure it is well-drained and the plants won't rot by constructing ridges inside the bed.

The crowns are spread out so they look like the rays of the sun on the ridges, about 18 inches (45 cm) apart. Stagger them to ensure better plants. Cover them with soil to about 3 inches (7 cm). As they grow, keep adding soil so that only the tips are showing.

Give them plenty of water. A good mulch will help suppress weeds, which will also grow in the nice bed that you have prepared. Hand-weed – do not use a hoe as that might damage the tender crowns.

Year 1 – let them grow and cut the fronds down in autumn.
Year 2 – the same.
Year 3 – harvest.

After the harvest, let the fronds grow.

Let the foliage go yellow before cutting it down to 1 inch (2.5 cm) in autumn and burning it.

Feed after you cut the fronds down and again in spring.

Issues

- Slugs.

- Asparagus beetles. These are black with orange markings, but tiny, $^1/_4$ inch (0.5 cm) so tough to spot. The larvae are grey and are about $^1/_2$ inch (1 cm) long. Take them both off and kill them. They chew foliage and spears. Cutting the fronds back stops them over-wintering in the foliage. Covering the plants in a fleece in spring can help prevent the beetles getting to them.

Harvesting

Do not harvest for the first two years – the asparagus spears are not ready.

In year three, harvest before the tips (called bracts) start to open – when the spears are about 6 inches (15 cm) tall. Cut the spears cleanly using a very sharp knife under the soil (about 3 inches or so) to give the nice long spears we love to eat.

Cool them and use quickly, although they will last a few days in the refrigerator.

Keep cutting until about mid-June (Royal Ascot is the marker used by many) to allow the plant to build up its reserves for future years.

Citrus fruits

One of my greatest memories of North Africa (Tunisia) was walking along the pavement in January and seeing trees on every street corner laden with oranges just ready for plucking and eating. I always associate these fruits with very hot countries, but in fact they like fluctuations in temperature (but not too cold) as this helps them grow.

Many of them ripen at Christmas, when the whole house positively drips with the smell of satsumas and tangerines.

The UK climate, perversely, is very well-suited to citrus fruit. They do need protection in winter, but can stand outside for most of the year. Growing oranges, lemons, grapefruit and so on is not really viable in the open on allotments, but if you have a greenhouse you can grow them.

The family is Rutaceae, and the plants originated in South-east Asia. They are generally shrubs or trees, usually have five petals (generally white) and are often very strongly scented. The fruit is a hesperidium and has a hard pithy skin-covering (rind) holding the juicy segments (called liths, meaning 'stones' as in megaliths at Stonehenge).

The main family members are: bergamot, bitter orange, Seville orange, blood orange, clementine, grapefruit, lemon, lime, mandarin orange, orange, pomelo, satsuma, tangelo, tangerine and ugli fruit (which is).

As citrus trees cross-pollinate (hybridise) readily with others, all commercial citrus cultivation is with known cuttings grafted onto rootstocks, as with apples. The produce is eaten or used to make juices. It is also the key ingredient in marmalade (defined as jam using citrus fruit).

Although grapefruits and oranges are eaten raw, limes and lemons are too astringent for this and typically are used to make strong juices, in cooking, or as additions to, among other things, drinks such as gin and tonic (lemons) and cuba libre (limes). Lime segments are often a feature of Mexican beer and tequila.

The rind is often sliced thinly – known as zest – and is a feature of many recipes in cooking. Marmalade can be made with or without the peel. Lemon peel is a feature of Christmas puddings. Grapefruit was developed in the Caribbean in the eighteenth century and is so-called because they grow in clusters, like grapes.

The Royal Navy used limes to ward off scurvy, hence the nickname for British sailors in the USA – Limeys.

Citrus fruits must be exposed to a cool winter to give the fruit its associated colour. In warmer regions with no winter the fruits stay green, which is why you can see green oranges and lemons.

Although they need some exposure to cool days they are not frost hardy, being tropical. They prefer sunny, humid environments with fertile soil and plenty of water. Curiously, they are broad-leaved but evergreen at the same time. The trees flower in spring, but although the fruit sets quite soon thereafter, they only begin to ripen in late autumn/early winter – although grapefruit may take up to eighteen months to ripen.

Citrus fruits have a long association with royalty and gentry (as they could afford to look after them) and orangeries were developed to grow them in cooler European climes.

Kumquats look like citrus fruits but are not, as an inspection of the skin – which is edible – will tell you. They were originally from China but are now grown everywhere.

How to grow them

All citrus will grow much better in containers placed in a sunny position and then taken indoors when it gets cold. The best type of pot is unglazed terracotta. Put polystyrene in the bottom. This keeps the pot 'sound' and is lighter than bits of old crockery that were traditionally used – an important point if you have to lug them indoors when winter comes!

Key points

- Do not over-water – keep just moist.
- Keep well-fed at all times.
- Stand outside in the summer in sunny positions.
- Bring inside in the colder months.

I have grown citrus fruit plants from seed for fun – but that is as far as I have gone. If we are really seeing climate change, perhaps they will become an increasing feature of allotments.

(24)

Herbs

What is a herb?

There is no real definition. If you ask people to name some herbs they will rattle off parsley, dill, basil, mint, sage, etc and might come up with a few more such as tarragon, bayleaf, rosemary, allspice and so on. There is no commonality at all. Some are from one family, others from another, some are plants, some are bushes.

Herbs have many different characteristics or features:

- Some are grown for their fragrance.
- Others for their flavours.
- Some are believed to have healing and/or health properties.
- Others have an aesthetic appeal.

Definition
A basic definition, therefore, is a plant that has become associated with a particular use or a specific purpose – flavouring, medicine, aromatics, etc. This is perhaps not very helpful as there hundreds of herbs or quasi-herbs – many familiar, some unknown – and many originally from overseas, now thriving in the UK; but it is probably the closest we can get.

The study of herbs and herblore is called herbology, as in Neville Longbottom's – of *Harry Potter* fame – best subject (in Old English it was wortlore).

What is a spice?

If the definition of a herb is difficult, then that of a spice is slightly easier. Herbs are usually the leaves or stalks of a plant. Spices on the other hand are the berries (allspice), seeds (caraway) or bark (cinnamon). Spices are usually thought of as being more pungent or piquant. Many of them originate in far-off climes that are very much hotter than the UK and have names that are redolent of those lands – cinnamon, cloves, nutmeg, saffron, vanilla (from Mexico). Zanzibar is a well-known producer of spices. I have been there and visited a spice farm, which was fascinating. The spice trade made many people very rich as people sought spices to improve the flavour of food, and also to help to preserve it.

The expeditions to the west that resulted in the discovery of the Americas were attempts to find a route to the spice islands of Africa and the East Indies that would break the monopoly of the Arab traders.

Popular herbs

Below are some of the more popular herbs grown in gardens and allotments.

Basil (*ocimum basilicum*)

Basil likes the Mediterranean warmth of its original climate and thrives in a greenhouse or outside as an annual in sunny spots in UK gardens. It is an essential ingredient in spaghetti Bolognese and Italian cooking generally. Sow under cover (in greenhouses or slightly later on in cloches or polytunnels) in March. Plant out when warmer. Frost will probably kill it. Pinch out flowers to encourage the leaves. Our local Italian deli owner recommends it as a tomato and basil salad. There are lots of different types – classic or Italian basil; sweet (which we grow); Thai basil, which smells of cloves; purple and dwarf basils; and even scented basil which comes in several types, including cinnamon, lime and camphor.

Bay (*laurus nobilis*)

Bay is an evergreen shrub; more a miniature tree really. It is hardy and can grow to over 10 feet (3 m). It likes sunny positions with well-drained but moist soil. Prune it in summer to keep it to a manageable size. Usually bought as a plant.

Borage (*borago officianalis*)

Borage has beautiful delicate blue flowers and is adored by bees. Easy to grow and self-setting as well. We grow it mainly for bees but also for putting in Pimm's (when we remember). You can also chop it up and put it in salads. It tastes a little like cucumber. If you put a flower in each section of an ice-cube tray before freezing, they look fantastic and add a new dimension to drinks!

Chives (*allium schoenoprasum*)

Chives are small onion-like spears. A hardy perennial which is delicious sprinkled over soup, especially smoked haddock – one of my favourites! Easy to grow in any soil. The reddish-purple flowers attract bees and the leaves can be eaten. Sow *in situ* in late spring (can be raised under cover, but not necessary). Once it is established, the clumps can be divided to give new plants (autumn). After flowering (autumn) cut it down to 2 inches (5 cm) to promote new growth. Grown from bulbs.

Coriander (*coriandrum sativum*)

Coriander is an annual grown for both its leaves and seeds. An essential ingredient in curries. Sow outdoors in late spring. If you want lots of seeds, choose the sunniest position that you can; for leaves, it can be grown in most places. If you want lots of leaves, sow a few plants every few weeks or so. We grow it as a pest repellent, not to use. It is sometimes called cilantro in North America. The leaves are best used fresh.

Comfrey (*synphytum x uplandicum*)

Comfrey is grown for use as a fertiliser, and not for any other use of which I am aware. Best grown in a contained area as it can spread. Cut leaves can be used as a mulch or you can make comfrey tea (see Compost). It has very deep roots which bring minerals such as potash to the surface.

Dill (*anethum graveolens*)

Dill is an annual herb with feathery leaves. It is hardy and likes the sun, but needs to be kept moist. Sow directly *in situ* in spring – it doesn't transplant readily. Its leaves are used in salads with potatoes and with fish (gravadlax is salmon served with dill sauce – absolutely delicious!). Its seeds are used in pickling spices. It self-seeds easily. Keep cutting a few leaves at a time. It runs to seed very easily so succession sowing is a good idea if you want lots of leaves. You can store the leaves dry or you can freeze them. To harvest seeds, take them off when they have turned light brown, then gently, tap them into a paper bag. Store in an airtight container. Leave a couple of heads to self-set next year.

Fennel (*foeniculam vulgare*)

Fennel is a hardy perennial which can be grown from seed or propagated from existing plants by dividing the roots. It has a liquoricey flavour and is usually used with fish. It can grow 5 feet (1.5 m) high and its leaves look like feathers. It can grow in sun or partial shade and attracts lots of beneficial insects.

Lavender (*lavendula angustifola*)

Lavender is one of our favourite plants. Not only does it smell lovely, but bees and hover flies love it too. It needs dry soil and lots of sun. It can be sown under cover in early spring, or *in situ* late spring. It flowers all through summer and autumn. The flowers are edible, and of course you can gather it to make lavender pillows to aid sleep and breathing at night and to deter clothes moths. It can also be put under running water for scented baths. It can be blue, mauve, pink or white. Give it a good prune in autumn to encourage new growth. It is an ingredient in potpourri. Very easy to grow from seed or cuttings.

Marjoram (*origanum marjorana*)

Marjoram is similar to oregano, but slightly sweeter in taste and not so hardy. It likes good sun and very good drainage. It is tender and either grown as an annual (it is a perennial in warmer climes) or moved into shelter in winter. Let the soil get quite dry before watering sparingly, but if the plants look very sad, give them a good watering. It is difficult to grow from seed so most are propagated from cuttings. It is nice to put in a hanging basket. The plants need trimming to keep them from getting straggly. Bees love them – but so do butterflies. Chewing the leaves is reputed to help in toothache.

Mint (*menthe*)

Mint is a plant or group of plants that have countless uses, from flavouring toothpaste, chewing gum and mint imperials to cooking and herb-pillows. They are very hardy indeed and rapid-growing. There are several types: spearmint (*menthe spicata*), peppermint (*menthe piperita*), lemon mint, orange mint, pineapple mint and apple mint. I think that we have all of these except orange mint on our plot. It is the most popular herb that we sell at our fund-raising days.

It is a bruiser of a plant, sending out a mycelium of roots that push everything out of the way. It is therefore invasive and should be grown in a container and chopped round to control it. It self-sets so easily that it will appear everywhere. You only need one plant! We use it in vinegar as mint sauce with lamb and redcurrant jelly, and in new potatoes and peas. Many people make mint tea which is very refreshing. You can also rip up a few leaves and throw them into a bath as it runs for a refreshing, tingling experience. A cut-and-come-again plant, it can be stored dry or frozen and in jars with vinegar as mint sauce.

Oregano (*origanum vulgare*)

Oregano is a bushy perennial plant which has a distinctive scent and is much used in Italian and Mediterranean cuisine, especially pizzas. It is a member of the marjoram family (which curiously is called *origanum* in Latin). Bees love its flowers. It likes full sun and dry soil, reflecting its origins in sun-kissed Greece. If the soil is wet, mix sand in to help drainage. It can be cut often and this stops the flowers, so you encourage lots of leaves. It can be grown from seed easily or divided in autumn. It will need protecting over winter in the UK. Take the leaves off when you want to use them. It goes well with tomatoes. The leaves can be stored dried after separation from the stems, but it is best stored on the stems in glass jars in the dark after drying.

Parsley (*petroselinum crispum*)

Parsley is a hardy biennial that can be tricky to grow. Often bought in pots and planted out. If growing from seed, it is best to soak the seeds first. Sow in spring for early use, and then again in summer for a crop to last into winter. It has many uses in soups, sauce, in bouquet garni and as a garnish. It also gets rid of garlic breath if chewed raw and attracts beneficial insects to the plot when it flowers the following year. Sow each year to continue to enjoy the flowers and leaves. The leaves can be stored dried or frozen.

Rosemary (*rosemarin officinalus*)

This evergreen shrub is grown in many gardens and allotments. It grows to about 4 feet (1.2 m) and can be harvested all year round. It is used to flavour many dishes including roast lamb, often along with thyme as stuffing. Its blue flowers are attractive to bees and other beneficial insects. Some are hardy, but not all, so winter may kill it depending on what you have – covering it will help protect from frost. Prune in spring. Don't overwater: brown leaves are a sign of that.

Sage (*salvia officinalis*)

Sage is a very pungent herb used in many dishes and for sage and onion stuffing. It likes light, poor soil with plenty of sun. It grows to about 3 feet (1 m). Prune in spring to get new tender growth. The plants need replacing every four years or so. Bees like it.

Thyme (*thymus vulgaris*)

Thyme has a peppery flavour but there are some lemony types as well. An essential ingredient in many dishes, it can be gathered all year round. It will thrive in poor gravelly soil in full sun. It is a member of the mint family but is not invasive. It becomes woody after a few years so replace it as that happens. Prune it after it has flowered.

Other herbs include:

Chervil, feverfew, horseradish, hyssop, lemon balm, lovage, marshmallow, orris, tansy and tarragon.

25

Cereals and Grasses

Grass is a most remarkable family. It feeds the whole world. Without this family we (and many animals that also crop grasses) would not have survived. It was the hybrid cross of two grasses to form emmer wheat (which has larger heads) that fuelled the expansion of farming and led to the development of civilisation within the Fertile Crescent. Grasses sustain the largest herds of animals in the world (gnus, cows, elephants, bison, etc).

Not many of you will be growing cereals. If you do you will probably grow maize or sweetcorn, and perhaps some others as green manures. You may also have a nice bit of grass on which to sit.

Give us this day our daily bread

It takes an area 5 feet by 4 feet to produce enough wheat for one loaf. To provide 100 loaves for a family of four for a year would require a plot 20 feet by 50 feet. That is about a third of the ten rods of a normal allotment. I wonder if it would be worth it? Then you would need to grind it, mill it, etc. But what about an allotment site setting aside a whole plot or two for wheat? Could that be a good idea?

Major members of the family are:

- Oats.

- Barley.

- Rice.

- Wheat/corn.

- Rye.

- Buckwheat.

- Maize/sweetcorn.

Most of these need huge fields to be commercially viable, but some allotment holders do grow a few members of the family. I just deal with the most common – maize/sweetcorn.

Maize/sweetcorn (*zea mays*)

Characteristics

Maize/sweetcorn is from Central America. It was developed, we believe, by the Mayans or Incas from a wild grass. It has been grown in continental Europe for some time and is now becoming more widespread in the UK. We grow it on our allotment as part of the 3 Sisters system. I am not sure if this reflects more hardy strains that can grow well in our climate or climate change or a bit of both.

It is a crop that almost everybody likes. Whether boiled, grilled or barbecued it is very popular.

How to grow and when to plant

It needs full sun. It has long been grown on the Continent and when I was working in Hungary every hotel, café and restaurant had masses of dried cobs around the walls as decoration. Although normally yellow, it comes in a whole host of colours from white through orange, red, purple and verging on black.

It will be killed by frosts, so do not plant it out until they are past.

It should be planted in blocks rather than rows (which is probably where we went wrong!) and in a good summer will deliver an excellent crop. It is wind pollinated and the blocks help in the process by ensuring lots of pollen falls down onto the female flowers which will produce the cobs.

It needs warmth to germinate but doesn't transplant well as it doesn't like root disturbance (you could try using root trainers, as for sweet peas). It also doesn't like heavy, wet soils, so if your soil is like ours dig in plenty of organic matter. We dug a trench for ours and filled it up, planting courgettes underneath it (see 2 $^1/_2$ Sisters).

May or June is best for outdoor sowing as this is when it is warm enough. Sow three seeds to each station and then thin to the strongest. Leave 14 inches (35 cm) between stations. Give the plants plenty of water until they are established and then again when the cobs start to grow. It should take four months from sowing to maturity.

The plants have shallow roots so mulching is very good. Hand weed as well.

Issues
- Weather.
- Mice.
- Birds.

Harvesting
Once the silky tassels start to turn brown then it is nearly ready. If a milky juice comes out of a kernel when pressed it is ready. Eat as soon as possible as the sugar starts to turn to starch immediately. Best to chuck them onto a barbeque straight away! It also doesn't store well fresh, but freezes very well. The cobs can be dried as well, in which case leave them to start drying on the plant and then harvest them and let them continue drying by hanging them in a warm dry place.

Popcorn

You can make popcorn from them after thoroughly drying them. Leave them to dry and try a few occasionally as they dry, to see if they 'pop'. Once they are ready, store them in an airtight jar.

Baby corn

Baby corn is used in stir-fries. Plant the crops (special varieties have been bred for this) much closer together, about 8 inches (20 cm), and more deeply in the ground. Pick when it is a few inches long.

26

Flowers and Trees

Why grow flowers?

Why should you grow flowers? Aren't allotments about fruit and vegetables? Yes they are, but there are several reasons for growing flowers.

Firstly, they bring colour to the allotment and can be used to separate out different areas. They look pretty and smell nice and add an extra dimension to your plot.

There are, however, several more practical reasons for growing them. If you like that sort of thing, then many parts of lots of flowers are edible (thanks to Gloria Kitson, one of my fellow allotment holders, for this) including: calendula, cowslips, daisy, marigolds, nasturtiums, pansies, roses, sunflowers and violas.

Many flowers have beneficial points that help an allotment greatly:

- They attract pest predators (see The cavalry).
- They attract other beneficial insects, such as pollinating creatures.
- They deter pests.
- As companion plants they help other plants to grow better.

- They 'disguise' your vegetables by confusing the enemy. A lot of pests fly randomly looking for large areas of specific crops. When they land on a plant that is not what they are looking for they will often move on elsewhere. We planted several plants among our crops, such as coriander, nasturtiums and marigolds, and it seemed to work.

- By breaking up your crops with others it can help slow the spread of plant-specific diseases.

You can buy flower plants or you can sow them *in situ* from seed. Alternatively, you can do what we do and raise them from seeds in seed trays and then pot them out. This has a few advantages:

- You know where they are because you can see them. With seeds sown *in situ* you won't know where the plants are until they come through and if you don't know what they look like you will probably weed them out.

- They will be more developed and therefore will not provide such easy meals for predators as seedlings will.

Why grow trees?

Trees are a vital component of the UK landscape. What would Britain look like devoid of trees? I can tell you that places such as Kazakhstan with their flat desert landscapes are bleak godforsaken places with nothing to lift the soul. Also, trees are excellent harbingers of the seasons. Nothing does this for me more overtly than the horse chestnut (conker) tree. In spring the green leaves burst from the empty branches; in summer the blossom covers them; in autumn the leaves turn to those beautiful yellowy-brown dappled colours, with conkers everywhere before they fall lazily to the ground; and in winter the trees stand stark and proud against the skyline. I often think how fast autumn has come round when the leaves change!

Trees provide natural habitats, shade, cool greenness and make towns much more pleasant. They also provide the oxygen for our world, taking in and processing carbon dioxide. In some instances they act as pollution absorbers. The London Plane was created in a genetic masterstroke by our Victorian forbears. It is deciduous and its leaves absorb dirt and soot then fall off – as do many other trees of course – but much pollution is also absorbed into bark, and it also sheds that, so even more pollution is neutralised.

Trees on allotments

It is not permitted to grow trees on our allotments. This is because the shade from a mature tree will stop anything growing, the roots will suck up all the moisture, and also many trees are poisonous to other plants.

But if there are trees growing nearby then you can make use of them. Our site is surrounded on three sides by trees and this provides several advantages:

- They act as a fantastic windbreak, giving us a great deal of shelter from the worst effects of the weather.

- They make the site very secure. Vandalism is an increasing problem but the trees seal the site, along with fences and gates, making it very secure indeed. We are lucky in this respect as many other sites are open to anyone and therefore vulnerable.

- They provide a haven for wildlife. We are fortunate to have a fantastic nature area next to us (Cox's walk and Dulwich woods) that is home to very many useful creatures. It is not, however, without its draw-backs, as the trees also provide homes and roosting for pigeons, crows, squirrels and others – you can't have it both ways!

- The trees provide handy branches for many uses.

- The leaves can be gathered and mulched.

- We have several sloe trees that can be harvested.

- The trees also provide some shade, which is very useful at the height of summer.

One way round the prohibition is to grow trees in containers. This restricts their growth but still enables you to enjoy them.

Of course, if you are allowed to you can grow fruit trees. Apples, pears, peaches, plums and damsons are grown on trees in many allotments.

Maintaining Your Allotment

Introduction

An understanding of the plants you wish to grow, what they need, and how they grow is useful, but of course running an allotment comes down to the real practicalities of actually *doing* things.

In Part III I will look at the practicalities of running an allotment, such as the problems that you will encounter; protecting your tender crops; composting; crop rotation and how it works; and harvesting, storage and seed collecting. There are also some useful tips, contacts and a vademecum to help in planning your year.

Couch potatoes?

Once you have an allotment, one of the things that you almost invariably find yourself doing is watching a whole new set of television programmes on gardening. Although many of them are terrible and more like reality shows, there are some very real nuggets among them, packed with interesting and useful tips. The recent increase in public interest in growing one's own food has shifted the emphasis of these programmes away from flowers and more towards vegetables than hitherto and this is helpful.

The Victorian Kitchen Garden was a very gentle series – first shown in the 1980s – which re-created a kitchen garden from a large country house as it might have been in the nineteenth century. It is packed full of tips and advice and coincidentally in many respects, by going back to pre-industrial growing when there were few, if any, pesticides, foreshadowed today's focus on organic approaches to gardening.

The two presenters were Peter Thoday, a lecturer in horticulture from Bath University and a scion of a long line of head gardeners, and Harry Dobson, a life-long gardener who had been apprenticed to a real Victorian head gardener in a Victorian country house and learnt from him the tips of the trade.

In *Heaven's Kitchen,* an organic garden was created from scratch to provide food for the Pot Kiln pub in Berkshire.

More recently, the BBC produced *Grow Your Own Veg* with Carol Klein, which is excellent – she has a passion for gardening. There was also a mini-series on allotments, contrasting two sites in Wales and London. Unfortunately it was presented in a rather patronising and pedestrian way, and a lot of what could have been interesting was lost. It still had some useful tips in it, though.

(27)

Planting

Your allotment needs to be well-planned and ordered. This is so you know:

- what is where;
- what was where, to ensure adequate rotation and no repeats;
- you can grow the crops in the right area;
- you won't 'lose' crops – or walk over them accidentally.

This means that you need to prepare the soil in different ways for each crop and then plant the crops.

This may be by:

- sowing seeds *in situ*;
- sowing them under cover for transplanting out;
- taking or propagating plants;
- moving plants; or
- buying them from a seed/plant merchant.

Round about autumn the catalogues will start dropping through your letter box. They contain a sometimes bewildering range of many (often too many) seeds and plants, tools, solutions to pests, sheds, wheelbarrows and other items. Once you have had transactions the catalogues will come to you – you do not need to order them every year – they are like perennials. Indeed, on the day I wrote these words two fell through the letter box!

Before buying anything, plan out what you want to grow – and when. Then check what you have left over from last year or have harvested yourself; only then order your seeds and plants.

You may also want to look over your tools – they do wear out and break from usage. We were on our second fork and had worn out several trowels by the end of only our first year!

Winter preparation

Not a lot happens during this period of dormancy and hibernation, but the winter months are a great time for sitting down and planning what you are going to do (see Part I) and for preparing the soil (see Digging). Little grows during the winter and it is not until the warmth of the spring sun that growth will once again break out. You can, however, use the time profitably.

In the northern hemisphere our winters are (usually) cold with strong rains, winds, frosts and occasionally (less frequently than even I remember now) snow. You can use this to your advantage. Autumn is the best time to dig over your plot. This means that you can leave the winter weather to do a lot of work for you. The weather will:

- Break down the soil that you have turned over and left in clods and sods.

- Kill many pests.

- Ensure that, as there are few plants around that will feed creatures, they will eat the pests that are around instead.

- Replenish the water in the ground (water table) to help you get through the (increasingly) dry summers.

- Help some hardy plants to develop.

- Help root crops turn their starches into sugar and therefore make them taste better.

Spring, after the weather has done its work on the soil, is your opportunity to plant. Different plants need planting out at different times – see each chapter for specifics – but in general there is commonly understood way of sowing seeds or planting out.

Sowing from seed

Most plants that we grow are sown from seed, either *in situ* – that is, where they are going to grow – or elsewhere for transplanting later. There is a fantastic sense of achievement in saying to someone, 'Yes, I grew it from seed myself.' Later on, of course, in many instances you can also harvest the seed for use – even better.

Always sow in the best conditions for the plant. Those sown later on when it is warmer will be more successful than those sown earlier. It is, however, better to plant at the wrong time than not to plant at all. You cannot guarantee that conditions will be 'just right' Goldilocks, so in some instances you just need to carry on sowing regardless.

Buy organic seed – it might be more expensive but you should start as you mean to go on.

Packet contents

Sometimes the packet will tell you the number of seed enclosed, and other times it will tell you the distance its contents will cover, eg a 30 foot row. I think the firms do that so that it is harder to make price comparisons! The number of seeds you get varies. With some plants, eg courgettes or tomatoes, you may only get twenty or thirty, but with others such as peas or celery 300–400 may be more typical; swede and carrot packets may contain a couple of thousand tiny seeds. For sprouting seeds such as fenugreek, lentil and alfalfa, you may get between 10,000 and 45,000!

Rows

Many seeds are planted out in rows – also known as drills. 'But seeds don't grow that way naturally do they?' I hear you say. No, of course not. But you are trying to maximise both the yield and the ease of maintenance, and rows do both these things. Planting in rows gives serious benefits. Of course, some plants (eg maize) need to be planted in blocks for various reasons, and others at stations (not St. Pancras!).

Rows allow you to:

- Distinguish your crops from the weeds – anything growing between the rows is an intruder (weed) and can be taken out.

- Pull out stragglers more easily as you will not walk on others.

- Avoid breaking plants by leaning across them to reach others.

- Water more easily without wetting foliage, if that is a requirement of the plant.

- Thin out as you can guarantee the correct spacing between plants and rows to maximise utilisation of soil, sun and water.

How to plant in rows

- Firstly read the instructions on the packet! If it says how far apart to plant rows – heed the advice.

- Pick a day that is neither windy – small seeds will fly about in the slightest breeze – nor raining.

- Dig over the area lightly (assuming it was dug over in the previous autumn).

- Rake it smooth, flattening out the lumps by bashing them with the back of the rake; for large ones use the back of a spade or fork.

- Take out very large stones – if there are any – not usual on an allotment. You do not need to remove small stones.

- Take out all weeds.

- Lightly water the soil if not moist – do not over-water.

- Using a piece of string and two twigs or equivalents, mark out the line where you want to sow and pull the string taut.

- Using a draw hoe, make a small line or trench in the soil to the required depth. This is usually one and a half times the size of the seed.

- Sow seeds more thinly the larger they are. It is difficult to sow very small seeds other than thickly, but large seeds such as pumpkins or beans can just be pushed into the soil with your fingers.

- Cover them up with a little soil.

- Put markers at each end of the row and also put labels at either end. Try using several combinations of markers and pencils – they fade very easily when exposed to wind, rain, sun, frost, sleet and snow! I often make a couple of holes in the packet and thread one of the row markers through it before sticking it into the ground.

Nothing is guaranteed of course – even when you take all precautions – but if you follow these instructions you will be increasing the chances of success. Some people give some types of seeds extra attention, for instance by 'nicking' peas or soaking broad beans. Berries are sometimes placed in sand in a pot over winter – a process known as stratifying.

Station sowing

This is a variation on row sowing. Prepare the ground as before, but instead of making a drill, plant two or three seeds at the specified or recommended distance, called the station. Allow the seeds to grow and thin to the strongest. Sometimes called space sowing, station sowing is usually used for the larger and more easily handled seeds such as runner beans, broad beans, peas, pumpkins and sweetcorn.

Broadcasting

Surely this is something that the likes of Alan Titchmarsh do? No, it is a method of sowing over a wide area. It is effected by walking along and throwing the seed gently by hand from side to side as you go. It is remarkably simple and also highly effective. It is used for covering large areas, eg cornfields. I use it for planting green manure where I want the whole area covered. It is also how you sow lawns and mixed flowerbeds.

Pellets and tapes

You can buy seeds that are pelletted or strung onto tapes. These are expensive but do give the advantage that the taped seeds are already correctly spaced out and you just lay them into the trench, though of course this doesn't allow for gaps caused by non-germination. The pelleted seeds are easier to handle and are wrapped in a ball of 'fertiliser'. We don't use this method. We like to make life more challenging.

Succession sowing

Don't sow all your lettuce or radish at the same time. If you do they will all mature at the same time and you will have masses for a few days, then nothing. It is much better to sow a few at a time, say a 6 foot (180 cm) or so or a row first, and then another 6 foot row a fortnight later, and so on. That way they will mature progressively and you will have food over the course of the season, rather than all in one go.

Thinning

When you plant lots of seeds, you hope that the majority will germinate. If they do, then you will have too many plants growing in too small an area. This means that they will compete for air, light, water and food. As a result, you will get thin, straggly, poorly developed plants rather than the full-sized crops you want. Help the plants to grow strong by thinning. You do this in a couple of stages by removing the weakest plants periodically to leave the strong healthy ones to grow big and fat.

The ground heats up by 1°C a week in spring. Sowing four weeks early under cover can steal a month on nature!

The fluid sow method

Some claim that by using this method the seeds emerge two or three weeks earlier than by dry sowing. It is particularly good, it is claimed, for those tricky little blighters, parsnips and carrots. The steps are:

- Germinate the seeds in a warm place, usually by placing a paper kitchen towel inside a plastic box or punnet.

- Moisten the paper and scatter the seeds over it.

- Cover it and place it in a warm place such as a propagator or airing cupboard.

- Check for roots every other day.

- When they appear on most seeds, make a gel to 'carry' the seeds. This can be a non-fungicidal wallpaper paste (yes, honestly) diluted by half with water, or made from cornflour (3 tablespoons in a pint of boiling water – let it cool completely before using it!). It should be thick enough so that the seeds are suspended in the middle rather than floating or sinking to the bottom.

- Carefully wash the seeds off the towel into a sieve, with water; then gently push them into the gel.

- Pour the mixture either into an icing bag or an ordinary plastic bag.

- Prepare a drill at the correct depth for the seeds.

- Water it – not too much.

- Gently squeeze the paste out (cut a hole in the corner of the plastic bag).

- Cover it in soil.

I haven't used this method as I can see all sorts of opportunities for it to go wrong, eg missing the root growth, damaging the seedlings as you put them in, but I am sure that it will work for others.

Planting out crowns

Some plants, eg asparagus, come as root crowns. These need to be planted in a slightly different way. Excavate a wide trench for the bed, make some mounds along two or three lines, and then neatly lay the crowns on them before covering them up. I asked my eldest daughter to lay out the crowns and she did it beautifully – I could never have done it so well!

Sowing in containers or under cover

Growing in containers or under cover is an excellent way of giving seedlings that extra start. With cover they can be started earlier than *in situ* and this can make a difference.

Generally you should match the container to the size of the seed. Sow very small seeds in trays, larger ones in separate modules and very large ones in pots straight away.

Seed-growing containers

There are several different types of containers:

- **Clay pot** The traditional pots are expensive and easily broken. The porous nature of the pot, however, does help drainage, but put a couple of pieces of broken pottery over the hole in the base to keep it 'sweet'. They are a little harder to clean than plastic pots.

- **Wooden seed trays** A traditional type of tray, nowadays expensive and rarely seen. They are reusable and let moisture in and out, being made of organic material. You could make them yourself.

- **Plastic pot** These are relatively inexpensive, reusable for ever and come in a wide range of sizes. Drainage is poor compared with pot.

- **Plastic tray of individual cells** Cheap but not very robust. They usually come with a drainage tray and covers can be bought to fit them. Plants soon need potting on though. (Not biodegradable.)

- **Biodegradable cell pack and pots** Reduces the transplanting shock as the plant stays in the cell/pot which (in theory degrades) when transplanted. Relatively expensive and can collapse if over-watered. Make sure it is the right size for the plant.

- **Plastic seed trays** Relatively inexpensive and I use them all the time. You often have to make holes in the base. Covers can be obtained for them, they are easy to clean and reusable.

Transplanting

You can, however, steal a march on spring by sowing under cover in a greenhouse or in trays left on the window sill. By sowing earlier in a warm environment you can gain a month or so, which means that when the ground and air temperatures are warm enough for growth, your plants will already be a month old and can use the heat for further growth rather than for germination.

Sowing in trays or pots is similar to sowing outside except that there will be no weeds (as long as you use 'sterile' potting compost), and you are in control of the temperature and water. Your plants must, however, be planted outside to reach full maturity – you cannot grow twenty-four squashes each 20 foot long from inside a 1 inch-deep layer of soil in a seed tray. They therefore have to be moved into the big, bad world. Do this in two stages. It is called 'hardening off'. Plants are gradually introduced to the outside world by taking them to a half-way house of some sort.

Pricking out

The plants are usually pricked out of their trays and into individual pots. It is best to do this after the true leaves have appeared, by which time they will usually be strong enough to be handled. You can use anything to remove them gently from the tray and into a pot. Some use chopsticks, others use swizzle sticks – but I find that a children's spoon is best as it scoops the plant out nicely without affecting the tiny roots. I always use modular trays rather than open trays as this gives them a unique amount of soil to grow in, which can then be lifted out together with the plant and its roots.

Hardening off

What you use to do this depends on your own situation and preferences. Some use cold frames, others small unheated greenhouses, yet others use cloches or polytunnels. Whatever you use doesn't matter as long as the plants are taken progressively from the cocoon of warmth in which you have raised them into the real world. This is just to get them accustomed to the change in environment.

After they have been allowed to get partially used to the real world, they are then transplanted into their final sites. This varies from plant to plant (see Part II) but by then they should be tough enough to withstand the normal things that nature will throw at them (weather, pests, diseases, etc).

Buying plants

In some cases you will buy in plants. This is typically for such plants as leeks and fruit shrubs, but you can just about buy any plant if you can't be bothered or haven't the time to grow from seeds. They are, of course, more expensive – a lot more expensive. This is because:

- Someone else has put the effort into sowing them, raising them and pricking them out.

- They have to be packed in a more secure way, as they are usually sent by post (unless you buy them from a garden centre locally – but you can't always get vegetable plants).

- They are already through the thinning-out stage and well on the way to developing into plants.

Plants v seeds

To give you an idea of the price differential, I have put some examples together. I have shown the difference in the cost of seeds v plants and given a price per unit:

	Plant cost	*seed cost*	*multiplier*
Beetroot	0.20	0.01	20
Broccoli	0.20	0.02	10
Cabbage	0.23	0.04	6
Cauliflower	0.20	0.005	40
Courgette	1.40	0.20	7
French bean	1.20	0.01	120
Leek	0.17	0.015	10

I make no comment as to which is better value – that is entirely subjective – it all depends on whether you wish to pay for the extra convenience, the more rapid take-up; the reduction in waste, etc. We buy leeks, and apart from potatoes, onions and garlic we grow the rest from seed. We hope to, where practicable, grow everything (except potatoes) from seed, wherever possible from our own seeds saved from the previous year.

Bulb and tuber crops

In other cases you buy the tubers or bulbs, eg onions, garlic, potatoes, etc. You can now even buy pre-chitted potatoes, but I prefer to chit my own. I like to see the little sprouts coming up as I wander into the study – it makes me feel that I am involved in all the stages of growth and it is more of a challenge.

Propagating

Once you have established plants, you can start to take cuttings: note that you can't do this with annual or biennial plants – they just don't work that way.

You can take cuttings from many parts of the plant – stems, leaves and roots. In many cases the plant helps by sending out runners (strawberries) or suckers (blackberries and many others), or by growing off-sets – baby plants that grow up next to the parent (cardoons, globe artichokes). You can also peg down branches and cover them in soil to make new plants (thyme), and divide the roots (asparagus) or divide up the tubers (Jerusalem artichokes).

Catch cropping

This is when a crop is planted on soil that has either been used for another crop which has been harvested, or a quick crop is put in before you plant out the main crop. You are therefore using the ground twice.

Make sure that you do not grow the same family of crop in the same area or you will be a) taking out the same nutrients and b) increasing the probability of pests and disease. Rocket is a very fast-growing crop that can be used in this way, as can radish. Note that catch cropping requires very careful planning!

Intercropping

This is not the same as catch cropping. This is when two crops (or more) grow together. It is sometimes called interplanting. (See also 3 Sisters.) The idea is that:

- The plants may repel pests from the other crop.

- They use different aspects of the soil (nutrients, height, depth of soil, etc).

- They may work in harmony with each other eg by suppressing weeds or giving shade.

- They can make use of space that will ultimately be needed when a plant reaches its full size, but in the meantime is small.

- You can double your productivity.

Some examples include;

- Onions with carrots.

- Cabbages with an entirely unrelated crop (beans) to confuse cabbage pests.

- Planting different strains of the same plant, eg disease-resistant cultivars with non-resistant cultivars (still being researched).

- Squashes/pumpkins below beans or sweetcorn (also called undercropping).

- Radishes sown among carrots and parsnips – mark the rows and get a crop before the others mature, also spinach and lettuce.

(28)

Organic Matter

Throughout this book I refer to organic matter or manure. This is a vital ingredient for any gardener, and especially those who wish to be as organic as possible. It is a substitute for what would occur naturally in the wild. All organic living things eventually die and their remains break down to 'feed the soil'; also animals manure the soil with their droppings.

Manure v compost

These terms are often used interchangeably. There is, however, a very real difference between the two.

Manure

Manure is usually animal droppings of plant-eating animals (herbivores) (cows, sheep, horses – never carnivores or omnivores as their droppings contain pathogens (nasty organisms which may be dangerous) or poultry; or plant material that has been used as bedding for those animals and, therefore, is impregnated with their faeces and urine (and therefore rich in nitrogen). The best manure is, in fact, that which is mixed in with bedding material – usually straw and hay. When mixed, it provides not only goodness to help growth, but bulk to improve soil structure as well.

A well-fed horse will produce some 12,500lbs (5,700kg) of manure per year, so there is plenty, especially if you live near stables.

Manure is often composted before use to allow the nutrients to stabilise, otherwise it may rob the soil of goodness as it breaks down. The result is sometimes called 'mature manure', as opposed to 'fresh'.

If there is a stables near you, become friendly with the owner; all that manure has to go somewhere and it is often very cheap if not free! Usually it is not mature so it might need to 'stand' for a while – but it is excellent for the soil (if a bit smelly for a while!).

Compost

Compost, by contrast, is the aerobically decomposed remnants of any organic material (and may include manure). It generally has a lower fertility than manure (see Compost heaps).

Green manures

These are slightly different as they are plants that are grown solely to be dug back into the soil to provide bulky organic matter, rather than food. They are not composted but are allowed to deteriorate under the soil. Many of them are nitrogen-fixers.

They also protect soil from erosion by weather (the plants cover the soil and the roots bind it together) and prevent weeds from taking hold and establishing themselves and taking goodness out. Some, such as rye, have deep roots that can help break up heavy soils. A side-effect can be that pests are deterred by the crop – and pest predators (eg beetles and frogs) like to hide in the shelter of the green manure.

Some are rapid growers, others take longer – see below. The longer-growing plants give your soil a good rest by lying fallow. By and large they grow on most soils, especially the nitrogen-fixers. Good examples include:

Name	Growth period	Nitrogen-fixer
Alfalfa	12 months	Y
Buckwheat	3 months	N
Field beans	3–6 months	Y
Clovers	12 months	Y
Mustard	2 months	N
Rye	3–6 months	N
Trefoil	3 months	Y

Dig in the manure some weeks before you want to use the site. Planning is therefore of the utmost importance as some, eg rye, will inhibit seed germination for a few weeks after they have been sown. The most common time to plant is late autumn, so that they can grow and over-winter, before digging them in during early spring.

Composting

Referring back to the phrase from the beginning – 'Look after the soil and it will look after you' – brings us to compost. There is no finer way of looking after the soil than by continually putting organic material into it. The best way of doing this and of recycling all organic waste is by composting.

What is compost?

Producing compost is merely tapping into a natural cycle of growth, death and decay. All living things are organic. When they and plants die they start to decompose virtually immediately (and start to smell too!). It is nature being super-efficient and ensuring that all the energy and goodness contained in the once-living entities are quickly transformed into nutrients to feed the earth. The hotter the weather, the faster things decompose. In building a compost heap you are seeking to replicate this natural occurrence.

We dig earthworms – and they dig the soil!

The real beauty of compost is that it does it all itself. The changes are wrought by two things – earthworms and micro-organisms. All you need to do is pile the contents up and, hey presto, it happens. It might need a little bit of input – a bit of water if it is too dry, a turn every now and again – but by and large you can sit back and let those worms do the work.

In the ordinary course of things the organic matter that is compost would take a long time to break down completely. The beauty of a (hot) compost heap is that it speeds the process up considerably. Instead of months or years, it is often only a matter of weeks.

How to make compost

Making compost from garden and organic household waste is one of the most important and also one of the easiest things an allotment holder can do.

Making compost will help you reduce pollution – cut down that landfill! And your plants will grow healthier and look happier for it. It will save you money on fertilisers too!

What can be used for compost?

Basically, if it can rot then it will compost, but some items are best avoided as they attract vermin or take a long time to decompose, or contain unpleasant chemicals, etc.

There are three kinds of compostables that can be used:

- 'Hotter-rotters'.
- 'Slower-goers'.
- 'In-betweenies'.

Hotter-rotters

Some things, like grass mowings and soft, young weeds, rot quickly. They work as 'activators' or 'hotter rotters' and are also called 'greens'. These are often the main things that many gardeners have, and precious little else. While they will get the compost heap kick-started, on their own, unfortunately, they will rapidly decay into just a sludgy, smelly mess called silage, which is also what farmers do with grass to make winter fodder (although through controlled fermentation) in a silo.

For best results you must mix the grass and weeds with 'tougher' more 'woody' items – the 'slower-goers' – often called 'browns'.

Luckily, as an allotment holder, you will have many slower-goers that can go into the heap – the by-products of your crops.

Slower-goers

The slower-goers – sometimes called browns – are the longer grown and tougher plant materials and stems that are slower to rot down, but which will give body to the finished compost. Older hedge clippings (as opposed to the new younger green shoots) are a good example. Woody items such as these and small twigs, straw and thick stems decay very slowly. For the best results you should chop them into smaller pieces with a spade or loppers/secateurs, or shred them. This exposes a greater surface to the rotting or decay process and hastens the composting.

If you have the space, leave some of the woody items to rot down in a separate pile. Although they will decay much more slowly than in a 'hot heap', they will provide places where useful and beneficial wildlife can hide and survive. Keep the heap dry, however, so as not to give hiding places to slugs and snails. That is very much part of the organic way – using nature to help you.

We have a part of our allotment at the very back, near the boundary fence under the trees, where it is too shady to grow much – although brambles and ivy seem to like it there. We pile lots of the really thick old woody items there (such as bramble stems, and overhanging branches that I trim back) to allow useful and helpful creatures (spiders and toads) to find little nooks and crannies from where they can sally forth and attack slugs and other predators.

In-betweenies

There are some items that don't fall into either of the above categories. I call these the 'in-betweenies'. They include tea bags and egg shells.

Compost components

Key items in each category include:

Greens – hotter-rotters	In-betweenies	Browns – slower-goers
grass	rhubarb leaves – chopped	straw
immature weeds	tea leaves/bags	cardboard
fruit/vegetable remains	coffee grounds	egg boxes
nettles	cut flower leaves/stems	vegetable stems
comfrey leaves (stinky)	cow manure	newspaper
flower petals	crushed egg shells	paper bags
failed seedlings	young, soft prunings	bedding plants

For the best results you need a good mix of all three categories to provide both heat and body. I also chuck in a couple of spadefuls of soil, to make sure that there are worms on the top as well as underneath. I have also spoken to our maintenance man and I let him put the grass cuttings from our paths in my bins; as that provides masses of 'hotter-rotters' which otherwise I wouldn't have, not having a lawn.

I am also friendly with the local Italian cafés who give me their coffee grounds from time to time. These can either go into the compost or be used to keep slugs at bay by scattering them around the plants.

Seaweed

Seaweed is also excellent as it contains many essential nutrients and minerals, but do not take living, rooted weed – only that which has been washed up onto the beach. It must be mixed in with the other items as well. Hose it down to get rid of the salt and flies! We collect it when we visit the family in Hants. We bring it back in black bin bags. It is amazing how many different types of seaweed can be seen on a stretch of beach a few hundred yards wide!

Do not use: Meat, fish, cooked food, coal and coke ash, cat litter, dog faeces, disposable nappies, glossy magazines.

Note that you can now buy all-in-one composters that purport to compost everything. I haven't tried these, but if they work they would be jolly useful, and very good for the allotment, your bank balance (as we move to extra council charges for recycling) and the environment.

The compost heap

All organic allotment holders (in fact, all allotment holders and gardeners) should have a compost heap. In fact, they should have as many as possible (we have three on the go at any one time).

You can make a compost heap very easily. Either use a container (looks slightly better – and keeps the smell in) or just make a heap in the corner of the garden, like my and your parents probably did. There are two types of heap:

- Hot.
- Cold.

Hot

In a hot heap the mix is intended to break the ingredients down much faster. It is created by using lots of green 'hotter-rotters' mixed with others (see above).

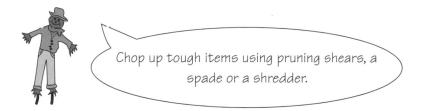

Chop up tough items using pruning shears, a spade or a shredder.

Try to gather enough material to fill your compost container in one go. Use manure, raw vegetable scraps, grass cuttings and so on to make up the bulk. Make sure you have a mixture of soft and tough materials.

We have a small separate bin in the kitchen for all our peelings and cores of fruit, vegetables, teabags and coffee grounds. Try doing this yourself and get into the habit of placing all your organic items in it. Also put in eggboxes, loo rolls and other brown cardboard. You will be amazed at how much is useable and by how much it reduces the need for rubbish collection! Make sure that you take it to your compost heap regularly however – especially in hot times – or you will generate a pungent smell and an (un)healthy crop of flies!

Mix the ingredients together as much as possible before adding to the container. In particular, mix green items, such as grass mowings, that tend to form heavy dense piles which exclude air, with browner or in-betweeny items that will help to dry out the greens. Fill the container as above, watering as you go.

You can make compost simply by adding compostable items to a compost heap when you feel like it. It will all rot eventually but may take a long time, may not produce a very pleasant end product, and could smell. If you are short of 'browns' you can add crumpled-up newspaper which will act in a similar manner.

Give the heap a good mix and within a few days – it is amazing how it works – the heap is likely to get hot to the touch (in winter you will see the steam coming off it!). When it begins to cool down, or a week or two later, turn the heap. This involves removing everything from the container, or lifting the container off (as we do) and mixing it all up, trying to get the outside to the inside. Add water if it is dry, or dry material if it is soggy, and replace it all in the bin.

The heap should heat up again; the new supply of air you have mixed in allows the fast-acting aerobic microbes, ie those that need oxygen, to continue with their work. You can repeat this as often as you wish, at regular intervals. When it no longer heats up again, leave it undisturbed to finish composting.

Compost can be made in six to eight weeks, or it can take a year or more. In general, the more effort you put in, the quicker you will get compost – depending on the composition.

When it has turned into dark brown, friable, earthy-smelling material, it is ready. It is then best left for a month or two to 'mature' before it is used. Don't worry if it isn't perfect. Even if it is lumpy, sticky or stringy, with bits of twig and things showing, it is fine.

Compost bins

You can buy or make a compost bin. We have bottomless green bins which I take off from time to time then turn over the contents and put the bins back – usually (but not always) remembering to place twiggy bits in the bottom for aeration.

Easy-to-make compost bin

You will need:

- Four 4 inch x 4 inch (10 cm x 10 cm) wooden posts, about 1 yard (1 m) high.

- A mallet, hammer and strong nails.

- Enough planks or boards of wood to nail onto three sides – using old recycled wood is excellent.

- A piece of old carpet or tarpaulin to cover the top and the open side: 8 feet by 4 feet (2.5 m x 1.5 m) should do it.

Method

- Mark out an area a yard square (1 m^2) and flatten the soil down.

- Hammer the posts in at each corner, making sure they are very firm (at least 6 inches (15cm) deep).

- Cut the planks or boards to 3 feet (1 m) lengths (the width of the bin).

- Nail the planks or boards around the posts on three sides only, neatly.

- Put the compost in – in layers if you can – if not, chuck it in as you get it.

- Cover with the carpet or tarpaulin.

Cold

The cold heap is just a pile of material left to rot down slowly. For example, a pile of branches or a heap of leaves will eventually rot down, but it takes a long time.

Leaves can take up to three years to break down – depending on their type and local conditions – so they are best left in a pile on their own to break down; or you can chuck a whole pile into a black bin bag, prick it with a few holes and leave it quietly to rot down, after which it makes a good mulch. It is worth remembering, however, that leaves usually contain little or no value, as it has been sucked back into the tree ready for winter dormancy.

Pine needles take ages to break down but are very acidic, so they make an excellent mulch for fruits.

What is a mulch?

The word comes from the old Anglo-Saxon or Middle English word meaning 'soft' or 'mellow' – presumably as the half-rotted matter is soft to the touch. Essentially it is any – usually, and ideally, bio-degradable – material that is placed on soil and/or around crops to keep them moist by retaining water. It is usually 'poured' on to give a covering of about 3 inches (7.5 cm).

Typical mulches include:

- **Grass cuttings** Especially useful around potatoes. Note that dried grass is also called hay. It has a high propensity to set seed and grow from cuttings – so be careful. Laying it over paper can help reduce this.

- **Leaf mould** Adds bulky matter of sorts to the soil as it rots down – but of course leaves do not contain much of value as the tree sucks the goodness back into the tree before the leaves drop off for winter.

- **Bark chippings** Usually used in gardens rather than allotments as they are quite expensive.

- **Wood chippings** Shred your prunings from home and allotment – ideal as mulch and free.

- **Straw** Best not used on crops as it steals nitrogen from the soil as it breaks down. Needs to be twice as thick as other mulches because of its nature (6 inches – 15 cm).

- **Compost** If not added to soil directly, it can be used a mulch.

- **Pine needles** Very good for around fruit crops to keep the acidity that they like.

- **'Living mulches'** Not for around crops (see Green Manures).

Using a mulch:

- Clear the soil in the area of weeds.

- Water the soil well.

- Add bulky organic matter and dig in as necessary.

- Put your plants in.

- Add the mulch around them – to about 3 inches depth or more – trying to keep it clear of the stems.

- Inspect it from time to time, pulling out annual weeds, cutting off perennials and adding more mulch as/if required.

Membranes

A membrane is slightly different from a mulch. Mulches are piles of loose items, whereas a membrane is a continuous sheet with no gaps in it. There are two types – natural and man-made. Organic gardening obviously demands that you only use natural membranes. They are usually used to clear weeds rather than conserve moisture, as they exclude light – but can sometimes be used in combination with a mulch.

Note that while annual weeds will be killed off fairly rapidly by a membrane, perennials may need *several years* before they die off completely!

Natural membranes include:

- **Paper** From a roll – good for vegetables, but expensive.

- **Newspaper** Lay it out ten sheets thick around plants. Often covered in other items (leaf mould, grass) to keep it in place. Plant through it. Much cheaper than a roll of paper – essentially free. Will rot down.

- **Cardboard** Cover the ground and plant through it. Will rot down.

- **Coir matting** Peg it down. It will last about five years or so.

- **Pumpkins and squashes** Can also serve as weed suppressants, functioning as a living membrane as their extensive foliage spreads out and excludes light from beneath them (see 3 Sisters).

Man-made membranes – not recommended for organic gardens:

- **Polythene** Will clear weeds but will damage the soil if left too long.

- **Synthetic fabric** Needs to be covered with a mulch.

- **Woven plastic** Again, cover with mulch.

- **Carpet** Not allowed on many sites and is a pain to get rid of if left. (We found a lot on our site and it had become entangled with plants, partly rotted, was generally disgusting and falling apart and providing homes for slugs.) Rubber- or foam-backed carpet should never be used under any circumstances!

Planting through a membrane:

- Clear all vegetation from the area.

- Water the area.

- Add manure/compost if necessary.

- Spread out the membrane, covering the edges with soil to hold it down.

- Cut crosses in the membrane with a propagating knife.

- Dig out holes in the soil through the gaps in the membrane.

- Put the plants in, pulling the membrane back over the soil, and adding more soil if necessary.

- Water them in well.

- Place a mulch over the exposed membrane.

It is likely that perennial weeds will try to grow through the cuts that you made for your plant. Deal with them by cutting them off carefully, so as not to damage your plants.

Note that planting through a membrane is quite labour-intensive. I helped a friend lay out his relatively small front garden with box plants through a membrane and it took two of us a whole day.

Trenching

You can also use compost in a trench, which is especially useful if you are growing beans, pumpkins, courgettes/marrows and squashes, which are very hungry.

- Dig a trench one spit deep and as long and as wide as you need for the crops.
- Line it with cardboard – pizza boxes are ideal for this, as are the boxes that white goods, wine, etc arrive in.
- Fill it with compost to about 2 to 3 inches deep.
- Cover it up with earth.
- Sow the seeds directly into it (or for tender plants, grow them on in pots then plant them out after the risk of frost has gone).
- Watch them zoom away!

29

Dealing with Pests, Diseases and Weeds

This chapter considers the downside of gardening. There is no getting away from it. If you grow crops you will encounter problems – that is, pests, diseases and weeds.

If you were to go into a bookshop (or your library – public or home) and idly leaf through the gardening books and look at 'problems' it would be easy to get very depressed and give up. This is because, in my view, some books labour the point. I feel that this is often because they have got into a vicious spiral of using pesticides and herbicides which therefore kill the beneficial insects; who then don't eat the pests; which results in plagues of pests, etc.

Organic gardening, on the other hand, promotes the natural ways and means of controlling pests by working with nature rather than against it. We do this by rotating crops, companion planting and encouraging natural predators. You have to accept some losses, but on the whole it is better all round.

There are, however, still many potential pests (and diseases) that can affect each plant, but it is not all doom and gloom. Careful husbandry, organic principles and knowing what to look for, all help to minimise the effects. Also, there are good creatures – the cavalry that can 'ride to the rescue' – if you follow basic principles.

Pests

It is not possible to cover all pests here – there are hundreds, if not thousands.

Sorry to all the vegetarians out there, but in a garden it is carnivores that we like. Herbivores/plant-eaters are the biggest menace we encounter.

Slugs and snails

Slugs and snails are the number one pest. I hate them – and I really mean it. They destroyed so many of my plants that we declared war on them and virtually every trip involved a slug/snail hunt.

Kill them without remorse, relentlessly. They show your crops no mercy and breed like wildfire.

Look for tell-tale signs – slimy silvery trails that show you where they have been, and eaten crops. They are such a menace that there are many different ways of trying to deal with them. It is difficult, though, as they are successful and well-adapted predators.

The ways to deal with slugs and snails fall into several categories:

- Encourage predators.
- Kill them.
- Put up barriers.

Slug and snail predators

Frogs and toads, song thrushes, mistle thrushes, redwings, ground beetles, hedgehogs, shrews, marsh flies, slow worms, centipedes, newts. Other birds and the crow family (magpies, crows, jackdaws, etc) also eat them but not in any big way.

Killing slugs and snails

Slug pellets You can use slug pellets. This is not allowed in organic gardening – but they do work. The issue with them is that they kill animals higher up the food chain, and that is undesirable.

Patrol The best way of killing them is to go on patrol. Using sharp sticks or half bricks works a treat. This is time-consuming although very cathartic. They lurk in damp shelters – under bits of wood and piles of leaves.

Salt Salt also works very well and you can hear them fizz!

Beer Many people recommend yoghurt tubs with beer in them sunk into the ground with a small lip showing. But they can trap other animals and, in my view, are a waste of good beer. Also the smell is disgusting!

Oatmeal I have recently heard that slugs will gorge themselves on oatmeal and then explode. I haven't tried this yet, but it sounds good and is on my agenda for next year.

Organic slug and snail repellent I bought some of this. The smell alone is enough to put anyone off, but I am not yet convinced of its effectiveness. It is based on egg shells and I think it is more of a barrier than an effective killer. It is also expensive. After using it in late summer/early autumn, however, there did appear to be plenty of slug corpses around, so I will try it again and see how it goes.

Barriers

As slugs and snails slime their way across the ground, barriers that inhibit this are helpful – but you need a lot to give proper protection. Rain will also wash a lot of these away or they will get disturbed by wind, other animals, etc, so they need constant attention and replacement.

Some examples:

- Coffee grounds.
- Soot.
- Ash.
- Fresh dry lime or dry ground chalk.
- Dry sharp sand.

- Grit.

- Crushed egg shells.

- Lots of sharp pointy leaves, such as holly or thistles.

- Pine needles – recommended to mulch fruit as they are acidic; and fruit shrubs generally prefer that in any case.

- Dry straw.

- Sawdust.

- Shredded bark .

- Oak leaves – the tannin in them is a deterrent.

- Aromatic herbal mulch – mint, tansy, lemon balm, etc.

- Large plastic bottles, without top or bottom, can be used as do-it-yourself cloches.

- Petroleum jelly around the rim of flower pots or containers.

- Thin metal edging, the upper edge bent outward & slightly down.

- Copper bands are toxic.

Insect pests

There are many of these. I deal with just the more common here.

Butterflies, moths and caterpillars

I like butterflies; they pollinate plants and have an ethereal beauty that is inherently appealing to humans and actually I don't mind sharing a little of my crops with them – but sometimes they go too far. It isn't of course the butterflies and moths that cause the problem, but their offspring – the caterpillar.

Caterpillars hatch from the eggs of butterflies and moths. They have voracious appetites and spend their entire life eating. And eating your crops! They gorge themselves, then spin a cocoon and hibernate to emerge as fully grown adults (imagos) next year.

The best way to keep them away is not to allow eggs to be laid. Netting keeps the parents away and deters them from laying eggs on your plants. Keep an eye on crops and if you see any eggs, crush them. After that, hand searching and picking the caterpillars off is the best way.

The main culprits are the cabbage white butterfly, which attacks brassicas (they can strip a whole plant, leaving only a strange skeleton), the codling moth that attacks apples, and the pea moth.

Millipedes

This distant relation to the lobster and shrimp is usually regarded as a nuisance rather than a pest. Millipedes are herbivores. In fact, the correct name for them is detritovores; as they feed mainly on dead and decaying plant matter (detritus) and as such are a crucial part of the organic gardening cycle.

Where they become a nuisance, however, is when they eat living plants, especially seeds and young seedlings. In addition, they will often enter wounds in roots, tubers and bulbs that were caused by other pests, such as cutworms or wireworms, and enlarge them. The garden plants most commonly attacked are pea and bean seeds, potatoes, carrots and cucumbers. Once the damage has been done, however, and they have enlarged the wounds, the continued seeping out of essential liquids will ensure attention from millipedes for some time.

Millipedes breed when it is warmer, in spring and summer. They can lay up to a hundred eggs, which hatch after about 2–3 weeks. As they grow the number of segments in their body increases until they reach the full adult number of about fifty. They hibernate during the winter and may live for 2-3 years. Like their aquatic cousins, they need water or moist conditions to breed, but apart from that have adapted to living on the land.

Each body segment has two pairs of legs and when they walk each pair of legs is lifted at the same time which gives them their wave-like motion, which is a bit creepy. Their shell is impregnated with calcium for protection – therefore they are more common on alkaline soils.

Toads, frogs and starlings eat them, and in general the jury is still out on them as to whether they are pests or friends. We see hardly any on our allotment – probably as allotments tend to be slightly acidic.

Do not confuse millipedes with centipedes, which are wonderful allies in the fight against pests. These latter have only one set of legs per segment, fewer of them, and are faster-moving – to catch their slower-moving prey!

Others

Aphids

Commonly called greenfly or blackfly, these are small (3–5 mm) red, green, orange, yellow, black or brown insects that feed off the sap of plants and can easily kill them. They also deposit a sticky substance called honeydew on which disease spores can stick. Note that some types of ant 'farm' greenfly and 'milk' the honeydew! Aphids can also spread virus diseases. They can lay eggs when only a week old!

Don't panic, however, if you see them on your plants – in an organic garden the natural predators will soon dispose of them. Do not worry about them if they are on non-crop plants – they will act as 'nurseries' for predators such as ladybirds, which will lay their eggs on those plants.

Apple saw-fly

The larvae burrow in and leave marks on the skin of the fruit, and the fruit tends to fall early. They over-winter in the soil and come out in spring. Digging the soil over exposes them to predators and weather. Pick up any fruit that has been attacked and compost it.

Asparagus beetles

These hibernate over winter, then emerge and lay eggs. They feed on the spears and foliage. They may lay two or three clutches in a year. It's best to hand pick them off and kill them. Prevent them from over-wintering by removing the fern fronds and burning them, or putting them in a very hot compost heap.

Cabbage root fly

These are about $\frac{1}{2}$ inch (0.5 cm) long and look a bit like horse flies. The larvae (maggots) feed on the root and the pupae over-winter in soil. Signs of infection are wilting plants and a lack of growth. Pull up infected plants and look for tunnels in the roots. You can use special collars of felt or cardboard to stop the fly laying its eggs on the roots. Intercropping with beans can also help.

Carrot fly

They attacks all members of the carrot family, including parsnips, Hamburg parsley, celeriac, celery, chervil and parsley. As with many pests, it is the larval stage that is the problem. The adult fly is attracted by the smell of the carrots and lays its eggs.

Note that when thinning carrots, the stems are 'bruised' by the pulling-out action, which releases the scent, and this attracts the fly. It is recommended that thinning out is done towards dusk when the fly isn't active or when it has less time to find the plants. Also intercropping with onions or strong-smelling herbs can help. The fly travels very close to the ground so physical barriers can help, as can growing carrots in raised tubs.

Cutworm

A catch-all name for several varieties of caterpillar that are soil-living pests. They feed at night, are fat and can be any colour depending on the types (usually moth larva). They feed on roots and stems of plants. Keep all areas weed-free to stop egg-laying. Turning the soil over is a good way of exposing the worms to predators who love this useful source of protein.

Flea beetle

This is a small, shiny, black beetle that gets its name because it jumps when disturbed. It attacks young seedlings and soft-leafed plants, especially brassicas – look for small holes in the leaves. Planting out more mature plants helps prevent attacks.

Gooseberry saw-fly

As usual, it is the larvae that cause the damage. They are green with black spots and a shiny head. They attack berry and currant bushes and can strip plants in days, leaving a green skeleton. Attacks usually start in April or May and go on until late summer. They start at the centre of the bush and work outwards. Eggs are laid under leaves in the centre of the bush. Inspect the plant regularly and pick off any eggs or larvae found.

Raspberry beetle

The larvae of this pest attack all briar fruit (rosaceae family such as blackberry, raspberry and loganberry). The eggs are laid on the flowers and then the larvae feed on the ripening fruit. Each larvae becomes a pupa in the ground. Gently forking over the soil at the end of the season will expose them to birds. If infested, cut all canes right down to the ground.

Pea moth

The tiny caterpillars live in the peas. Eggs are laid when the pea flowers, before it sets the fruit (pods). You can sow peas earlier or later than the usual season (late June/early July) to 'fool' the moths, or you can cover the peas when in flower. When we harvested our peas we found on average one caterpillar in every other pod. We just sorted them out and threw them away. There's not much evidence that the caterpillars are there until you open the pods. We just live with it.

Wireworms

These are the larvae of the click beetle. They usually live in weeds and grassland. They eat virtually anything, but especially potatoes, brassicas, beans, onions and carrots. Often you can see their depradations as small holes on the surface. We found some of these in our potatoes. The problem is usually worse on newly cultivated ground. Digging in winter therefore exposes the worms to predators and leaves the soil undisturbed for the rest of the year. If you think that you have an infestation, be careful to turn your compost over in the air before use to expose any wireworms to birds, etc. Keeping your site free from grass is a big factor in keeping wire worms away.

Larger pests
Pigeons and crows

They will eat fruit and young seedlings. They will dig up peas and other large seeds. Netting crops helps, as they do not like to get entangled in it.

Note that although we built one, scarecrows don't actually work!

Rabbits

These eat plants. They are difficult to keep out – you could try keeping a fox handy!

Moles

These are not that much of a pest, and the soil they leave in piles (mole-hills) is very good for the garden – nice and friable. They cause more damage on lawns than to vegetables. They may damage roots occasionally. Humane repellents include devices that emit noises to scare them off.

Rats and mice

These eat anything, in my experience. Even if you can't or haven't seen them, be assured that they are lurking around somewhere. Do not do anything to encourage them, eg do not leave food lying around and keep the compost heap closed.

Diseases

These are a real menace. They are persistent and extremely difficult to eradicate. In addition, the use of pesticides not only weakens plants' ability to resist diseases, but also; by killing off the weaker viral strains, encourages pesticide-resistant disease strains to evolve, thus continuing the vicious cycle!

There are many diseases – too many to address here. I will concentrate on the main ones.

Best practice for reducing disease

The incidence of disease can be greatly reduced by following good organic practice:

- Always ensure that your soil structure is good – do not walk on it too much.

- Rotate different types of plants that break or use different parts of the soil.

- Dig in plenty of organic matter to give body, help drainage and encourage the right organisms.

- Choose plants or strains that are best suited to the site.

- Ensure adequate ventilation/air circulation around plants.

- Take out disease-infested or 'sad'-looking foliage.

- Dig up and burn infected plants as soon as practicable.

- Keep the site clear of plant rubbish and debris.

- Rotate crops to ensure that disease does not build up.

- Do not overfeed, as this usually causes plants to develop masses of vegetation which will attract disease-bearing pests.

- Try resistant cultivars.

- Take care when trying to identify problems – if in doubt, get help.

The vast majority of diseases are fungal and caused by poor ventilation around plants and poor soil drainage. Addressing these issues considerably reduces the likelihood of disease – but sadly does not eliminate it altogether.

Blight
What is it?
The devil's own disease (*phytophtora infestans*). Devastating. Attacks members of solanaceae (potato and tomato). Caused the great famine in Europe in the nineteenth century. Spreads like wildfire.

Symptoms
Brown marks on the leaves or stems. Spreads across the whole plant, eventually affecting the fruits and tubers. Lots of grey/white spores on underside of leaves. These are then washed down into the ground, where they affect the tubers. This weakens the plants and other infestations also join in a general free for all. Foliage goes black and shrivels and rots. Common in wet summers and later on in the year. Smells terrible.

Treatment
None. Planting earlies avoids the problem. Burn any infected leaves. Rotate the crops away for many years. Grow plants in pots or growbags with spore-free soil. Good ventilation/airflow and reducing moisture helps. Earthing up and mulching helps to prevent spores from being washed down.

Cut down all infected foliage and do not compost it. Burn it.

Do not leave any potatoes in the soil after your harvest. They will grow and can help spread the disease. Always buy new certified stock.

In my view this should also be applied to tomatoes – but it isn't.

Celery rot
What is it?
A fungal disease that attacks celery crowns. The spores live in damp soil rich in compost and can survive for years. It enters through wounds in the plant, eg made by hoes or by pests.

Symptoms
Stunted growth; plants go yellow; lesions appear.

Treatment
Grow in well-drained soil. Use rotation to prevent build-up. If it is present, harvest the unaffected plants and store in cool conditions. It doesn't spread to non-growing plants.

Clubroot
What is it?
A fungal disease and a survivor – up to twenty years in infected soil. Particularly affects brassicas. It thrives in acid conditions which provide the moisture for it to develop.

Symptoms

Wilting on hot days; stunted growth; red-tinted foliage (not rose-tinted); galls on roots.

Treatment

Avoidance is best. Rotate the crops, ensuring that brassicas never follow each other. Liming the soil helps. Remove all infected foliage immediately and burn it. If it is present, then use pots or growbags to ensure the soil is clean.

Mildew
What is it?

A fungal disease that can affect just about any plant when they are young.

Symptoms

Yellow patches on leaves and patches of mould on the underside, particularly in damp weather or damp conditions – even in stores.

Treatment

Ensure good ventilation and good drainage. Take off infected foliage or uproot plants.

Botrytis (grey mould)
What is it?

Fungal disease caused by damp summers.

Symptoms

Leaves, buds and flowers rot. It is fluffy and when disturbed jets out masses of spores.

Treatment

Keep good spacing between plants and ensure air circulation is good. Clear away rotting vegetative debris which can harbour it.

Canker
What is it?
A fungal disease that attacks parsnips. May be brought about by carrot fly holes which provide an entry point.

Symptoms
Roots discolour (brown, black, purple or orange) and go soft.

Treatment
Protect from carrot fly; ensure site is well-drained.

Mineral deficiency
What is it?
A lack of or imbalance in the minerals in the soil, eg boron, calcium, iron, manganese, magnesium, nitrogen.

Symptoms
Depends on the type of deficiency. Often poor growth, yellow leaves.

Treatment
Usually caused by the wrong soil pH for the plants in question, or lack of organic matter. Make sure the pH is right. Dig in plenty of organic matter. Rotating crops so that a nitrogen-fixer is present every three or four years is critical, as is liming before brassicas.

Do not be tempted to add the mineral yourself. You will probably cause more harm than good. Get help instead.

Onion rust
What is it?
A fungal disease that affects all alliums (leeks, onions, shallots, garlic).

Symptoms
Reddish spots appear on the leaves in summer. Leaves turn yellow and die. Declines as the weather cools – Indian summers will increase its longevity.

Treatment

Ensure plants are well-ventilated. Well-drained soil. Rotate crops to stop build-up.

Root rot (violet)
What is it?

A fungal disease that can last for years dormant in the soil. Acid soils help it. Affects root crops and tubers as well as asparagus and celery.

Symptoms

Violet/purple strands (hence its name) with darker spots cover the roots. There may also be a felt-like mass. Roots rot. Plant goes yellow and growth is stunted (roots can't function properly). Cooler, northerly areas less likely to be affected.

Treatment

Dig up and burn before the spores are released. Ensure good drainage of soil. Rotate affected type of crops away for at least four years.

On our site we cannot currently grow tomatoes in the soil. This is because a few years age there was an outbreak of tomato blight. As a result tomatoes were banned. It is permissable to grow them in growbags, however, as the soil is disease-free inside them, and we are trialling them in the open on two plots – one at the top and one at the bottom – to test for blight.

As tomatoes are part of the same family as potatoes (solanaceae) and everybody grows them, it was the right course of action to follow. History tells us what can happen with potato blight.

Weeds

The bane of any gardener's life. Whether you are a farmer, an allotment holder or a home gardener, you will have weeds. They need attention – all the time. Weeds do not go on holiday!

What is a weed?

Put simply, a weed is any plant that is growing where you don't want it to grow. Nature doesn't differentiate between weeds and non-weeds – they are all plants. Weeds are not just the usual suspects such as buttercups, convolvulus (bindweed), dandelions, docks, nettles, plantains and thistles. They can also include self-setting potatoes; trees growing up and stealing light and food; bamboo; blackberries (brambles); which are all weeds when growing up through your asparagus bed, or lettuce patch (or lawn) – as is grass on a vegetable patch or allotment. Even herbs can be weeds. For example mint which, if not controlled, will spread like wildfire.

Weeds can be divided into two types:

- **Perennials** Those that develop a strong root system and stay forever, coming back year after year (brambles, buttercups, grass). Some also send out suckers which root as soon as they touch the ground; and they make seeds as well.

- **Annuals** Those that grow, then flower, set seed and die, coming up again as new plants from the seeds. Each plant can often produce hundreds, if not thousands, of seeds and they are very successful!

It is not possible to get rid of all weeds. It is silly to think that you can. They are crafty, well-adapted and extremely hardy. The effort increases expoentially as you try to increase the level of eradication (see graph).

Even if you reduce the plot to a sterile bed by 'nuking' it, it is only a respite, as the next breath of wind will blow hundreds and probably thousands of new seeds in to fill it (nature abhors a vacuum – which is why it is so untidy!) and there will not only be no competition for them, but also there will be no good organisms to maintain the soil nor to attack them. The weeds will have a field day. In addition, deeply buried bits of perennial weeds will slowly but surely grow and push their way up through the surface, surprising you with the depth from which they have come – as you will find when you try to dig them out! When we were digging over the plot after having just taken it over, some of the roots I pulled out were over three feet long! Suckers and underground roots will invade your plot from next door by creeping through or over the soil.

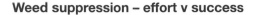

Weed suppression – effort v success

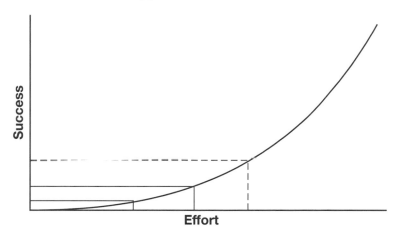

A cardoon produces several seed heads, each of which produces thousands of gossamer-like fairies which drift everywhere on the wind and self-set. A cardoon is a vegetable if you planted it – a weed if you didn't.

Weed control

Weedkillers are, by and large, indiscriminate, often killing all plants, and also killing insects. The decline in so much of our native flora and fauna can be laid in large part at the door of indiscriminate, unnecessary and over use of herbicides and pesticides. Organic growers do not use weed-killers, preferring natural remedies and approaches.

It is sad to see that in a book published by the RHS (*Growing Vegetables*, 2006), it still talks about using chemical weedkiller throughout.

The aim, therefore, is to *control* weeds *organically* – ie to do just enough so that they are no more than a minor nuisance – rather than fight a running war of extermination.

You do this by using a number of stratagems:

- **Double digging** (see later) and excavating around perennial roots to remove them.

- **Riddling** (sieving) Putting soil in a riddle (I prefer the word my grandfather and father used to use) or sieve and taking out all the weeds. A time-consuming process but effective (see also 'Basics – Tools'). Do this in small bites. Because of the motion involved it can hurt your back to do it for extended periods of time.

- **Hoeing** Sowing crops in lines allows you to hoe between them. When weeds are small and it is sunny you just chop them off and leave them to die in the sun. You must pull large ones out by the root or they will just grow again. If it isn't sunny then you need to pick them all up and throw them away.

- Using **cleaning crops** such as potatoes. As they require earthing-up, weeds are cleaned out, and it is easy to pull them up from between the rows. The foliage also acts as a suppressant when fully grown as the tips touch and give complete ground shade.

- Using **natural weed suppressants**, such as pumpkins or squashes, that produce masses of foliage and spread out and therefore push the weeds out by denying them light, water and food.

- Growing **green manures** which act as suppressants; keep the earth used (to stop weeds growing there), prevent soil erosion over winter, and can then be dug in to provide goodness for the next crop (see Green manures).

- **Mulching** Covering the earth in various substances which exclude light and therefore suppress weeds (in theory). My experience is that the practice is somewhat less than perfect.

- **Membranes** which exclude light and suppress weeds.

- **Berlin walls** built around plots to exclude sneaking roots and creepers. They go into the ground and extend above it.

Never rotovate – it just chops up perennials into lots of pieces, all of which will grow.

And of course there is always good old hand-weeding – which is a never ending task.

When you have taken the weeds out, you must be careful what you do with them. Perennials must not be put into the compost heap – unless you are really sure that it will be hot enough to kill them – or they will start to grow. It's best to place them in a plastic bag and let them die off slowly. If allowed to, you can burn them. Annuals, if small, and if they have not yet seeded, can be put into the heap. If they have seeded then, again, place them in a separate heap/plastic bag or burn them.

On our site one of the plot-holders decided that enough was enough. He had his entire plot excavated down to 3 feet (1m), put in a membrane, and then replaced the soil with weed-free topsoil. That is over the top for anyone – not to say expensive – especially as the plot was 20 feet by 100 feet! Needless to say, however, his plot was then perennial weed free and very fertile. But of course annuals still visit with clock-like frequency and these still need to be dealt with. If you ignore a plot, of course, eventually the perennials will creep back as well.

Why are weeds so successful?

There are several reasons for this:

- Often they are indigenous/native plants that have adapted to our environment over thousands of years.

- They tend to grow in conditions that favour them. The plants that we grow, on the other hand, are, by and large, growing where we want them to rather than in their natural habitat, eg potatoes from Peru herbs from the Mediterranean.

- They are great survivors and can lie dormant in the soil for years and years. Poppies are a great example of this. They only grow on disturbed ground. That is why they are symbolic of the First World War – the battles and high-explosive shells disturbed the ground, enabling them to germinate and grow. You can also see them where new construction is taking place or where roadside verges have been built and soil turned over or headed up. As I was travelling to my publishers to deliver this book I passed a field where the tracks of a vehicle were clearly and strikingly marked out with a swathe of poppies.

- Some weeds have been introduced and found our shores very much to their liking, eg the giant hog-weed and Japanese knot weed. The latter is the biggest nuisance of all and it is illegal to plant it (see panel below).

Weeds Act 1959

Under the Weeds Act 1959 the Secretary of State may serve an enforcement notice on the occupier of land on which injurious weeds are growing, requiring the occupier to take action to prevent the spread of injurious weeds. The Weeds Act specifies five injurious weeds: common ragwort, spear thistle, creeping of field thistle, broad-leaved dock and curled dock.

Note that neither Japanese knotweed nor giant hogweed are covered by the Weeds Act 1959. They are dealt with under the provisions of the Wildlife and Countryside Act 1981.

Possibly, however, the most irritating things about weeds, are that pests don't seem to eat them, and they never seem to suffer from the diseases that blight crops!

Why get rid of weeds?

Weeds are vicious and deadly competitors in a Darwinian world of survival, better adapted in many cases to the environment and to the conditions on your allotment. They will:

- **Steal the light/sun** from your crops by absorbing it, and often by growing faster and shading them out.

- **Steal the nutrients and water**.

- Sometimes live off the crops as **parasites**.

- Grow up your plants and progressively **throttle** them.

- Often **host pests**, which will delight in eating your crops.

- in some cases be **dangerous**. The sight (or rather sound) of a young child falling into a bed of nettles is a terrible thing to see and hear, and brambles when they are old and large have incredibly vicious thorns which cause great damage. I and most other allotment holders bear the scars from encounters with man-eating brambles. Our patch was particularly overgrown with them when we first obtained it, and even thick gloves do not keep bramble thorns out!

Note that heavy weeding is tiring so take it in easy stages, resting or doing other things in between. Watch your back!

Tools for weeding

- A **container** – bucket, bag, or tub-trug for putting weeds in.

- **Hand fork**.

- **Hoe**.

- A **garden fork** for big perennials.

- **Gloves** are a must as there are many weeds that have thorns, stings or nasty, spiky hairs. This is another reason why weeds are successful – the thorns stop them being munched by passing herbivores.

- A **kneeler** can be invaluable and not just for old people. I bought a very useful one from the National Trust that has measurements on it for planting distances and identifies key weeds.

Pest-eaters

There are many natural things that you can encourage to help in the (often seemingly hopelessly one-sided) battle with pests.

As mentioned previously – we like carnivores. They eat pests. This is good. One of the principles of organic gardening is to encourage nature to manage pests. Many animals will help you in this.

As a general rule, faster-moving animals tend to be predators – to catch their slower prey.

Ladybirds

Excellent little creatures (Coccinellidae). Called ladybugs in the USA and Canada, I think our name is much nicer. There are nearly a hundred species of ladybirds found in Europe and about forty of these are resident in the British Isles.

Apparently the name ladybird comes from the Middle Ages, when they were known as the 'Beetle of Our Lady', allegedly named after the Virgin

Mary, who in many early religious paintings was often depicted as wearing a red cloak. But they were also called 'Freya's Creatures' by Vikings and Anglo-Saxons, so it was probably a case of the Christian church changing a pagan goddess' name to a Christian one and post-rationalising it. The sevenspots on the UK's most common ladybird are reputed to symbolise seven joys and seven sorrows. In Turkey the ladybird is called 'Luckybug', and Ireland 'God's Cow'!

One ladybird can eat 500 aphids in one day. Great! Do all you can to encourage them. They like to shelter in dying vegetation and over-winter in snug places like piles of dead leaves (see Helping ladybirds).

Better yet, the ladybird larvae eat even more. When we found aphids on our runner beans we got rid of them by scouring our allotment plot for ladybirds and then gently taking them and putting them on the beans. Result – no more aphids, plenty of healthy runner beans and very happy and full ladybirds. Nature in full swing helping us!

You can buy ladybirds for release on the allotment if you do not have enough. We are lucky in that because we garden organically – that there are lots of ladybirds all over our site.

Lifecycle

Adult ladybirds hibernate in winter in sheltered places, so provide shelters for them. They only live for a year but during that time the adult will eat over 5,000 aphids. They lay eggs in small batches, usually on the underside of leaves infested by aphids to provide food for the larvae.

Ladybird larvae look nothing like adult ladybirds. In fact, they look like insect crocodiles. They can be grey or other colours with massive jaws that crunch aphids – yes! Do not mistake them for pests.

The larval period lasts about three weeks during which they grow and shed skin three times, after which they pupate and emerge as ladybirds a few weeks later. If you have aphids you can see the ladybird larvae. They are not very efficient at finding their prey and don't use sight or smell and sometimes the eggs were not laid near a food source – or it has already been eaten. If you come across one – move it onto the aphids!

Helping ladybirds

Create/conserve hibernation sites for ladybirds. They like to shelter in dead or dying vegetation/plant debris, so try to leave some for them until they emerge in spring. Hollow stems of carrot family plants such as fennel are favoured sites for hibernation. If you dead-head these types of plants it makes it easier for ladybirds to get in. Alternatively, cut the stems and stack them in a dry sheltered spot. They like nettles too, so leaving nettles in spring gives them food (nettle aphids). Once your plants have grown, get rid of the nettles (taking care not to harm the ladybirds, so that they will munch on the aphids on your plants).

Most aphid-killing insecticides are indiscriminate and will also kill ladybirds – so do not spray.

Hover-flies

These flies (Syrphidae) are easily recognised by their hovering ability – no, really! They feed on nectar, and therefore pollinate plants, so they are beneficial. They are a little similar in colour and size to bees and wasps, but after a while you can easily tell the difference. They do not sting or bite, however, and are safe: their colouring is merely mimicry of their stinging friends in order to deter predators. Do not kill them in error.

It is the larvae, however, that you want as they eat the aphids. The hover-fly larvae look like green or brown flattened maggots and they are quite hard to spot. Flowers encourage the adults who will lay their eggs.

Lacewings

Lacewings (Chrysopidae) are usually green, and you often find them indoors. I didn't really understand how helpful they were until I obtained my allotment and started looking into it – so I may have squashed a few in the past unintentionally. Some are brown lacewings (Hemerobiidae). These are smaller than the green lacewings. Both adults and larvae eat aphids – and lots of them.

Lacewing larvae look a bit like ladybird larvae (ie fearsome crocodiles – especially, I would imagine, to aphids!) but are brown, and some of them (and this is amazing) cover themselves with the dried remains of their prey to camouflage themselves and deceive the aphids into thinking they are aphids. Even better, they have two long, thin jaws which curve out like tusks from their head. They insert these sharp tubes into the aphid victim and sucks out the body fluids, leaving a dry husk – excellent!

Frogs and toads

When I found out that these creatures ate slugs and snails, they went up enormously in my estimation! We are going to put in a small pond to encourage them. We often see them in our tiny garden, but they seem to be rare on the allotment. They need water to survive – especially in summer. They also lay eggs in water before they turn into frogpoles and toadpoles, so again water is a prerequisite.

Even small pools help – but they need gently sloping sides for easy access and overhanging vegetation to provide shelter from predators (birds). A good idea is to contact local nature bodies to obtain frog and toad spawn.

Hedgehogs

These eat cutworms and slugs. They hibernate in winter and live in piles of vegetation. If you build a bonfire and leave it for some time, check it before setting it alight in case hedgehogs have moved in. Hedgehogs are full of fleas, so never handle one. Note that, despite the assistance given by Mr Badger to the lost young hedgehogs in *The Wind in the Willows*, badgers eat hedgehogs!

Birds

A bit of a two-edged sword, as many birds eat berries, peas, corn and seedlings. But many others eat insects. You want to encourage the right ones. Blue-tits, for example, eat lots of insects – a family will consume about 7,000. They feed on pests like apple sawfly and apple blossom weevil.

Nematodes

These are parasites. You water the ground with a special solution which contains these microscopic organisms, and the theory is that they feed on slugs. We did this and I have to say that I was unable to see any difference whatsoever in the slug population on our plot for the year. Perhaps others have had different experience – but we won't be using it again.

Centipedes

Centipedes feed on slugs and slug eggs. You can distinguish them from millipedes – who feed on your crops – as centipedes are often reddish coloured and have only one pair of legs per segment. They move faster than millipedes. You don't want millipedes – but you do want centipedes.

Beetles

These are slug predator number one according to the *Encyclopaedia of Organic Gardening*. I haven't seen many of these on our site so will be doing what I can to encourage them.

Spiders and harvestmen

They feed entirely on insects. They do not always only eat pests, but they are an essential ally in the fight against pests. Encourage them. Do not break webs unless you can't avoid it. One of the amazing sights is a web that has been covered in dew on a cold autumnal morning. It is like diamonds on string.

Create some nooks and crannies for them to live in. Most do not actually use webs, but hunt actively for their prey.

Lizards

Adult slow worms (a legless lizard – not a snake) eat lots of slugs and snails. They are protected by law and you want to encourage them.

Encouraging beneficial animals

There are many things that you can do to encourage the right types of animals. Ensuring that the plants that they like are present is a very easy step to take.

- Hover-flies and others like cornflowers, coriander, fennel, yarrow, brambles and alyssum.

- Bees (essential for pollination) like broad beans, rosemary, candytuft, blackberries and raspberries, heather, honeysuckle, old fashioned geraniums (blue) and wallflowers.

- Many birds that eat insects also like to eat fruit, so fruit shrubs and, if you have room, fruit trees are very good. They also like sunflower seeds. A song thrush eats thousands and thousands of pests in a season, so they are to be encouraged. We have an elderberry tree at the back of our allotment – thrushes love it as well as privet (uncommon on allotments). You will need to protect the fruit that you are growing, however, as birds feed indiscriminately – so net the crops you want to enjoy yourself. At the end of the season we take the nets off our fruit bushes to let the birds enjoy the tail end of the berries, etc.

Other things to do

- Insect hotels can be purchased or made by rolling up corrugated cardboard in a plastic drinks bottle with the base cut off and hung on a tree. Secure the cardboard so it doesn't fall out. You can also use a plastic food box; make a few holes in the bottom large enough for the insects to get in but small enough to keep predators out. Fill it with straw and put it on its side under a shrub to keep it dry. You can also use drinking straws stacked in boxes laid on their side.

- Leave a pile of leaf mould or a few logs stacked in a shady spot. The cool environment will encourage frogs, ground beetles and hedgehogs.

- Dry piles of largish stones, with gaps in between them, will also attract toads, spiders and slow worms.

- Leave some mulches undisturbed. Centipedes and beetles like them very much.

- Put a hedgehog box in a sheltered place.

- Build a pool. It should be in a sunny spot, but with at least two sides full of plants to give shelter. The minimum size is a yard/metre square with a gentle slope for access. Once it is full, it will be colonised by wildlife. If it goes green it is just algae – put some barley straw in it to stop this. Never put fish in – they are predators. Some may appear as if by magic, as stickleback eggs can be carried on bird's feet (hitch-hikers). Ignore them – the pool life will adjust to the right numbers. If using tap water to fill it, let it stand for 48 hours to remove the chlorine before putting anything in. Good plants include iris and water starworts (for newts). Floating plants like golden club will give animals homes. Oxygenating plants should also be put in the pool.

(30)

Crop Rotation

Why rotate?

Crop rotatioin is an essential component of both good husbandry and organic principles and was popularised by the British agriculturist Charles Townshend in the eighteenth century.

In essence it is growing dissimilar crops on the same part of the allotment in successive seasons. So where potatoes were grown one year you might grow cabbages the next year. This is to avoid the possible (probable) build-up of diseases such as clubroot (known to scientists as pathogens) and pests (e.g. carrot root fly) that can occur if you grow the same crop in the same space year after year.

It also alters the fertility demands of crops as each has different require-ments – surface-feeder, deep-rooter, nitrogen-fixer, etc – and therefore helps to reduce depletion of soil nutrients.

Crop rotation can also improve soil structure by, for example, alternating deep-rooted and shallow-rooted plants, or leaving one part to lie fallow for a season, or grassing it over before using it the following year. The grass or other green manure is dug in to provide a natural manure for the next crops.

A four stage rotation could be:

1 Potatoes, tomatoes, squash, pumpkins

2 Legumes

3 Brassicas

4 Onions, carrots, parsnips

The pattern for a plot divided simply into four parts (quarters A–D) would look like the diagram below:

Simple pattern for four stage rotation

	Year 1	Year 2	Year 3	Year 4
Quarter 'A'	1	2	3	4
Quarter 'B'	2	3	4	1
Quarter 'C'	3	4	1	2
Quarter 'D'	4	1	2	3

Animal and mixed rotation

Rotation has long been used of course with animals. Moving a different type of animal, say sheep, to fields previously grazed by cattle is a very good thing. The new animals ingest any parasites that might infect the other animals – and as they are a different 'host' the cycle of host/parasite is broken and the parasites are killed.

On mixed farms, placing animals on fields previously used for crops ensures that they are well manured for the next crop. This is not usually an option that is available to allotment holders – hence the need to use compost (see Composting) as a substitute.

Benefits

There are a number of benefits from using a system of rotation on an allotment:

- **Soil fertility** Artificial fertilisers are not required as different types of plants put back nutrients taken by previous plants and take out different ones.

- **Variation** Many vegetables thrive better in soil that was previously used for a different crop than in soil that was used for one of their own kind.

- **Pest and disease minimisation** Soil pests and diseases tend to attack specific plant families, so by rotating crops, pest/host life cycles are broken and build-up is reduced.

- **Weed control** Some crops (eg potatoes and squashes) 'clean' the soil by suppressing weeds or allowing easy weed clearance. For instance, ergot in weed grasses is difficult to separate from harvested grain. Planting a different crop breaks the ergot's cycle and allows you to identify and remove the weeds.

- **Soil structure** Alternating between deep-rooted (parsnips) and shallow-rooted (sweetcorn) crops improves soil structure and 'rests' different layers of the soil.

- **Risk spreading** A general effect of crop rotation is that there is a geographic mixing of crops, which can slow the spread of pests and diseases during the growing season – and they grow at different times, breaking the insect breeding cycles as well. Different crops can also reduce the effects of adverse weather as a drought or a deluge at one time does not affect all the plants in the same way as would be the case in a monoculture (single crop, eg a field of wheat or potatoes).

What sort of rotation is best?

There are no hard and fast rules. It depends on space but you can use anything between a three-year rotation and a six-year rotation. Often during the longer rotation cycles an area is left fallow, or a green manure is planted and then dug in.

The diagram shows a simple five-year rotation plan, which is explained below.

Five-year rotation plan

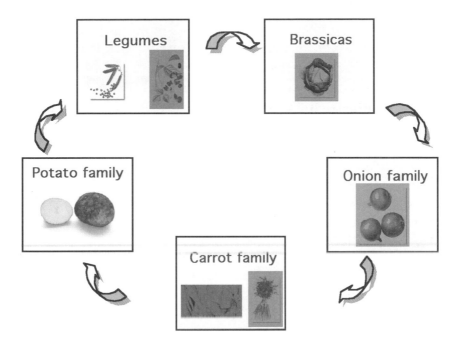

A simple order would be as follows:

- Legumes (peas and beans) like lime, so add some to the soil. Peas and beans fix nitrogen in the soil and should be followed by brassicas.

- Brassicas (cabbages, brocccoli, sprouts) are also lime-lovers. After the brassicas the soil will be quite firm. Follow them with the onion family.

- The onion family (onions, garlic, leeks) also like firm ground. This is an easy option as you don't need to dig the soil over – you can just put the onions where the brassicas were.

- Next, vegetables such as carrots and parsnips go in. These are root vegetables and therefore you break the soil up getting them out, which prepares it nicely for planting potatoes! I always dig the soil over very well before planting potatoes and ensure that I dig in lots of compost or manure.

- Potatoes take a lot of goodness out of the soil, so putting goodness back in is important, either before or after. Many people use grass clippings or compost when earthing up, which increases the humus content.

- Then it's back to the beginning of the cycle for more peas and beans.

Note that for a six-year rotation you could leave an area fallow, or plant a 'green manure' after the carrots.

Successful rotation requires planning and record-keeping. You must be sure where you planted what. It is highly likely that you will forget exactly where you planted some things – so a diagram is essential.

Plot plan

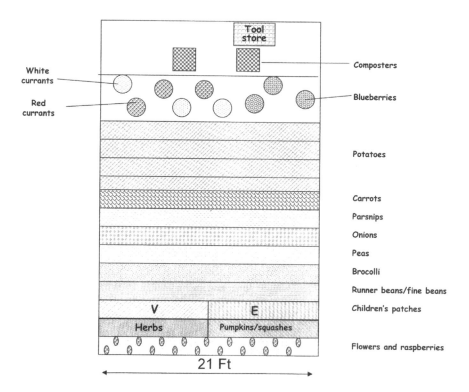

It is more difficult using raised beds and a no-dig approach, but many people do and have no problems with it.

Non-rotating crops

Some crops are not rotated. These are 'anywhere' crops and permanent crops.

'Anywhere' crops

Some crops are lucky enough not to suffer from the vicious diseases that affect most plants and they can be slotted in almost anywhere. These crops include:

Asparagus	Aubergines	Chicory	Courgettes
Cucumbers	Endive	Fennel	French beans
Lettuces	Marrows	Peppers	Pumpkins
Runner beans	Squashes	Sweetcorn	

We plant squashes as we take out potatoes. The soil has been weeded and they mature later than the earlies that we have harvested. Our rhubarb – as well as providing almost the first crop of the year – just sits happily in the same place. Some crops grow well with others (see 3 Sisters).

It still makes sense, however, to change the crops that you grow in the same part of the allotment – even if it is only to put back nutrients.

Permanent crops

These are those plants that you do not move, either because they need to mature *in situ* – or because they do not need to rotate. These crops include:

Asparagus	Berries	Fruit trees
Rhubarb	Currants	Herbs

They can still suffer from diseases, of course – not to mention pests – so you do need to keep an eye on them. You also need to water and feed them as required. Many of them will require pruning as well:

- to improve the yield (eg raspberries); or
- to control them (mint);
- or both (blackberries).

31

Protecting Your Crops

Protection starts even before you sow. It takes many forms, depending on crop type and location. General protection includes fertilising the soil to ensure good growth, crop rotation to ensure no build-up of pests and aerating the soil during digging. It also includes propagation.

The reason for propagating is two-fold. Firstly, given the length of the growing season in the UK, to give crops a good start by ensuring that they can germinate in the right conditions – even when it is too cold outside, and secondly, to give greater protection from pests and weather.

It is much harder (through not impossible) for a pest to eat your delicate little seedlings when they are inside a greenhouse and, in this way, when you plant them out they are robust plants and not the thin weedy seedlings that are easily terminated by a couple of well-placed bites from slugs, snails, pigeons or mice.

Once the seedlings are out in the big bad world, however, that is not the end of the protection racket. Some plants, notwithstanding the head start that you have given them, will still need protecting – and at different stages.

Fruit plants, once established, in general do not need protecting from pests, but once they start fruiting it is a different matter and every pest will try to eat your fruit – including small boys.

Even when seeds have been propagated, in many cases you cannot just put them outside. Taking small plants and setting them in an allotment where there is a sizeable temperature difference and they are exposed to the merciless ravages of the elements can kill them from shock! So protection continues.

Plant covers

There are several ways of protecting plants with covers and they work on the same principle letting sun in but keeping the cold, rain and wind out. If you can, put them in place a month before sowing. This will warm up the soil.

Cloches
Cloches used to be made of glass. Nowadays they are plastic. Glass is much more expensive – and is prone to breaking, with dangerous results! All allotment holders have found the very sharp remains of cloches or cold frames lurking in the soil. Plastic is also very light and therefore easier to move around.

Polytunnels
Not, as you might imagine, for parrots but effectively a long form of cloche. It is a row of wire hoops supporting a polythene sheet. The hoops can be any size – some you can walk through. They are really the same as mini greenhouses. Make sure that they have good anchorage, but are easily lifted for watering. They let sun in but also keep rainwater out!

Bell-shaped cloches
You can buy these but there is little difference – and a huge saving – if you make your own out of large translucent plastic bottles. Cut off the bottom of the bottle and then place it over the plant or seed to be protected. Leave the top of the bottle open to let air in and out – it also makes watering easier. Make sure the bottle is big enough for the plant!

Greenhouses

These grew out of Victorian lean-tos and gradually came to be built as separate structures. They can be heated or unheated. Few have them on allotments – they are expensive and take up quite a lot of space. Nowadays you can buy quite small plastic mini-greenhouses which are immensely useful. They provide a constantly higher temperature than the ambient outside temperature – even if unheated – as they absorb and retain the light and heat.

Nets

Useful for keeping animals off. They give no elemental protection, however. Birds do not like to get their feet tangled in them so they stay away from them.

Fleeces

These provide protection from marauding snails, as well as letting in heat and light. They also allow water in, so have many good points. Fleeces are also known as a floating mulch. They protect everything – weeds as well – so make sure that the weeds have been killed before you cover your plants with a fleece.

Cold/hot frames

These are permanent cloches with lids. They provide a secure environment for plants – especially in allowing them to harden off. If you pile manure around a cold frame you can make it into a hot frame. However the manure is usually put into a pit, covered with a few inches of soil and then the plants are put into the frame.

Cloche hopping

By careful planning you can maximise the use of cloches. Linking in succession sowing with later maturing crops means that you can use your cloches on one crop and then a little while later move them onto the next sowing or another crop sowed after the preceding one.

Windbreaks

If your allotment is in a windy location, you should if at all possible position plants so that they have the protection of a windbreak such as a wall or a hedge. Be sure that the windbreak will not cast a shadow – or at least do not plant anything in the shadow. If the break is a hedge, this will affect the fertility of the soil, so make sure you plant at least 6 feet away from hedges.

Walls provide a high degree of protection, as well as absorbing heat, especially if made of or lined with brick rather than stone – hence their use in walled gardens.

Windbreaks

Permeable barrier

Effective 'shadow' of protection

6'

60'

Being a solid barrier though, walls force wind upwards and thereby will create greater turbulence than a natural barrier through which the wind blows and thereby dissipating much of the force. A windbreak should be around 50 per cent permeable to be effective without turbulence.

As a rule of thumb, windbreaks give protection up to a distance equivalent to ten times the height of the windbreak – with diminishing effectiveness. So, for example, a hedge 6 feet high will provide protection from wind for a distance of up to 60 feet.

Multi-breaks

You can also erect smaller windbreaks, for example by piling up loose stones, to provide protection further away from the main break. Or you could plant a lower hedge some distance from the first to further improve the protection.

After protecting your crops and making their journey to fruition as easy as possible, you can now do what you started out to do – enjoy the fruits of your labour!

(32)

Enjoying the Fruits of Your Labour

The main reason for growing food is to eat it. This is called harvesting. It is no coincidence that harvest festivals are important in all cultures. Growing food is a chancy business and, until the growing season is over, you are never really quite sure what you will get. It was even more important in times gone by, when you couldn't pop down to the local supermarket and buy what you wanted. If you didn't grow enough crops to get you through the winter (non-growing season) you and your family would quite simply starve.

One of the key issues is how to keep crops. Some of course can be left in the ground, eg parsnips, while others need to be harvested and stored. You can do this by several methods, depending on your own preferences, capabilities and the type of food:

- **Storing them as they are** This is only practicable for some crops as others, eg berries, will start to 'go off' straight after they have been picked.

- **Leaving them in situ** eg parsnips, cabbages.

- **Preserving or processing them** Pickling, making them into chutneys or jams, canning them for industry, or storing them in alcohol such as sloe gin or rumptofts.

- **Freezing them**.

Storage

I have dealt generally with storage of crops in Part II. This section augments that.

The best place to keep produce is where it grows. While this works well for many items (parsnips, etc) of course it is not practical for all as the produce rots, grows, goes to seed, or will be eaten by other creatures. Therefore, storage after harvesting is essential for most crops.

Successful storage of fruit and vegetables starts early, before the harvest has even begun. Plants that have been grown in optimum conditions produce the best crops for storage. Crops that are not ready or those that have had a difficult growing season – suffering from lack of water, sun or food (nutrients) – will not keep well. By and large, any that have suffered from pest or disease attacks must not be kept in case they infect others.

Careful handling is essential: once harvested, crops become inert and stop growing. Therefore they have no means of repairing any damage. Quite tough crops can easily be bruised or damaged, even if it doesn't show up immediately, but once damaged in any way, the chance or probability of rotting is greatly increased.

Store only the best-quality crops. Anything that has broken skin or shows any sign of pest or disease damage should not be stored.

Although no longer actively growing, crops in storage are, surprisingly, still 'alive' and need air. Air circulation is important to provide oxygen and carry away the heat and moisture produced. Crops have different requirements for temperature and humidity. Providing the correct conditions for each crop ensures the best results.

Vegetable storage

Root-type crops such as carrots, parsnips, celeriac, beetroot, turnip, swede, etc require the same conditions. They usually last well, as they are in fact designed for that purpose – most are the storage units of plants, so would naturally stay dormant in the soil during winter, ready to revive the following spring as conditions improve. They should be harvested carefully. Do not wash them.

Harvesting is best carried out on a cool day; where this is not possible, cool the crops before storing them. We usually put them in a trug and let them lie in it for some time to 'acclimatise' and get over the trauma of being uprooted. Remove the leaves by twisting them off close to the crown. Place them in layers in shallow crates/boxes separated with a damp packing material such as sand.

Ideal temperature: 0 °–4 °C.

Potatoes

These require slightly different conditions from other root crops. They must be kept in the dark to prevent the light from turning them green and, because of their origins in warmer climates, they must be protected from low temperatures. We left some potatoes in our trug for a few days without thinking and they all went green and had to be chucked away.

If stored below 5 °C the starch turns to sugar, giving them a sweet taste when eaten. Harvest in dry, cool conditions if possible. Remove any damaged tubers and store the good ones in thick paper or special hessian potato sacks closed at the neck to conserve moisture. Do not use plastic sacks – the potatoes will sprout and/or rot.

Ideal temperature: 5 °–10 °C.

Clamping is a well-established method of storing potatoes. They are piled up, covered in straw and covered in earth. This protects them from the ravages of winter and allows easy access for use. It is less used now than formerly.

Onions and garlic

Lift garlic when between four and six outer leaves have turned yellow. Leave onions longer, until the tops have completely died away. Do not bend the tops over prematurely. Both need to be dried until the skins 'rustle', either in the sun or under cover. Store in nets, old tights or make into strings, and hang in a cool, dry place where air can circulate.

Pumpkins, winter squashes and marrows

These crops which originated in the warmth of the subtropics are not hardy to winter (or even cool autumn). The vagaries of the weather will affect them greatly because, as they mature towards the end of the growing season (ie Hallowe'en), they are susceptible to poor conditions as they need a few weeks of warm sun in August/September to develop the tough skin that makes for successful storage.

2007 was especially bad for ours, due to a lack of sunshine at the right time and unexpectedly cold nights in September. We managed to harvest a few, however, and that was a marvellous moment when I brought the first (acorn) squash home. A beautiful deep green colour, and perfectly formed.

These crops must be harvested before the first frost, or be very well protected from the initial frosts to enjoy the remains of the autumn sun. Leave the stalk as long as possible as it is from here that rot starts – the longer the stalk is, the longer the rot will take to affect the produce (think of a long slow-burning fuse). Check for skin blemishes. Use any damaged crops straight away. Then store the remainder in a dry, airy place, preferably on slatted shelves or hanging in nets to allow the air to circulate.

Preserving

In the UK (and other countries) we have developed many ways of storing food to keep it from going bad – or rotting – to help see us through the hungry period of winter. We call this preserving. It usually involves using some natural preserver such as salt, sugar, alcohol or vinegar, which protects the produce from deteriorating. The produce is often cooked as part of this process.

Preserving is a very good way of dealing with gluts (which tend to happen at harvest times). It allows you to make many different products (jam, chutney, jelly, pickles, etc) and enables you to use the crops long after they would normally have been available. It fell rather into disfavour as freezers and convenience food came along, but has recently enjoyed a resurgence, along with the upsurge in interest in growing your own produce.

Nowadays we can freeze just about anything – so soup is an excellent way of preserving crops to be eaten later, which can be easily frozen.

The objective of preserving food is to take it at its peak of perfection and preserve this for as long as possible. Therefore, for many types of preserves only the best fruit or vegetables are used. Jams, jellies, marmalades, chutneys, pickles and bottling fruits and vegetables are all types of preserving.

Pickling

Pickles are vegetables preserved in vinegar or brine. The name comes from the Anglo-Saxon or German for 'brine': *pekel*. In Britain, however, it was usually vinegar that was used – but some vegetables need to be salted first, which was known as brining – hence the name. This reduces the moisture content, making the vegetable crisper. It has long been a tradition that vegetables and even flowers were preserved by pickling for use on salads and cold meats.

The vegetables are preserved in a spiced vinegar – usually keeping the original shape and texture of the crop. White vinegar shows the fruit best, but malt vinegar is usually used. Spices are added to make the flavour more interesting. The vinegar should have an acid (acetic) content of at least 5 per cent. Many stores sell specific pickling vinegar.

Chutney

This is from the Hindi word *chitna* and usually involves fruit rather than vegetables, but can be either or both. The fruit is usually cooked slowly into a pulp and mixed with lots of spices. The chutney must be left for at least three months to mature before eating. We usually make damson chutney each year with the produce of Catherine's parents' damson tree.

Sauces

Sauces are indispensable. Some are made on the spot (hollandaise, onion sauce) – others are a form of preserving. Ketchup is thought to be derived from a Chinese word meaning the brine of pickled shellfish, and is usually the juice of two vegetables preserved and blended with vinegar and spices. Sauce is technically speaking liquidised fruit or vegetables again with added vinegar and spices for preservation. A ketchup is usually more highly concentrated and used more sparingly than a sauce – although you may not think that next time you see your children ladling tomato ketchup all over their chips.

Jams, jellies and marmalades

Jam

Jam is fruit that is boiled with sugar as a preservative. Pectin, which occurs naturally in fruit (although at different levels) and reacts with acid when boiled, is the setting agent. It is thought that the word 'jam' dates from Elizabethan times but the etymology is uncertain – perhaps from 'jamming' the fruit in?

Jelly

Jelly is fruit boiled with sugar, but strained so that only the pulp juice is used and set. You get a lower output therefore from jelly rather than jam – but it is easier. It only works with high-content fruit such as blackberries, bilberries, rowans and damsons.

Marmalade

Marmalade was originally a jelly made from quinces introduced in the fourteenth century by the Portuguese and named after their word for it (in Portuguese 'quince' is *marmelo*). However, it quickly came to be associated with citrus fruits, especially oranges. Marmalade contains every bit of the fruit except the pips. Despite them being very acidic fruits, they have little pectin, so this must be added.

Pectin

High-pectin fruits include redcurrants and blackcurrants, cooking apples, damsons, quinces, gooseberries and some plums.

Medium-pectin fruits include apricots, early blackberries, greengages, loganberries and raspberries.

Low-pectin fruits include blackberries, cherries (sweet), elderberries, strawberries and sweet apples.

Some fruits also have low acid and this must be added in the jam-making process. They include apples, cherries, quinces, bilberries, raspberries, peaches and pears. Lemon juice, citric or tartaric acid or redcurrant and gooseberry juice can be used for this purpose.

Two vegetables are used to make jam. Rhubarb and marrow are low in pectin and acid respectively.

Alcohol

Alcohol has long been used to preserve fruits, both as wines and as a preservative. The fruit is either fermented to produce wine, during which process the sugar is turned into alcohol, or the fruit is placed in a container and alcohol is poured in to preserve it. Incidentally, Nelson's body after Trafalgar was preserved by being kept in a tub of brandy!

Cooking the produce

Although many fruits and vegetables can be eaten raw, a lot benefit from being cooked – especially when blended with other ingredients. In the following pages I include some recipes for cooking the produce of the allotment. I am grateful to Catherine for sharing some of her family secrets with us.

Squash soup

On a cold winter's day there is nothing nicer than a wonderful mug of hot soup as you stretch your back, lean on your fork and contemplate the area that you have just double dug.

You will need:

2 large onions

A large squash (any sort, it doesn't matter, if they are small use two – they can even be different kinds!)

2 large potatoes

Home-made stock (approx 2 pints)

Seasoning

Steps

Peel, slice and dice the onions.

Peel the squash and chop the ends off.

Take out the seedy bit in the middle of the squash – I use a strong spoon. (Save the seeds for harvesting later on.)

(Place all peelings and ends in the compost bin.)

Cut the squash into one inch cubes (doesn't have to be exact).

Clean the potatoes and chop them up whole into similar-sized chunks.

Heat 2 tbls of oil in a large saucepan; add onion and cook until softened (about 5 mins); add in squashes and potatoes, the stock and seasoning.

Bring to the boil, cover the pan, and then let it simmer until nice and thick.

Liquidise it all.

Add more stock if necessary.

You can take it (as my aunt always described eating soup) straight away, save it for a couple of days or freeze it. It thickens up further, so you can dilute it to make a bit more after you defrost it.

Replace the squash with a pumpkin for pumpkin soup.

All-in-one damson chutney

My favourite chutney. It takes a lot of effort (picking out the damson stones, and you always miss a few) and you have to put up with the smell for a couple of days or so (vinegar mainly), but it is definitely worth it. We eat it with cold meats, salads and sausages.

You will need:

6 lb damsons (2.75 kg)

2 lb cooking apples (0.9 kg) (from your tree – if you have one – or a fellow allotment holder's – we swap blackberries for cooking apples)

6 large onions (from your allotment)

6 crushed cloves of garlic (from your allotment)

24 ml (4 heaped teaspoons) ground ginger

2 lb (0.9 kg) raisins

2 lb (0.9 kg) each of soft brown sugar and Demerara sugar

4 pints (2.5 l) malt vinegar

4 cinnamon sticks

2 ounces (50 g) of whole allspice berries

60 ml ($\frac{1}{4}$ cup) salt

20 ml (2 dessertspoons) whole cloves

This makes 12 lb of chutney so you will need the equivalent of twelve 1 lb jars. We naturally use the jars that we have saved from jam, tomato sauce, peanut butter, mayonnaise, etc, so they are all sorts of sizes and shapes. If you want to sell them or give them as presents then you can buy jars, tops and fancy coverings that are all the same size that make them look very professional. We make our labels on the PC.

Steps

Tie the cinnamon, allspice and cloves into a piece of gauze with a long piece of string attached so you can tie it to the handle of the pan and fish it out later. Slice and dice the apples with the peel on (take out the core) and place them in a (large) pan. Peel and dice the onions and put them in the pan. Put the damsons in whole. Put all the other ingredients in then add the vinegar. Bring it to the boil, stirring all the time. Let it simmer for about 3 hours.

After about an hour or so, take a wooden spoon, a small metal spoon and a saucer and start fishing out the damson stones. This is a bind but it is better than discovering a stone when you bite down hard!

Stir and bring the damsons up. Place one on the wooden spoon and gently tease the mush from the stone and back into the chutney with the metal spoon – place the stone on the saucer. The stones will be a lighter colour than the chutney so fairly easy to spot.

Put all the jars and tops into the dishwasher and wash them beforehand and then place them in a gentle heat in the oven.

While still warm, pour the chutney carefully into the jars and put the tops on. When they have cooled (next day), label the jars and store in a cool, dark place.

The chutney will thicken further in the jars, and you must leave it for at least three months. Making it in early September (which is when damsons are harvested) means it is ready for presents at Christmas.

Courgette moussaka

It is difficult to grow aubergines on open allotments – but a lot easier to grow courgettes. This variation on the traditional Greek dish is an excellent way to use all that green produce. It can be frozen.

Prepare exactly the same way as for normal moussaka – but use courgettes (from your allotment). Note that you still need to use salt to draw out the bitter juices.

Chuck it in carrot and lentil soup

This is a really tasty and filling soup. Catherine knocked it up one day when we found ourselves with a lot of carrots that needed using. It is very easy and quick to make!

You will need:

4oz (100g) of lentils

2 pints (1.2 litres) of chicken/ham/vegetable stock

3 tablespoons of oil

2 medium onions

1 lb (450g) of carrots

Steps

Preparation
Peel and chop (slice and dice) the onions
Peel and chop the carrots

Cooking
Heat the oil

Saute the onions for 5 minutes

Add the carrots, lentils and stock

Half cover the pan and simmer until the carrots and lentils are tender (about half an hour)

Liquidise

Ready for eating.
Add pepper to taste

For the more sophisticated you could add a swirl of cream!
You could also add in garlic and parsley for a slight variation (1 garlic clove, chopped, 2 heaped teaspoons of chopped parsley).

This freezes really well for later on!

Apple and blackberry pie
My favourite pie!

You will need:
For the flour

6 oz (175g) plain flour

1½ oz (40g) lard

1½ oz (40g) cooking margarine

pinch of salt

For the filling

1lb (450g) cooking apples

8 oz (225g) blackberries

3 oz (75g) of granulated sugar

plus

a 1½ pint (900ml) pie-dish

a little milk

caster sugar

Serves 4

Steps

Preparation
Make the short crust pastry first.

To make the pastry, place the flour, sugar, butter and salt into a bowl and mix until the butter is thoroughly blended in. It should look a little like breadcrumbs.

Next add the water and mix it until starts to form a ball. Add more water if required.

Put it in a plastic bag or cover it in clingfilm and put it in the fridge.

Filling

Peel and slice the apples straight into the dish

Add in the blackberries and granulated sugar

Roll out the pastry to give a 1" margin over the dish (place the dish upside down on the pastry and score round it – then add another 1" further out)

Cooking

Wet the rim of the pie dish with water and fix the outer rim of pastry to it so it fits snug; damp it with water.

Lift the pastry on to the pie, pressing the edge firmly on to the pastry rim.

Seal it [called 'crimping'] with your thumb and finger, or by pressing down with a fork.

Make a couple of slits in the centre of the pie to let the steam out. Some put in a 'pic support'.

Brush the pastry sparingly with milk and sprinkle on a little caster sugar.

Cook it for about 35 – 40 minutes at 190° C.

Great with custard or vanilla ice cream, or cream.

Chicken in a whole pumpkin

A fantastic way to serve chicken. I can't remember where it originally came from but it is a brilliant thing to serve to guests at supper. You use the pumpkin as the cooking utensil! Serve it with green vegetables (eg broccoli, mange-tout) and new potatoes. Even better if you have grown the pumpkin, garlic, green vegetables, new potatoes and onions yourself!!

You will need:

A large eating pumpkin (say 8lb (3.5 kg)) – but do make sure it will fit into your oven!

sunflower oil

sea or ground salt

8 garlic cloves

4 oz (100g) of mushrooms

8 cardamon pods

2 fresh green chillies

8 skinless chicken breasts – boneless

4oz (100g) of butter

$\frac{3}{4}$ pint (450 ml) of milk

2 oz (50g) plain flour

peeled fresh ginger – 3" long

3 or 4 large onions

Serves 8

Steps

Preparation
Peel and slice the onions thinly

Cut the top off the pumpkin, about $1\frac{1}{2}$" down, to make a 'bowl' and a 'hat' – keep the 'hat' – it is the lid of the cooking pot – use a sharp knife! Using a strong spoon; scoop out the stringy bits and the seeds – leaving only the useful flesh behind - note that this can be tricky and can hurt your arm. (Save the seeds for planting later on!)

Take the seeds out of the Cardamon pods and grind them.

Cut the chillies open, take out the seeds (keep them for planting too if you wish) and chop them up very small.

Slice the mushrooms – or use small button mushrooms

Slice the ginger finely – or grate it

Slice the chicken into $\frac{1}{2}$" strips

Slice the garlic thinly

Cooking
Melt 3 oz of the butter in a large pan, and cook the onions gently until they are soft;

Add in the cardamon, garlic, chillies and ginger.

Put the last of the butter in and when it has melted add the chicken and mushrooms and thoroughly coat them.

Stir in gradually the flour and milk and add the salt to taste.

Bring it to the boil, stirring constantly until it is nice and thick.

Take it off the heat.

Heat the oven to 240°C or equivalent.

Put the mixture into the pumpkin shell and put the lid on.

Place it on a shallow roasting tin and coat the pumpkin all over with the oil.

Put it in the oven.

After about half an hour turn the heat down to 180°C and leave it for a further $1\frac{1}{2}$ hours.

When cooked, carefully take it off the tray and put it onto a large serving plate and take your triumph to the table.

The chicken and the pumpkin will have blended into a wonderful creamy, tasty mixture.

Scoop out the mixture onto plates.

Traditional onion soup

A tasty and traditional English and continental soup. (The French version uses lots of cheese and croutons and is filling and fattening!)

You will need:

$4\frac{1}{2}$ lb (2 kg) onions (from your allotment)

Cooking oil

1 teaspoon chopped herbs – to your taste – thyme or basil or oregano (from your allotment herb garden)

1 teaspoon sugar

1 tablespoon sherry

3 pints (1.5 l) chicken stock

1$\frac{1}{2}$ tablespoons plain flour

150 ml dry white wine

3 tablespoons cooking brandy

Steps:

Peel and slice the onions.

Pour some oil into a flat large pan, coat the onions slightly and cook them over a medium heat until they soften (about 8 minutes).

Reduce the heat to very low, cover the pan and cook for 20–30 minutes, stirring frequently, until the onions are very soft and golden yellow, then add the herbs.

Uncover the pan and increase the heat slightly. Stir in the sugar and cook for 5–10 minutes, until the onions start to brown. Add the vinegar.

Increase the heat again, then continue cooking, stirring frequently, until the onions turn a deep golden brown. Stir the flour into the onions and cook for 2 minutes.

Boil the stock and gradually pour it in, adding the wine and brandy.

Add salt and pepper to taste.

Note that if you replace half of the stock with milk and cream it becomes cream of onion soup.

(33)

Food for Free

Having grown your crops one year, there is now an added bonus as, in many cases, you will not need to buy them in the future. You save money by saving the seeds from your crops. Many crops produce seeds in abundance (pumpkins, peppers, etc), and from just one fruit or vegetable you can save enough seed to grow all the crops you want and give them away to the rest of the site!

Once you start growing on an allotment, you get into the habit of saving seed from everything. Suttons, the seed company, started out on an allotment.

Be warned – growing from collected seeds is both extremely satisfying and intensely addictive. You will soon run out of space, with every nook and cranny filled with developing plants, seed trays, pots, etc.

Always label the seeds with the crop type and date the seed was saved. You will never remember later on whether those seeds were kabocha squash, pumpkin, melon or little gem squash!

Use them in date order – oldest first.

You can also arrange seed swap days when you and your fellow allotment holders can swap packets of seeds. It is a good way to get together, and if linked to a work day and a few drinks, makes a great social gathering.

N.B. – seeds from F1 hybrids will not germinate 'true'. They will revert to one or other of the 'parents'.

Harvesting seeds

Below are a few examples, but you can save seed from most plants.

Squashes/pumpkins/melons When slicing these up, scoop out the seeds. They are usually wet and covered in flesh. Put them in a sieve with small holes and rinse them thoroughly to get the flesh off. Spread them out on paper to dry, turning them every few hours so that they do not stick. When completely dry, store them in envelopes or paper bags. Throw away any that are damaged or very small.

Peppers Slice the peppers and extract the seeds. They are usually quite dry, but I spread them out on a plate for a day or so to ensure they are completely dry. Note that you can handle sweet peppers with bare fingers, but for hot peppers – **always wear gloves!**

Sunflowers The seeds are contained in the flower head. In the centre of the brightly coloured petals lie hundreds of seeds. When the plant has finished flowering, cut off the flower head, let it dry out and then gently scrape the seeds out. I store them in envelopes, clearly marked with the type of plant, name and the date I stored them.

Cardoons These triffids hold their seeds in the large thistle-like tops. They are very heavy and solid when growing, and if you bash them with your head accidentally (as I did once) they are lethal. When the plant has finished, cut the heads off. Each plant produces several heads and all contain thousands of seeds. They look like 'fairies' when they dry out – and float lighter than air on the most gentle of breezes. One head is more than enough to supply all your cardoon needs – probably forever!!

Runner beans Once the main season is over (September) we leave the last few pods to become seed pods. Let them grow long, at which stage they are too hard to eat, and then harvest them. Open them up and you will see lovely purply beans with interesting patterns on them. When I opened the first one up I felt as though I was Jack from 'Jack and the Beanstalk', they looked so magical; and I had to stop myself from running out and planting them straight away (fee fi fo fum!).

Apples, pears, oranges, limes, etc The pips are the seeds. Let them dry out before storing them and planting them. The plants will not be recognised varieties but will give you nice apples after a few years.

Plums, damsons, peaches, etc The stone in the centre is the seed. Eat the flesh and then wash and let it dry. Store in paper bags.

Onions and shallots Let one plant go to seed. It will produce a large head of seeds to harvest. Store them in a dry place for a few days then extract the seeds.

Peas, broad beans, etc Take them out of the pod and let them dry, removing any with maggots, etc. Store in envelopes/paper bags or in airtight jars.

Members of the carrot family

These plants produce seed heads that look like umbrellas (umbels). Choose the largest as they will have the best seeds. Pick when ripe and put them into a paper bag and let them dry. Then you can remove the chaff and keep the seeds. This is called winnowing and is also what is done with corn and wheat. Their seed heads are 'threshed' using a flail for large seeds, but that is not for small plants. The chaff is lighter than seeds so the mixture is tossed and the chaff blows away.

You can do this by putting the gently crushed heads on a plate and gently blowing across it – the heavier seeds will stay and the chaff floats away. You could also use a hairdryer on a soft cool setting (no heat). Wear a face mask as the chaff gets everywhere.

If you are really sophisticated you can use a sieve with holes at just the right size to let the chaff through and keep the seeds – maybe!

Lifespans of seeds

Seeds last for different periods – some for years, others for only a season. Examples are given below:

	Up to 3 years	*3–5 years*	*Over 5 years*
Basil	✓		
Beetroot		✓	
Broad beans		✓	
Cabbage		✓	
Carrots	✓		
Cauliflower		✓	
Celery		✓	
Chicory/endive			✓
Cucumber			✓
Leek	✓		
Lettuce		✓	
Onion	✓		
Parsnip	✓		
Pea	✓		
Pepper		✓	
Pumpkin			✓
Radish		✓	
Rocket	✓		
Runner bean	✓		
Squash			✓
Sweetcorn	✓		
Tomato		✓	
Turnip		✓	

These are only guides – you may be lucky or unlucky. Quite often seeds surprise you by lasting very much longer than normal expectations – but you can't bank on it.

There are tales of people discovering seeds that belonged to their fathers –
or even their grandfathers – and sowing them. I doubt that they had very
high germination rates – but seeds are very hardy really.

We tend to keep seed for ever, and we haven't had too many disappoint-
ments yet.

If you use glass jars with an airtight seal you can keep the dried seeds in a
fridge or freezer. We don't bother, but it can allegedly increase the lifespan
by up to ten times!

In general, keep seeds in dry, cool conditions, ie not in a greenhouse or
airing-cupboard. Usually a cool room is fine, or an outside shed that is dry
and protected from frost and predators!

Drying

The critical factor in successful seed-saving is removing the moisture.
Without moisture they last much longer. If damp or wet they will start to
rot almost immediately.

It is very important, therefore, to thoroughly dry all seed before saving it,
even if you are only going to save it for a short while.

Drying agent

You can use a desiccation or drying agent – I don't though. Silica gel is
usually used. This also has the advantage of changing colour when it has
absorbed the moisture – from blue to pink (just like anhydrous copper sul-
phide from chemistry lessons) – and can be dried and re-used. Remove the
silica gel and place the seeds in a different container before storing. The
silica gel can be dried out in a (low temperature) oven or microwave.

Using stored seeds

If seeds have been kept in paper bags or envelopes at cool but ordinary
temperatures, then you can sow them straight away. If, however, you have

kept them in jars in the fridge or freezer, then leave the jar, unopened, in a room for a few days or so, so that they acclimatise to normal temperatures. This also stops moisture condensing in the jars if you open them straight away, which will spoil the seed.

Note that seeds can harbour pests, eg in the form of eggs or viral diseases.

Always take out any that look a bit dodgy – discoloured or imperfect. These are much more likely to be infected or infested. You don't want to spread whatever they might have. Be ruthless – it's better to have twenty good seeds than hundreds that may be suspect.

You can also take some extra steps to kill off pests. Putting thoroughly dried seeds in a freezer for a couple of days will kill off many pests. Also, soaking them in water at 50 °C (122 °F) will kill some diseases – but not all.

34

The Allotment Society – Getting Involved

Typical structure

Most allotment societies are unincorporated societies – just like many clubs. That is, they are not limited companies and do not have the benefits of that. Neither are they a legal entity, so that also poses problems. You require special mandates from banks for operating bank accounts, and they are not as flexible as with ordinary accounts.

Committee

There will usually be a committee that runs the society and deals with the day-to-day chores such as setting and collecting the rents, ensuring that plots are kept up to scratch and used for the purpose for which they are intended, and dealing with maintenance issues (grass cutting, water, tree pruning, etc). The committee is unpaid and volunteers at the annual general meeting (AGM). Have some sympathy for them as they are usually trying to run the society, as well as their own jobs and household – often with little understanding and help from some plot-holders.

The commitee will also liaise with the landlords with respect to lease issues and maintenance contracts, as well as insurance. There will usually be a chairman, treasurer, lettings officer, secretary and one or two other officers depending on the size and nature of tasks. Larger sites often have a 'water' committee who are on call to deal with leaks – essential if you are a small group with a water meter and limited funds!

Work days

A good committee will also organise work days where activities that are for the common good are carried out – usually with reluctant help from plot-holders who resent the extra work and have to be inveigled or dragooned into it, but will not pay for someone else to do it – and organise social events.

We typically have four work days a year, when we mend broken paths, cut hedges, tidy the communal shed – rescue dead plots and so on. These things are to ensure that the site is kept up to the standards required by the lessor, and that weeds do not get out of hand on unused areas that will infect all plots.

Fund-raising

An essential part of allotment activities, as income is limited (rents are low) and expenditure is often larger and can involve unexpected calls, eg when the landlord decides that, all of a sudden, your society is responsible for tree pruning or an access road needs to be made up.

Fund-raising can be undertaken in a number of ways. The NSALG website has a lot of good ideas on this. We usually attend a couple of local events per year. We sell produce, plants, jam, etc and raise money that way. In addition, this raises our profile in the community, providing people with information on what we do and where we are – to encourage new members, and also allowing us to develop a rapport with local people so that in the event of any issues arising (such as landlords wishing to close the site – which has hap-pened all too often) we can garner and mobilise support.

Children

Although some people have issues with children on allotments, this is usually because they have had a bad experience with some that are poorly behaved.

Well-behaved children are always welcome on our allotment and at least half of the plots are family-run so there are always children there. This is in my opinion a very good thing.

Children bring an extra dimension to allotment holding that augments the experience. They see things with different eyes – typically with childish wonder. Nevertheless, it is incumbent upon holders to ensure that their children are well-behaved and looked after.

Children also do not work in the same way as adults. They have a lower boredom threshold and are obviously not there to put in the back-breaking work of double digging. We approached our allotment from the first as a family thing. It has proved to be great fun. We allocated a patch to each child so that they could grow what they wanted. We helped them plan it out and to dig it and plant it.

The success was variable of course (they soon get bored of weeding) so we made them both monitors – one of watering, the other of the diary. We make sure that they don't go too often and we often have lunches there so we share in several things. Everyone loves the bonfires!

We bought special seeds with wonderful names like sally sunflower or perky pumpkin to keep the fun element; and held a 'grow the biggest sunflower competition' which the eldest one won by a short head from the youngest (both mine and Catherine's were eaten before they got out of the starting blocks!).

For us it has been a great family thing. Others on the plot also take the same approach. It means that when you are working on the allotment you do not need baby-sitters as the children are there with you. You still need to keep an eye on the small ones of course.

There are a lot of things that can be done on allotments to encourage children:

- Keeping their interest is vital – you don't want it to seem a chore.
- Competitions are great – tidiest plot (no chance), biggest pumpkin/sunflower, prettiest flowers, most weeds collected in a trug.

- Give them responsibility – not too onerous but something that makes them feel important and something that is only theirs, eg writing labels, water monitor, etc. If you have a pond, put one in charge of the water level, or counting the tadpoles.

- Give them their own set of tools (gloves, trowels, fork, etc).

- Let them choose their plants.

- Make sure whatever you do is fair between them.

- Let them get dirty – it doesn't matter.

- If you can cycle there together do – it is a great way for all to keep fit and makes it much more of an exciting adventure.

- Reward and praise them for whatever they do, even if it wasn't quite what you wanted – they will respond better.

- Let them get involved in the things that they like – sowing seeds, for example. It is not difficult and makes them feel that they really are being productive. You will probably have to dig the soil over, rake it, etc – though they don't usually mind raking as it is easy and the results are immediately obvious.

- A good thing to do is to let them carve out their name in the soil and fill it with fast-growing seeds (radishes or sprouting crops). When they see their name it will give them such a thrill.

- When they are old enough, and under supervision, let them light bon-fires or garden torches or candle lights. It is great fun for them.

There are a whole range of educational things that you can get children involved in without telling them what they are:

- Measuring rates of growth, or relative sizes of plants.

- Learning to keep records of what you did and observation – keeping a diary.

- Making the plan of the allotment – very successful with ours.

- Making things – ours loved making the scarecrow (see how to make a scarecrow).

- Making windmills (whose movement helps keep pests away).

- Studying insects – How many different kinds can you find? Why are they different at different times of the year?

- Slug hunts – very popular again.

- Explaining about crop rotation and why it is important.

We have arranged for the school to come and visit as part of their science work. There is a lot that they can do – insect hunts, bird counts, looking at different crops, quizzes, etc.

How to make a scarecrow
(thanks to my daughter Victoria for this)

Things you will need:

- Clothes. You can let it wear anything you like, although it can't be your best dress as it will get rained on, animals will climb on it, etc. So old clothes that don't matter are best.

- PVA glue.

- Water.

- Balloon.

- Rubber bands.

- Strips of newspaper.

- Stuffing – straw, newspaper, etc.

- Wooden pole, about 9 feet (3 m) long, depending on how tall you want your scarecrow to be.

Steps
Collect all of the clothes together (trousers, shirt, coat/waistcoat, hat).

Cut up the wooden pole. You will need one long piece, which will make the body, and one short piece, which will make the arms.

Blow up the balloon. Use a balloon that is about head-sized and -shaped.

Cover the balloon in strips of newspaper, which you soak in the mixture of PVA glue and water (papier-mâché). It should be quite runny, so don't put loads and loads of glue in, you can always make more.

Let the head dry. This might take quite a while depending on how many layers you put on the balloon.

Pop the balloon once the head is thoroughly dry; it is now ready to paint. Paint the head with whatever kind of face you like: scary, smiley, angry, sad, etc.

Tie the poles together. They need to be very sturdy so, cutting indents and using both superglue and string is a good idea.

Put the clothes carefully on the scarecrow once the glue has dried. They will be loose and baggy. Tie string to the trousers, to act like braces; the string can then be hung over the crosspiece.

Stuff the clothes with newspaper until the scarecrow is as fat as you want.

Tie the rubber bands to the ends of the arms and legs and tuck the shirt in (if it's wearing a shirt), otherwise the stuffing will fall out.

Your scarecrow is complete! When you plant it, make sure it is deep enough so as not to fall over or blow over. Put a clear plastic bag over the head so that the paper doesn't dissolve in the rain. Put his hat on.

Safety

It is important that although you don't make too much of it, you do ensure that children are safe. It depends on how old they are. Ours are old enough to understand that secateurs are dangerous – a four-year-old probably isn't.

We keep a first-aid box in our toolbox, and there is also one in the communal shed. Key items are sterile dressings, cleaning tissues, plasters, ointments for nettle stings and thorns, bites, etc.

Cover all stakes/canes with plastic bottles or something similar – to protect adults as well – and make sure tools are not left lying around.

Pick up any glass immediately. Make sure that ponds or pools do not pose a danger to very small children.

All in all, an allotment is a great place for lots of fun and relaxation as well as a learning experience for children. We also allow them time to play with the other children as well – letting off steam is important, as long as it is not too vigorous and doesn't disturb anyone.

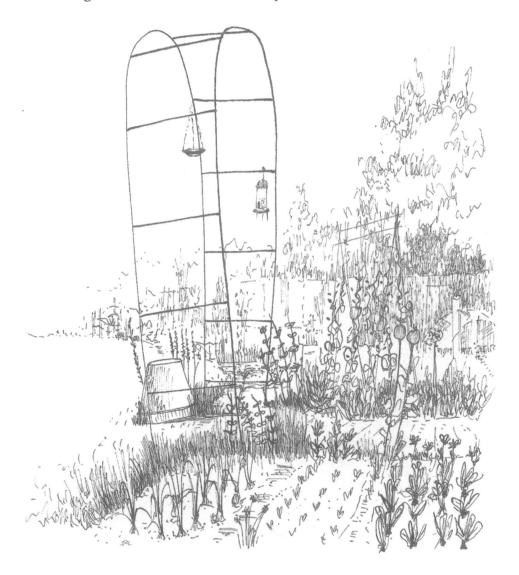

(35)

Allotment Tips

This chapter is really a catch-all for a few items that didn't fit in elsewhere. Mainly it is useful things that will I hope help you with the day-to-day running of your allotment.

Health and safety

Although allotments are not especially hazardous or dangerous places, bear in mind there are some common-sense things you should bear in mind:

- Don't leave tools lying around where anybody can trip over them.
- Put all tools away when you have finished with them.
- Always close your knife before putting it down.
- If you have sharp blades that do not fold away – get into the habit of putting a cork onto the tip when not in use.
- Cut down nettles, thistles and brambles *before* they grow large.
- Make sure that your paths stay level and even. As earth moves they can shift and leave 'lips' for people to trip over.
- Do not use metal for raised beds – it will rust, flake and become sharp.
- If you have a large pool, fence it off.

- When putting wires up for raspberries, etc, tie something like ribbon or silver Christmas baubles onto it so you don't walk into it and garrotte yourself or someone else.

- Place something over all sticks/canes that you use – it is amazing how often you bend down near the ends.

- Anchor your wigwams securely.

- Always wear gloves where practicable, eg when weeding. Sharp pointy things lurk everywhere!

- Have a small first-aid kit in your shed or toolbox.

- Make sure that you are up to date with tetanus if there are rusty metal things about.

- If your children are small – keep an eye on them – they may wander off, or come near just as you are swinging that scythe!

- When cutting large branches from trees or brambles, etc, make sure you do not stand underneath them as they come free.

- Do not overfill wheel barrows – they are unstable at the best of times and prone to tipping up.

Diaries

A diary is a record of such things as:

- The weather on a particular day/or week.

- What you planted when.

- What came up.

- What didn't!

- When and what you harvested.

- Problems that you encountered.

- How you resolved them – or learned to live with them.

Why should I keep a diary?

There is an old Chinese proverb: 'The faintest ink is better than the most retentive memory.' In other words, if you write it down it will be an accurate record of things – rather than a random collection of items half-remembered, out of order and probably rosy-tinted with retrospective nostalgia.

There is no compelling need for a diary, nor is it a requirement. However, it is a really useful record of what you did and what happened, and in the depths of winter it is great to look back and learn from the things that didn't happen.

We started keeping a diary from day one. It is a bit of a pain – and sometimes you forget or don't have time (or are too tired!) and have to fill in several days in one go. But as a family we shared the tasks with my children and me mainly taking it in turns to fill it in.

There are some things that you will be keener to record than others (the first strawberry or the initial potato plant that you dig up), but the other more mundane things will be almost as interesting when you look back – and probably more useful for future planning. There isn't an entry for every day – as of course we don't go every day.

Our diary
Below are some extracts from our allotment diary. They cover a whole year, more or less, to show how the seasons affect the allotment.

December

Well. We have been allocated an allotment after only a short wait. Lucky really – a nice Christmas present. We went and viewed it and started clearing it.

January 4th

Cold

Finished digging over the soil and putting in manure. Finally filled the last trench. Raked over all the soil. Took out the rose. Marked out the plot with string as per the plan. Made two paths out of brick. Dug up buttercups, weeds, grass, bramble roots broke trowel! Took large bags of things to the dump.

January 20th/21st

Cold/dry

Bought a greenhouse and seed potatoes (maris peer) from Harold Hillier Gardens (Hampshire) along with some more seed propagating trays. Also bought two blueberry bushes. Collected seaweed from Calshot beach (two bin bags).

Bought a small shed.

Erected the greenhouse and started putting plants in it.

January 24th

Fine

Chitted potatoes; took kitchen compost to allotment and put it in bin – casual weeding.

February 8th

2 inches of snow

Stayed home – in front of fire!

February 13th

Cold; but clear and dry

Planted out onions – 1 row of Brunswicker and 1 row of Stuttgarter Riesan. Planted out the blueberry bushes after hardening off. Constructed the bean support. Slightly re-dug E's bed. Weeding!

Turned over one compost bin. Seaweed has attracted lots of flies! Planted five parsnip tops as experiment (Note – didn't work!)

March 3rd

Wet

Sowed Hamburg parsley and perky pumpkin in trays. Uncovered more path.

Marked out second row for potatoes (note this row either wasn't planted or all died). Assembled a wheelbarrow – rubbish construction/quality – had to re-drill the screwholes. Put masses of rubbish in the site skip.

Planted out currant bushes (three white and three red), mulched the currants. Built second wigwam for beans. Turned over one compost bin.

March 19th

Very cold. Snow and thunder and lightning!!

Took kitchen compost up, some weeding. Hamburg parsley has grown too weedy and spindly – lack of adequate light is I think the cause!

April 13th

Overcast – patchy sun but mainly dry

Dug trench for three sisters; lined with cardboard and filled with compost from bin. Riddled the soil back into the trench and raked it over. Covered parsnips, turnips, beetroot and carrot seedbed with sharp and spiky things. Weeding and watering. Sowed coriander seeds at end of root rows. Covered lamb's lettuce with sharp sticks – heard a woodpecker in the trees. Rocket showing, potatoes starting to show! Discovered old asparagus bed – not where we want it! Moved strawberry plants into new bed.

April 15th

Warm day for April

Cycled to allotment

E planted her plants in her plot

AGM of Society – I was voted in as Hon Treasurer. Catherine also voted onto committee as member ordinary. Inspected all plots with the committee. Agreed that letting officer would write to several about the appalling state of their plots. Agreed that on next work day we would clear several areas and create some more plots. Watered everything.

May 2nd

Chilly but dry

Cycled to allotment. Watered and weeded. Rearranged cloches over the brassicas. Propagated tumbling toms and honesty (lunaria). Potted on many plants.

June 7th

Overcast

Raspberries starting to ripen – need to net this weekend. Red sunflower seeds through. Filled large pots with tumbling toms and other plants. Ordinary tomatoes (Gardener's Delight) now ready for growbags. Several potatoes flowering. Watering and weeding.

June 9th

Hot

Harvested lamb's lettuce, rocket, Tom Thumb lettuce. Catherine ate 5 raspberries – delicious – and tried some peas. They need a few more days – but will be ready this weekend. Dug up some potatoes. Cooked them and ate them for supper with the salad, home-made damson chutney (from last year) and gammon – absolutely delicious. Moved polytunnel from brassicas (getting too tall for it) to cover new sowings of parsnips, carrots and Hamburg parsley. Put netting over brassicas. Planted out more pumpkins, squashes and courgettes in second three sisters trench. Cleared the long grass at front of plot.

June 13th

Fine with rain forecast

Rest day (working on book!)

July 9th

Took scarecrow to allotment – looked fine!

July 20th

Thunder, lightning and four inches of rain!! Too wet to work.

July 21st

Intermittent light and torrential rain

Harvested peas, broad beans, a marrow, courgettes, runner beans, turnips, onions, lots of potatoes, some blueberries, lots of blackberries, cut down peas and broad beans as they are finished (left roots in soil).

Lots and lots of weeding following our week away.

August 4th

Intermittent cold and sunny

Masses of weeding – convolvulus rampant as well as others!

Cut down bamboo totally. Will dig it up later on.

August 28th

10 days of torrential rain and cold weather in last two weeks. Sweetcorn devastated. Squashes eaten (those on next-door site looking excellent and not eaten! – will ask them what they did/do). Harvested courgettes (3 large), potatoes, onions, turnips, last of blackberries, few raspberries and masses of runner beans. Garlic has disappeared completely from the wet! One sunflower 12 feet tall, other two 8 feet. Red cabbage still looking OK – rest slug destroyed. Berries and currants finished. Leeks still OK so far. Tomatoes looking poor.

Not enough sun!!!!!

Harvested cardoon heads for seeds – for sale at our open day. Will now take them out completely.

Despite the colossal rainfall – the ground was dry and we needed to water!

September 5th

Chilly in am – very warm in pm (24°). Autumn is here! Harvested potatoes and remaining few beans. All other runners will now be left to go to seed for next year. Blackberries still producing. One squash still left uneaten. Plenty of others setting. Put down organic slug repellent – the smell was terrible. Planted endive and rocket seeds – optimistically! – note must get some green manures.

October 3rd

Our wedding anniversary!

Weather has suddenly turned really cold, very wet and of course it is now very dark in the mornings. The allotment plot looks very sad. I took the runner beans down – I felt like I was losing a good friend – and dismantled the frame. The blackberries are still producing very fat large berries. A few squashes to go – but the weather has killed off the courgette plant. I put some more organic slug repellent down and collected a few more sweet peas – they have been a very good producer, despite the trickiness of germination. Leeks looking good – will harvest a few next week I think. A few potatoes left; plenty of onions. Time to double dig it all!

Three Ws

You will note that the three Ws of weeding, weather and watering feature constantly throughout!

General tips

Learn to work with the seasons. You can't plant or grow much in the depths of winter. Similarly, leaving your plot for three or four weeks at the height of summer will result in desiccation of your plants and major crop loss. 2007 had the wettest July for 95 years and it devastated our sweetcorn and garlic and others.

Take it easy – do not try to do everything at once. If your plot is large or difficult, then attack it incrementally. Draw up a staged plan and gradually bring it under control. Don't hang on to it if it is too much – downsize – there is no shame and it will ease your burden and allow someone else to enjoy it as well.

Revisit your plan throughout the year to measure the success of what you did/are doing and use it to make a better plan next year.

Think about what you will be doing in the course of the year. Think about how the allotment will look in winter and spring (bare), summer and autumn (packed with growth). Plants will grow and the space that you thought you had might be taken up with growth (eg on paths) making it difficult to get barrows through. Also, plants hold water and, after a shower, walking through overhanging branches, etc will soak you.

Only grow what you will eat. Nobody in our family likes Brussels sprouts (not even at Christmas) so we don't grow them. You will just give or throw away what you don't like – so why bother? Rather plant crops you will eat/use.

Plant a little and often to avoid gluts and ensure fresh food is available.

Think about what each plant needs in terms of light, food and situation. Like your children, make sure that you give them the best start. They want to grow, but need you to put them in the right place. It is your responsibility and – weather and external events apart – you take the credit for success and blame for failures.

Don't take up the lines that you used to mark your crops when they are growing. Later on in the year you will need to remind yourself where they are after the tops have died down, for example with garlic/onions/potatoes.

Plan what you are going to grow. With a little imagination it is possible to have crops all year round, though not the same ones obviously.

Companion planting

What is companion planting? At its most basic it is just using nature to help your plants. It has long been known that some plants repel some pests because of their smell or taste. Others attract beneficial insects like bees because of their colours or nectar. Some people believe (but there is little evidence to support it) that plants thrive when planted with specific others.

As organic gardeners we know that a diverse mix of plants – vegetables and flowers – makes a healthy and beautiful allotment by reducing pests and the incidence of disease; by taking and putting back different nutrients; and of course by making the allotment look pleasant as well.

How does companion planting work?

- **Companions help each other to grow** Tall plants for example provide shade for sun-sensitive, shorter plants.

- **Companions use garden space efficiently** Trailing plants cover the ground, upright plants grow up.

- **Companions prevent pest problems** Plants like onions repel some pests. Other plants can lure pests away from more desirable plants.

- **Companions attract beneficial insects** Every successful garden needs plants that attract the predators of pests.

Some of the earliest written documents on gardening discuss these relationships.

When selecting your companion plants, you will need to consider more than which pests are deterred. Think about what each plant adds or takes away from the soil and what effect the proximity of strong herbs may have on the flavour of your vegetables. Try to avoid placing two heavy feeders or two shallow-rooted plant types near each other.

While it is not known exactly how the plants benefit one another, some generalisations can be made. Companions often include plants with contrasting properties: sun-loving (sunflowers) and shade-loving; plants with deep roots and those with shallow roots; slow-growing (brassicas) and fast-growing (rocket, squashes); heavy feeders and light feeders or crops that incorporate nitrogen into the soil (legumes); aromatic plants, which often repel pests, and non-aromatic ones; plants with early flowers that provide pollen and nectar for some insect predators, and plants that do not bear flowers until late in the season; plants that are more attractive to a particular pest than others, ie as a trap-crop; and plants that stimulate biological activity in the soil with crops that are heavy feeders.

While companion planting is a lot if fun and makes the vegetable garden more attractive, both to the eye and to the nose, it has a more serious side. It represents an effort on the part of some producers to manage agricultural systems by studying the natural systems.

3 sisters

The Amerindians used to grow crops utilising companion planting techniques. They would choose plants that used different parts of the soil and allow them to grow together in harmony. They called it the 3 sisters system.

Typically they would plant sweetcorn (maize) with runner/climbing beans and squashes or pumpkins. The beans grow up the sweetcorn and, being leguminous, use different nutrients, and also fix nitrogen in the soil. The pumpkins or squashes grow underneath the sweetcorn, spreading out their foliage and suppressing weeds. They also benefit from the shade offered by the taller plants. You can see this system in use on our allotment.

36

The Allotment Year

There is always something to do on an allotment. Even in the darkest depths of winter there is a lot do to – ranging from planning the next year to tidying up or digging over parts of the plot. There are also the winter vegetables to harvest.

Weather of course constrains activity – but you can always plan inside when it rains; or plant seeds in trays; or even pot-on.

In the following pages I set out a handy summary of jobs and tasks by season. There are clearly a lot more things to do than I am showing here, but this is a useful working document around which to plan the detail. Each season is divided into early and late because the weather changes across all seasons.

Spring is the time when new growth comes through, hence its name in many languages – *primaverdi* (first greening). I think of it as from late February until late May.

Summer is when the ground really heats up and everything grows (including weeds) – long lazy days with strawberries and a host of fruits – from late May until late August.

Autumn, the 'season of mists and mellow fruitfulness' (or fruity mellowness if you have too much red wine), is my favourite time of year. The leaves are turning and so many crops are ready for bringing in – hence Harvest festival. Late August to late November.

Winter – that cold period – always known (before we could grow crops all year round under cover – or import them) as the hungry time. I always think of it as starting on my birthday – 20th November, (which was always foggy when I was a child) – until late February.

With careful planning you can be harvesting pretty much all year round. For our first year, as we had so much trouble, we had little to harvest during the winter months except for leeks and cabbage. For the second year we planned to have much more of the hardy vegetables for harvest (all things being equal and subject to the vagaries of weather, pests and diseases – not to mention cussedness of seeds!).

Conclusion

By way of a conclusion, I repeat what I said right at the beginning when discussing why you want your own allotment.

'Whatever people may say, it is important that you manage your allotment in your own way. Do what suits you and your likes, dislikes and objectives: within the constraints of what you can do, neighbourliness and the local rules. You will adopt and adapt what you see, hear and experience into your own way of doing things. Just because one person says do it this way doesn't make it right. Others will say something else. Use your common sense and develop a feel for things. Learn from your mistakes (learn also from the ones I made that I share here) and have fun and grow great food.'

After our first year, here is a list of our successes and failures:

Successes	Failures	50-50
broad beans	carrots	cabbages
runner beans	parsnips	Hamburg parsley
peas	pumpkins	blueberries
potatoes	sweetcorn	white/redcurrants
squashes		raspberries
courgettes		strawberries
blackberries		tomatoes
turnips		
lamb's lettuce		
rhubarb		
sweet peas		

I would just add that as a family we have had fantastic fun, masses of exercise (cycling and digging), some heartache when the plants just didn't grow, but above all else great food.

I can still taste the very first potatoes that we harvested and digging them up is always a magical moment. The first year was tinged with disappointment from our failures with carrots, parsnips and – despite early promise; but thanks to the attentions of the mice and adverse weather – sweetcorn.

I hope that your experiences are as good as (or better than) ours!

At the beginning of this book I suggested that you might want to draw up a list of pros and cons for getting an allotment. You might like (if you went ahead and obtained a plot) to revisit them and see how well you matched up to them. I hope that you are pleasantly surprised.

Summary (Vade Mecum)

	Spring		Summer	
	E	*L*	*E*	*L*
Introduction	As spring approaches the days get longer and it starts warming up. Frosts can still be a problem – as can bad weather – so keep an eye out. Do not plant out until soil temperature is above 46°F (7°C)	A time for lots of activity. Soil is warmer, days are longer and plants grow well now. Still possible to get cold snaps – so take care with tender plants. Seedlings will be ready for transplanting out, after hardening off	The start of the real harvest time which will extend well into winter. Many crops are now available and it is a time to enjoy the fruits of your efforts; but also a time to keep slugs, pests, disease and weeds at bay. The warmth favours them just as much	Usually very hot weather (but no guarantees). Plenty of watering, weeding and pruing. If you have them, fruit trees start to produce; fruit bushes similarly. Put in catch crops to use soil. Relax a little, and enjoy the harvest.
Tasks	Build frames for sweet peas	Feed plants	Continue to sow vegetables for later harvest	Cut herbs – either to use or to keep good growth
	Build frames for runner/ broad beans	In milder climates – sow tender plants such as sweetcorn	Earth up potatoes	Earth up potatoes
	Chit potatoes	Plant out asparagus crowns	Mulch as appropriate	Harvest runner beans
	Plant out onions and shallots	Plant out new herb plants	Pest watch!	Lift onions, garlic and shallots

Spring		Summer	
E	L	E	L
Protect crops if bad weather strikes	Put down organic slug/snail repellent/barriers	Plant out courgettes, cucumbers, squashes, pumpkins, runner beans, peppers and tomatoes	Net fruits
Put in new strawberries	Put in early potatoes	Plant out main crop potatoes	Pinch out tips of beans when they reach top of support
Sow early radishes under cloches	Sow broccoli	Protect crops with fleece to keep pests away	Place support under squashes and pumpkins
Sow peas and beans under cover	Sow more *in situ* (beetroots, cabbage, carrots, leeks, onion seed, peas, parsnips, radish, broad beans, etc)	Start winter seedlings for transplanting out later	Protect crops from pests especially after rain
Sow tender plants under cover ready for transplanting	Sow more tender plants out but under cover	Succession-sow peas, radishes, lettuce, etc	Sow spring cabbages
Start preparing asparagus beds	Start hardening off seedlings	Thin out crops	Sow squashes after potatoes
Start sowing more hardy plant *in situ*	Transplant out cabbage plants	Tie in climbers	Succession sowing
	Watering where dry	Weed and water	Take up broad beans once over (leave roots *in situ*)

Produce in season	Weeding starts again!		Watering Weeding
Broccoli	Broccoli	Asparaguss	Blueberries
Cabbage (spring/winter)	Cabbage	Beetroot	Aubergines
Kale	Chard	Broad beans	Broad beans
Leeks	Lettuce	Cabbage	Cabbage
Lettuce (early)	Peas	Carrots	Carrots
Parsnips	Radishes	Garlic	Courgettes
	Rhubarb	Lettuce	Cucumbers
	Spinach	Mangetout	Currants
	Turnips	Peas	French beans
		Potatoes	Garlic
		Radishes	Lettuce
		Shallots	Melons
		Strawberries	Onions
		Turnips	Peas (late)
			Peppers
			Potatoes
			Raspberries
			Runner beans
			Strawberries
			Sweetcorn
			Tomatoes

| | Autumn | | Winter | |
	E	L	E	L
Introduction	As the days start to draw in (after June) there are still plenty of crops to harvest – especially if you have succession sown. Many crops still need the lingering rays of autumn for ripening. As you reach the fag end of beans, leave some to fully mature so you can harvest the seeds for next year. Always keep seeds from the healthy plants such as squashes and pumpkins, etc	The beginning of the end of the productive year. Although with a well-planned allotment there will still be produce, the major portion of the bounty is over. Time to start tidying up and clearing the ground. Time for bonfires! Harvest the seeds	As the cold season begins it is time to consider what needs doing now and planning the next year's effort. General tidying up, as well as harvesting the winter crops. If you have planted them, then Christmas potatoes should be ready by December 25th	Even in the depths of winter there is plenty to do. After 23rd December days get longer – although you don't usually notice it yet. January and February can often be colder than December – so listen to the weather forecast and protect crops
Tasks	Cover tender crops with cloches or poly tunnels to protect them	Clean cloches	Clean stakes	Chit potatoes (earlies)
	Gather last of beans, take down frames	Clean seed trays, etc	Divide rhubarb	Finish double digging the plot
	Harvest pumpkins and squashes	Further pruning	Double dig the plot – especially for potatoes	

Keep an eye out for cold and protect as necessary	Harvest pumpkins and squashes	Examine seed stores and order them as necessary	Plant out onions
Lift onions for storage	Move tender plants inside if you can	Force rhubarb	Plant out shallots
Lift main crops	Order potatoes and onion sets	If severe weather is forecast – lift a few extra vegetables	Protect crops from severe frosts
Plant fruit bushes	Plant further green manures	Lime ready for brassicas	Start digging runner and broad bean trenches
Plant out cabbages	Prepare the soil for next year's crops	Plan next year's crops	Start marking out the plot for next year
Prune blackberries, but keep harvesting	Protect crops with fleeces, straw, etc	Plant fruit bushes	Start sowing crops under cloches
Prune raspberries and gooseberries	Sow some spring crops on mild days	Protect crops from severe frosts	Start warming soil by using cloches, black plastic, etc
Sow green manure – mustard or clover, beans	Start digging soil	Sow broad beans under cloches on a mild day	
Start planning next year's crops – look through catalogues	Tidy up plot; burn unwanted weeds, etc		
Thin winter/spring crops	Watering and weeding as necessary		
Watering and weeding – less required than before – but as necessary	Earth up plants for winter winds		

	Autumn		Winter	
	E	L	E	L
		Stake plants as necessary (eg sprouts)		
		Clear debris from below plants to remove pest homes		
Produce in season	Blackberries	Blackberries	Leeks	Leeks
	Cabbage	Cabbage	Parsnips	Parsnips
	Carrots	Carrots	Christmas potatoes	Christmas potatoes
	Cauliflowers	Cauliflowers	Sprouts	Sprouts
	Celery	Celery	Winter cabbage	Winter cabbage
	Chard	Chard	Last few pumpkins and squashes	Kale
	Courgettes (last few)	Potatoes	Kale	Swedes
	Cucumbers	Leeks	Swedes	Early broccoli
	Marrows	Parsnips		
	Peppers	Sprouts		
	Potatoes	Pumpkins		
	Pumpkins	Squashes		
	Runner beans	Turnips		
	Spinach	Strawberries (maybe)		
	Sprouts			
	Squashes			
	Sweetcorn			
	Tomatoes			
	Turnips			

ANNUAL CALENDAR (OUTSIDE)

	J	F	M	A	M	J	J	A	S	O	N	D
Beetroot				So	So	So	H	H	H	X	X	X
broad bean			T/W	T/W	W	H	H	D	P	S	S	
broccoli			Su	Su	Tr	W	W	M/W	H	H	X	X
cabbage (spring)		W	H	H	H	X	X	So	So	So		
cabbage (winter)	H	H	H	X	X	So	H	W	W			H
carrots			S	S/T	T/W/P	W	H	H	H	H/X	X	X
cauliflower			Su	Su	Tr	W	W	M/W	H	H	X	X
celery		Su	Su	Tr	Tr	E	E	E/H	H	H	X	
courgettes			X	S	S	W	H	H	H	X	X	X
french beans		X	S	S/T	T/W	W/H	H	H	H	D	D	
garlic	X	X	X/S	S	S	W	W/H	W/H	W/H	H	H	X
leeks	H	H/X	Pu	W/M	W	W/M	W	W	W	H	H	H
lettuce		Su	Su	T	Tr	Tr/W	W	W/H	H	X	X	X
onions	X	X	X/S	S	S	W	W	W/H	W/H	H	H	X
peas		S	S	S/T	W/H	W/H	W/H	H/D	D	D	X	X
peppers				S	W/P	W/P	W/P	H	H	H		
potato (early)	X	C	S	W/E	W/E	W/E/H	W/E/H	W/E/H	X	X	X	X
potato (main)	X	X	C	S	S	W/E	W/E	W/E/H	W/H			
parsnips	H	H/P	S	S/T	T/W	W	W	W	H	H	H	H
pumpkin			X	X	S	S	W/M	W	W/M	H	H	X
sprouts	H	H/P	S	S/T	T/W	W	W	W	H	H	H	H
squash	X	X	X	S	S	S/W/M	S/W/M	W/M/S	H	H	H	X
sweet corn	X	X	X	S	S	W	W	W	H	H/X	X	X
tomatoes				S/P	S/P	W	W	W/H	W/H	W/H	X	X

C Chit   **H** harvest   **Tr** transplant   **T** thin   **Su** sow under cover
D dig in roots   **M** mulch   **Pu** puddle in   **W** water/weed
E earth up   **P** protect   **So** sow in situ   **X** dig/prepare soil

Index